COUNTRY LIFE,
CITY LIFE

COUNTRY LIFE, CITY LIFE

Five Theories of Community

Linda Stoneall

PRAEGER SPECIAL STUDIES • PRAEGER SCIENTIFIC

Library of Congress Cataloging in Publication Data

Stoneall, Linda

   Country life, city life.

   Bibliography: p.
   Includes index.
   1. Community life—Case studies. 2. Sociology,
Urban—Case studies. 3. Sociology, Rural—Case studies.
4. City and town life—United States—Case studies.
5. Country life—United States—Case studies. I. Title.
HM131.S8257   1983   307   83-2427
ISBN 0-03-061712-X
ISBN 0-03-061713-8 (pbk.)

Published in 1983 by Praeger Publishers
CBS Educational and Professional Publishing
A Division of CBS Inc.
521 Fifth Avenue, New York, New York 10175   U.S.A.

© 1983 by Praeger Publishers

For my parents,
Madge and Rex Stoneall

Preface

In many ways, this book represents my personal odyssey. I was born at Grant Hospital in Lincoln Park where my parents lived before I was born, and I spent many summers in the Zenda, Wisconsin, area where I have a long family history. I became interested in communities during an undergraduate semester in Chicago, which exposed me to the community studies of the Chicago School and excited me with direct contact and study of varied urban life-styles. Later, graduate study of sociology, which suggested that loneliness, alienation, rootlessness, and a mass, mobile society dominate contemporary life, seemed inconsistent with my knowledge of Zenda. I watched Zenda over the years lose various stores and local institutions, yet the same families who had long histories there remained tied to one another and said they had a strong community. The discrepancies between what I knew to be true about the real live community of Zenda and how communities were portrayed in the literature made me curious to study Zenda. I spent a year there from 1975 to 1976 solely to collect data for a dissertation on Zenda (1978), and I have remained in close contact with people of that area.

Peter Manning and Barrie Thorne guided the fieldwork on Zenda, while Marilyn Aronoff taught me much about communities. Peter Manning also helped me choose the five theoretical frameworks and develop their parts. I was supported in the fieldwork in part by a National Institutes of Mental Health traineeship. I am grateful to the people of Zenda for their cooperation in the study.

Albert Hunter was instrumental in changing the dissertation into a book. He suggested adding Lincoln Park, which contrasts with Zenda, to extend my study of community to urban areas. Hunter also guided some of the reorganization of the book to include comparisons of the two communities within each paradigmatic section. Finally, he inspired many of the titles of the chapters.

I completed fieldwork on Lincoln Park in 1981, thanks to the people of that community, especially the Lincoln Park Conservation

Association members who gave me their time and many documents. Kenneth Fidel of DePaul University and Richard Taub of the University of Chicago also supplied many statistics and information on Lincoln Park.

The issues of communities both concretely and abstractly are becoming a stronger focus of the 1980s, as people turn away from the narcissism of the "me generation" and look to others to gain meaningful relations. Understanding how communities are formed and changed becomes important for creating senses of belonging. Furthermore, some have argued that events at the community level are most important both for determining worldwide changes and for feeling the impact of the changes. We no longer believe that any one community represents a nation or is a microcosm of society, and yet, local places form more comprehensible units than entire societies. These statements suggest that it is important to understand communities.

The five theoretical frameworks with comparable parts have proved useful to me in teaching the sociology of community over the past few years. From reactions of students to my lectures, I was able to revise the points I make in this book. The book is designed to clarify the confusion and evasiveness of the concept of community and, in turn, to make concrete communities more understandable and to facilitate community research. I assume the reader has some background in sociology.

I was able to complete the writing of the book as part of a National Institutes of Mental Health postdoctoral fellowship at the University of California, Berkeley, thanks to G. E. Swanson. Members of the Bay Area SWS Writers Group provided comments.

Finally, I appreciate the support of my parents, the help of my friend, Kay Hayden, and the encouragement of Steve Leadley and my daughters, Rosie and Lorna.

Contents

List of Tables

List of Figures

1

Introduction

Community may be defined as people interacting in a specific time and place. In local communities, significant proportions of the residential populations traverse the same space on a daily basis. I begin with this broad, heuristic definition, only to argue that a single definition of community is inadequate. Therefore, I start by discussing the inadequacies of definitions and the need for theories. Theories help make sense of definitions, and the elements I regard as essential to theories of community include people, time, and space. We inherit theories and the importance of communities from classical theorists, their reaction to the French and Industrial Revolutions, and their concepts of communities. Subsequent theorists have built on the classical theories and have applied the theories to communities in divergent ways. I have chosen five approaches or perspectives for extensive discussion in this book because they seem to encompass current work on communities. In each theory chapter, I delineate metaphors, methods, and three dimensions from our original definition — people, space, and time — using examples from two original case studies of a rural and an urban community. In this chapter, I rationalize my choice of these theories, their parts, and the case studies.

1

ISSUES IN DEFINING COMMUNITY

Despite the importance of community studies, sociologists continue to have difficulty in defining community. Besides the confusion over definitions, many different social phenomena have been called communities — cities, institutions, neighborhoods, villages, hotels, prisons, minority groups, religious organizations, military establishments, trade unions, and professions. It is questionable whether this list shares an inclusiveness, or whether some of the groupings are not better understood with other sociological concepts. Marcia Pelly Effrat, a community sociologist, describes the study of community as being like jello; the concept does not hold together, but falls apart with attempts to grasp it (1974). Innumerable and contradictory definitions of community abound (Hillery 1955), which can refer to almost any phenomenon.

What should a good definition be? A good definition* has both inclusive and exclusive qualities that distinguish one concept from others. Community, as a sociological concept, should have certain parameters that tell what is to be included and characteristics that simultaneously exclude it from other sociological concepts.

Sociologists often define community as whatever they happen to be studying, instead of being open to whether or not what they are studying is, in fact, a community.

> The community investigated is often such by predefinition rather than by empirical research. By not leaving "communityness" itself completely open to investigation, researchers make it difficult to ever

---

*Karl Popper, a social philosopher, suggests that scientific definitions exhibit methodological nominalism; that is, rather than looking for the essence or the indispensable qualities of a community, its parts are named and their functions described. "Instead of aiming at finding out what a thing really is and at defining its true nature, methodological nominalism aims at describing how a thing behaves in various circumstances . . . and regularities in its behavior" (Popper 1945, p. 32). The bulk of this book is devoted to looking at how communities "behave," how they differ from one another, and at the same time how they exhibit regularities.

completely characterize the fundamental components of a community, and hence, to clearly tell a community from a non-community other than on the basis of size. (Effrat 1974, p. 14)

The various definitions tend to obscure community's clear boundaries for inclusiveness and distinctness; they also indicate, however, that ccommunity is not a single item.

Examples of Community Definitions

Examining some of the most prominent community definitions will indicate the problems. Gideon Sjoberg's definition is similar to the one I am using: "a collectivity of actors sharing in a limited territorial area as the base for carrying out the greatest share of their daily activities" (1965, p. 115). Sjoberg draws from Talcott Parsons, whose definition says a "common" rather than a "limited" territory (1951, p. 91). Parsons also defines community as "that aspect of the structure of social systems which is referable to the territorial location of persons (i.e., human individuals as organisms) and their activities" (Parsons 1960, p. 250). Parsons believes that both population and territory are important components for a communal social system.

To territory and population, Robert Park adds commonality. Park's (1952) original formulation of community emphasized the aspects of behavior that could be understood with reference to the social similarities of people sharing identifiable, local geographic areas. As a fourth item, Leo Schnore (1967) includes local institutions.

Joseph Gusfield further expands the definitions to include the numerous characteristics of the social interaction that a population engages in: all-inclusive public interest, closeness of bond, and particular kinds of human relationships (1975, pp. xii-xiv). He also advocates looking at history as a critical component of community concepts.

We could keep on adding to this brief list of definitions, as Hillery did in 1955 when he discovered 95 definitions of community. He made 16 classifications of these and said that three central categories consistently emerge out of these numerous definitions: commonality among people, social interaction, and common land (1968). Updating Hillery's work, Sutton and Munson (1976) looked at community definitions published betweeen 1954 and 1973 and found that about 70 percent of all definitions emphasized community as a structural entity — a specific population, place, or location — while less than 12 percent also included interaction.

Jessie Bernard narrows Hillery's categories to two, what she calls "the community" (locality) and "community" (social ties) (1973, pp. 3-4). These overlap with Gusfield's (1975) divisions of territory and human relations. We have made a circle from Parsons's two parts — population and territory — all the way out to 94 definitions, and back to the same two — people and space, two essential components of the initial definition.

Criticisms of Definitions

Community researchers disagree not only on the number of parts required for a definition of community but also on which part is most important. For some, absence of one community element indicates the absence of community. For example, Michelson (1974) complains that the physical environment has been left out of many community studies; Macionis claims that friendship ties have been underestimated (1978); Pahl wants to see collective action in order to have a community (1974); and at the other end, Webber claims there can be "community without propinquity" (1963). The study of community includes a broad range of possibilities and continues to be fraught with disagreements and debates over what community is and whether we still have communities. For some, community is an anachronism (Stein 1960; Nisbet 1953), while others simply define it and say it cannot exist in modern life.

Community has become an omnibus term* and this has brought many criticisms. For example, John Walton says that definitions

---

*For example, communities have been portrayed as something else: as systems (Gusfield 1975; Warren 1978); as types (Gusfield 1975; Simpson 1965; Bell and Newby 1974); as utopias (Gusfield 1975; Kanter 1972); as territory (Warren 1978; Poplin 1979); as organizations (Poplin 1979); as wholes and processes (Simpson 1965); as distributions of power (Warren 1978); and as microcosms (Bell and Newby 1974).

convey little about the multiple levels of community organization, the variability in community integration and interdependence, or the interplay between local and extralocal factors that create the environment in which a community develops and acquires (or loses) an identity (1974, p. 177).

Conrad Arensberg also suggests that "definitions are too shallow and too full of verbal traps" and ignore many complexities (1955, p. 1145). In a harsher tone, Bell and Newby argue that all sociologists have their own notion of what comprises a community, frequently reflecting their ideas of what it should be (1974, p. 27). Margaret Stacey goes one step further and says we do not even need the concept of community, but can look at what she calls "local systems" (1969).

How many definitions of community are there? How many phenomena can be called community? How many comparisons can be made with communities? These are not the right questions. As Hillery states, it does not make sense to look for the ninety-fifth definition; we do not wish, however, to eliminate the concept of community because of its broad usage.

This review of issues in defining community points out the complexity of the concept of community. Instead of asking whether community does or does not exist, we should approach the problem by asking whether this or that part of community is present and to what degree (Hunter 1974). The sociology of community may include a distinct body of knowledge, but shades off into unclear boundaries, which overlap with other sociological fields of study. Community as a concept has a definite center without a well-defined periphery. The core of the concept of community is around people interacting in specific space and time; but these dimensions vary and, in some extremes, blend into other sociological concepts.

Defining community appears less fruitful than tracing the theoretical underpinnings of the concept, which have selective, organizing principles, while still preserving the complexity of communities. Conceptions of community were important to the founding of sociology as a discipline. I discuss classical theories to provide background for the major theories presented in this book. The classical theories also reveal the initial controversies and ideas about communities.

CLASSICAL THEORIES OF SOCIAL CHANGE AND THE QUESTION OF COMMUNITY

Many theorists (for example, Nisbet 1966; Strasser 1976) link the development of sociology and the importance of the concepts of community to the French and Industrial Revolutions. These transformations made phenomena of community more noticeable by their disruption, but also less intelligible and, therefore, in need of explanation. The question of communities — their nature and continued existence — became a central issue that has since preoccupied many social observers and analysts. In reviewing history to understand the emergence of the concept of community, I paint an exaggerated before-and-after picture of the revolutions, which provides a setting for contrasting explanations.

Before-and-After Images of Revolutions

Before: Medieval Europe

Medieval Europe plays the "before" role. Prior to the mid 1700s, the majority of people lived in rural areas, with the exception of hereditary royalty who lived in walled castles and were attended by servants, knights, religious people, and craftspersons. Some nobility had their own country manors with servants. The larger population of peasants worked the fields in unspecialized labor, planting and harvesting, tending animals, and providing every aspect of their own livelihood. Whole families of women, men, and children worked side by side. People produced primarily for themselves, eking out a minimum surplus to trade for taxes, crafts, and religious favors. These families lived in the same place for several generations, with aunts, uncles, cousins, and grandparents all residing in proximity. The Catholic church and superstitions dominated beliefs, explanations, and education.

Two Great Changes

Into this primarily pastoral setting entered the Industrial and French Revolutions (between 1780 and 1850). Through a series of inventions, farm labor changed so that machines could do the labor of several people. Fertilizers, genetic engineering, and other techniques improved and increased crops, reducing the number of people required for agriculture. Those who no longer found employment began to move to cities, where they found jobs in the newly created factory system that had replaced craftspeople (such as weavers, cabinet makers, metalsmiths). Extended families became too large to move to where the work was. Families became divided as men worked in one factory, women in another, and children in yet another. Money and labor became the primary mode of exchange, as people no longer produced what they required.

Meanwhile, in France, another kind of revolution brewed, as peasants became dissatisfied with royalty and feudalism. They fought to install a democracy in which common people would vote for the ruler and share in decision making. Individualism developed, whereby people saw themselves as unique and separate rather than as part of a collectivity; equal opportunity and freedom increased the demand for literacy. In turn, rationality and secularism were fostered, as people returned to the scientific explanations of the Greek and Roman classics and built on them to create even more inventions. The role of the church was played down.

After the Revolutions

After the revolutions, by mid-nineteenth century, social life consisted basically of urban, large-scale societies organized into democratic nation-states, with individualistically oriented people working primarily in factories owned by capitaists. Private property and accumulation of surplus capital for investment and expansions became important. Scenes from Dickens's novels, with overcrowding, belching factories, and great poverty, complete the picture.

Explanations of Changes

Rational attempts to develop scientific explanations of the great changes divide into conservative and radical camps, according to Strasser (1976). Conservatives fear the changes and give explanations that idealize the past and the period before change. Radicals praise the changes and develop theories that promote further change. Both radicals and conservatives present ideal types of communities.

Ideal Types

Ideal types are not ideal in the sense of being best or perfect; rather, ideal types conceptualize the essential characteristics that all

share — like the "chairness" of Plato's forms. Classical theorists constructed models of ideal types primarily in terms of polar opposites —
communities of the past and communities of the present or future.
Ideal types represent attempts to explain the causes and consequences
of social change. Ideal types of communities became so important
because of fears that the changes had eliminated communities or
at least changed them beyond recognition.

Max Weber, Karl Marx, and Emile Durkheim are widely recognized
as the most significant founders of sociology whose works are still
read, cited, and tested. Toennies's (1887) ideal types of *Gemeinschaft* (community) and *Gesellschaft* (society) inspired the three
great theorists who elaborated his initial polar types. More recently,
the anthropologist Robert Redfield (1941) tested these polar types
in Mexico and found a continuum rather than dichotomies (Table 1.1).

Toennies: Gemeinschaft versus Gesellschaft (1887)

The German founder of community types, Toennies, developed the concepts of *Gemeinschaft* and *Gesellschaft* (1887), translated as community and society or association (1957) for the
before-and-after pictures of the great transformations. The *-schaft*
ending makes nouns out of the German words for "common"
and "social." Toennies analyzed social change, progressing from

TABLE 1.1
Classical Ideal Types of Communities

	Types	
Classical Theorist	*Before Transformations*	*After Transformations*
Toennies	*Gemeinschaft*	*Gesellschaft*
Weber	Traditional authority	Rational authority
Marx	Feudalistic peasant-noble	Capitalistic worker-owner
Durkheim	Mechanical solidarity	Organic solidarity

close communal ties to impersonal societal ties. The changes are based on differences in interpersonal relationships or orientations between people.

By *Gemeinschaft* Toennies meant that people had lasting, intimate connections; people helped, understood, and felt loving toward one another. *Gemeinschaft* seemed a nostalgia for an idealized old-fashioned town, village, or tribe. The importance of families and land brought people close in kinship, neighborhood, and friendship, the *Gemeinschaft* prototypes.

With industrialization, mobility, and large-scale society, *Gesellschaft* ties, the opposite of community, became prominent. People relate to one another in impersonal, cold, calculating ways, out to get whatever they can for themselves. People rationally weigh possibilities and seek ends beyond other people, with a sense of belonging to larger units like companies and nations, rather than just to families and neighborhoods. Bureaucrats fighting their way up corporate ladders, entrepreneurs vying for profits and goods, and contractual merchant-consumer ties exemplify *Gesellschaft*. *Gesellschaft* forces a formalization of relationships to counteract the chaos of self-seeking individuals; laws, rules, and bureaucracies, instead of traditions, morals, and customs, regulate relationships of *Gesellschaft*.

Toennies had in mind a contrast between rural villages (*Gemeinschaft*) and urban metropolitan centers (*Gesellschaft*). He also viewed his ideal types as extremes, with most of reality somewhere between the extremes.

Weber: Traditional versus Rational Authority (1905; 1922)

Another German, Max Weber, saw the essence of historical changes as increased rationality. Logical, orderly ways of thinking drew societies out of the dark ages of mysticism and superstition and thereby changed authority or legitimate power. Ways of thinking and beliefs influenced governmental and economic systems. In the past, people relied on a traditional authority, based on hereditary monarchies and ascendencies from sacred figures. With rational authority, codified laws and bureaucracies provided efficient ways of choosing leaders, as secularism provided a demystification of beliefs. Modern cities with markets, laws specifying weights and measurements as well as citizen responsibilities, and taxes exemplify the bureaucratic rationalism of the present and future. Weber influenced both conflict and social psychology approaches to community.

Marx: Feudalism versus Capitalism (1859; 1867)

Marx, a German radical, analyzed the development of capitalism in England. The mode of production changed, as did class relations — from peasant-nobility to worker (proletariat)-owner (bourgeois). The point of conflict changed from land as the means of production to the bourgeois control of commerce and industry. To benefit capitalism, workers, capital, and materials were brought together in one place, the city, from which spread markets that soon became worldwide. Products became defined as private property that could yield profits and for which individuals needed money. Marx saw ties among people not according to where they lived, but according to the nature of their work; that is, class ties more than community ties were a basis for belonging and for collective action. Marx initiated conflict theory.

Durkheim: Mechanical versus Organic Solidarity (1893)

Emile Durkheim, a French thinker, looked more at the division of labor, how work gets done and who does what, as societies evolved from small-scale communities to large-scale nation-states. Before the Industrial Revolution, work had a low level of differentiation, with most people laboring in similar ways. Each person engaged in a variety of tasks, working on whole products; for example, building a house and all its furnishings. People worked as self-sufficient, duplicated parts, which Durkheim called mechanical solidarity. Like parts of a machine, each doing work, people were held together by their similarity to one another.

Durkheim's other concept was organic solidarity, where, like the organs of a body, complementarity binds people. Population increase influences the division of labor or the degree of variety among what people do. Durkheim believed greater order ensued among larger populations when people specialized. Organic solidarity comes with a specialization in labor; individuals work on different aspects of a product rather than the whole. They depend on one another for various products, instead of meeting all their needs independently. One person grows grain, another produces flour, still another bakes, and yet another sells the bread. To eat bread, these four need one another and still other specialists for other needs. Society evolves from similarity among people to variety and interdependence. Durkheim is a major founding father of functionalism.

Redfield: The Folk-Urban Continuum (1941)

More recently, American anthropologist Robert Redfield carried out empirical studies of communities in Mexico. Rather than opposites between the old and the new, the rural and the urban, he found a continuum. In his studies in Yucatan he discovered several different types of communities between the heterogeneous city of Mérida and the smaller homogeneous villages of Mayan Indians. Smaller towns in between were less isolated than the villages, but not as cosmopolitan as Mérida. Redfield questioned the classical theorists' attempts to separate the past from the present in terms of rural and urban differences, and concluded that the difference between the polar types is filled with transitions of intermediary types, a gradual continuum rather than polar opposites.

To conclude this section on classical ideal types, we see that each theorist analyzed radical changes in communities. Continuing the theme of people and space derived from definitions of communities, we can see that classical theorists of community addressed issues of the spatial shifting of people over time, from rural to urban. They also questioned whether this shift entailed a loss of communities or created new communities.

Interest in communities, beginning in the 1800s with the studies of the great transformations, became strong because of the fear that communities were being lost, resulting in a kind of chaos. The loss occurred as rural communities gave way to urban life. Rural-urban differences and the question of whether communities continue and in what form continue to influence contemporary theorizing about communities. Inspired by classicists, I also offer a rural-urban comparison of empirical studies carried out to illustrate the theoretical points.

THEORETICAL COMPARISONS

Five theoretical frameworks form the core of the book (Chapters 3-7), which show different perspectives on community that are broader than definitions, yet also encompass and organize categories of definitions. These frameworks not only embody the major theories in sociology but also cover the majority of writings on American communities.

Issues in Sociological Theories

Sociological theories range from the grand to the mundane and sociologists debate how many theories there are, whether there are too few or too many, and whether they are theories at all. Sociological theories have not always generated hypotheses or propositions, but they do provide organizing principles that help explain various phenomena of community.

The five theories selected for more detailed analysis in subsequent chapters of this book — human ecology, structural functionalism, conflict theory, social-psychological approaches, and network-exchange analysis — are variously referred to as theoretical frameworks, perspectives, or paradigms. Each has its own set of differing assumptions, concepts, and metaphors that make it difficult to fit them together easily into one grand theory. Each chapter has been subtitled with a key word from the perspective: competition, consensus, contradictions, communication, and connections.

There are numerous ways of talking about the five perspectives. One way has been in terms of paradigms. Kuhn used the idea of paradigms, which were originally grammatical models, to describe the history of revolutions within science. He defines paradigms as "universally recognized scientific achievements that for a time provide model problems and solutions to a community of practioners" (1962, p. x). Sociologists have paid much attention to the paradigm idea and have debated over whether sociology can be considered to have paradigms, and if so, how many paradigms sociology has (Friedrichs 1970; Effrat 1973; Mullins 1973; Phillips 1975; Ritzer 1975).

Other phrases are also used to designate theoretical frameworks. One of these is school of thought. For example, one of the perspectives we consider, human ecology, is part of the Chicago school. The school-of-thought designation is more humanistic than scientific and connotes generations as well as groups of scholars, while paradigm is more scientific in its connotations. Ideologies (belief systems) or world views also describe the differences in perspectives. Regardless of what words are used to label different ways of thinking in sociology, most writers agree that sociology is pluralistic and that there is more than one paradigm or school of thought in sociology.

Just how many perspectives there are is a matter of dispute. I have arbitrarily delineated five theoretical frameworks which circumscribe most of the literature on communities. To some extent these overlap, but I emphasize their differences to show multiple ways of viewing communities. Each perspective has virtues as well as limitations, and none is considered primary. The order in which they are discussed is somewhat evolutionary within the discipline.

The paradigms represent different ways of looking at communities. They are like pairs of glasses, each of which has a different focus. Perhaps a more apt metaphor would be photography. The paradigms use different photographers, different film, different lenses, and different developing techniques and paper to present slightly different versions of communities. Paradigms are selective of reality, with variable conceptions of it. Sociologists construct their varied pictures of reality through their methods of data collection and their changing analytical perspectives for interpreting those data. A major purpose of this book is to delineate the five paradigms and their elements. Examples from two contrasting communities highlight the resulting differences in photographs from the five perspectives.

Five Theoretical Perspectives

What is the reason for choosing each of these theoretical frameworks? Why should competition, consensus, contradictions, communication, and connections all be parts of communities? Each framework has a tradition involving community studies.

In the United States, the study of communities had a strong impetus at the University of Chicago in the 1920s. Seeking a unique discipline, while at the same time taking the opportunity to study empirically the city of Chicago, Robert Park and his students developed human ecology. Comparing human communities to plant and animal communities, human ecologists borrowed from Darwinian thought to show the struggle and cooperation among groups to survive with limited resources. Different branches of human ecology evolved, but they all share an emphasis on the processes of cooperation and competition.

Another area of community studies relies upon one of the dominant theories in sociology, structural functionalism, which emphasizes communities as systems of institutions held together by shared values. Also borrowing from Darwin, structural functionalists applied evolution to the gradual growth and adaptation of communities from simple to more complex units. Another area of influence on the structural-functional approach to community are the British anthropologists' study of culture — the norms, values, morals, and folkways by which order governs collective life. A consensus or agreement about the components of culture functions to maintain social organizations, including communities.

Conflict theorists, in contrast, ask what pulls communities apart. They criticize the order and consensus of functionalism and investigate how political economic conditions create contradictions, pitting class segments against class segments in communities. Rather than competing for survival, groups conflict over the possession of property, status, and power. Powerful elites attempt to suppress class struggles through ideology, or when that fails, through the physical violence of the state. Communities often become battlegrounds with armed camps of contradictory forces.

The last two areas are newer and less well established, based more on a micro level then the first three theories. Nevertheless, studies in these fields are growing and are significant for the study of communities. The first of these includes social-psychological approaches that relate to the Chicago school, investigating social life within the ecological niches. The burgeoning of social-psychological studies in relation to communities is evidenced in new journals such as *Environment and Behavior.* A number of subtheories — predominantly symbolic interaction, phenomenology, and cognitive psychology — examine community symbols, attitudes, perceptions, and interaction patterns. These schools of social psychology emphasize especially the processes of communication, negotiation, and meeting of different minds, through which community is constructed. Communities consist of creative processes, which require direct experience of the researcher to interpret them.

Network-exchange analysis has blossomed even more than social-psychological approaches to community, though exchange theory is older. Network analysts see communities as crisscrossing ties among people, through which goods, feelings, and commands are passed in exchange. In situations of crisis, need, or power exercise, individuals activate connections for help. Exchange works contractually through the norm of reciprocity or distributive justice. Many of the network studies are of communities or have implications for communities: for example, by assessing the percentage of connections and exchanges that are local, network analysts can compare degrees of "communityness."

In each of the central chapters, these theories are delineated according to comparable elements. Five major elements and seven subelements show the variety in the theories. Metaphors, methods, and people, place, and time dimensions have all been chosen for their contribution to the study of community (see Table 1.2).

COMPARATIVE THEORETICAL ELEMENTS

The elements or theory parts show both how the frameworks are alike (by using each of the elements) and how the frameworks differ (each element used in varied ways). Metaphor and method pinpoint each theoretical overview, while the three dimensions — people, place, and time — help apply these theories specifically to the study of communities.

Metaphor

Metaphors seem inconsistent with scientific tenets of social science whose positivistic attitudes downplay superfluous language. Metaphors, similes, and other figures of speech are more often associated with poetry and beautiful art, yet metaphors have a long tradition in sociology. Many sociologists use them as heuristic devices to drive home meaning. Each metaphor provides symbolic and cognitive images as shorthand reminders of what community means by making the reader aware of phenomena in a new way. I use metaphors to mean two things — images and comparisons. I include metaphors in community paradigms to help readers to grasp their essential meanings.

Most models begin as metaphors, which then detail complex relations. Brown (1977), who explicates sociological "poetics," argues that an aesthetic view of sociology synthesizes and merges contradictions within the discipline. Many community studies and texts refer somewhat obliquely to comparisons, the similes and metaphors; I have only made them more explicit. Many sociologists, in attempts to emulate science, have created scientific metaphors, while others, more recently, have compared people in communities to dramas or games.

TABLE 1.2
Dimensions of Five Community Theories

	Human Ecology	Structural Functionalism	Conflict	Social-Psychological Approaches	Network-Exchange Analysis
Metaphor	Plant and animal communities	Organic and mechanical systems	War	Artistic creation; drama	Electronic connections; net
Methods	Surveys; census data and maps; statistical analysis to test relations among populations, organizations, technology	Participant observation; data on values and institutions; comparative analysis; demonstrate institutional integration; latent values	Historical documents, participant observation; data on income, housing, class composition; reconstruction of inequality, macro conflict	Participant observation, life histories, ethnography; data on perception, interaction, symbol use; reconstruction of typifications	Surveys and interviews; take a point and trace through links to test hypotheses about communities
People					
Institutions	Organization of subsistence activities; accommodations to populations and space	Integrated, based on consensus to hold communities together	Hierarchies dominated by political economy	Reciprocal typifications	Specialized networks
Stratification	Dominance	Reward systems	Class and power	Identification of self; various rankings	Unequal exchange; coalitions, distributive justice

TABLE 1.2, continued

	Human Ecology	Structural Functionalism	Conflict	Social-Psychological Approaches	Network-Exchange Analysis
Interaction	Mediated through environment	Roles	Exploitation, alienation, ideology	Face to face; validation and creation of community; negotiation	Form and content
Time					
History	Cycles of competition and succession; evolution of technological change	Evolution, adaptation	Revolutions; changes in mode of production	Reconstructed biography	Build up of reciprocity
Process	Shifts in populations through space	Equilibrium	Dialectics	Cognition; conversation	Activation of network exchange
Space					
Territory	Zones and natural areas; resource	Localization of systems	Scarce resource for profits	Tool of community construction	Liberated from
Boundaries	Physical restriction of movement; maintenance limits of subsistence organization	Boundary maintenance	Political; point of conflict	Changing with situations	Set by analysis; extent of links; boundless

Methods

Metaphors provide overviews of theories, suggesting what questions to ask, how to answer them, and how to make sense of the answers. Questions, techniques of data collection, and analysis comprise the methodology of each framework. A statement of a problem is necessary for beginning a research endeavor, but without some perspective in the area, stating a problem becomes difficult. Many data-collecting techniques are available to sociologists — observation, interviewing, questionaires, use of documents, and experimentation. Community researchers tend to be eclectic and draw from many techniques, although one or two often come to be associated with particular theories. With analysis, or making sense of the data, researchers return to the metaphor and present results representing particular world views.

While metaphors give world views from each perspective and methods raise questions and suggest answers from the overview, each theory also has a number of dimensions that vary. Recall the initial suggested definition of people interacting in a specific time and place, which was inspired by Effrat's suggestion that community is a multidimensional, ordinal variable. She means that community is a changing phenomenon consisting of several parts that vary by degrees — more or less rather than either/or (1974). Combining the definition with Effrat's insight, we consider three dimensions along which community varies by degrees. These three dimensions are common to all the definitions of community. They suggest what to look for in communities and they also represent continua that indicate the ranges of communities. The extent to which each of these dimensions is present in communities depends both on the theory and the empirical setting.

People

Something about people is indigenous to all definitions of community; without people communities do not exist. This is obvious. People must be part of any sociological phenomenon, but people can also involve variables that change along continua. Different ideas about people separate one theory from another and also distinguish the community concept from other sociological concepts. The people dimension is complex and is not considered in its entirety either in the study of community or by any one of the theories. Subcomponents of the people dimension most common to the study of community include institutions, stratification, and interactions. Three aspects of people consistently appear in community studies, though with great variety in what role they play and to what extent they are emphasized.

In general, community is a middle-sized concept, with respect to the numbers and heterogeneity of people, for most community theorists (but not all). Larger than families or small groups, communities are also smaller than regions or nation-states. Similarly with heterogeneity, communities seem to need a minimum of diversity — usually gender and age differences. Using the village or vill as the ideal type of community, Hillery (1968) argues that, as a minimum, communities require families, multiple generations, and multiple genders. This heterogeneity distinguishes communities from total institutions (prisons, mental hospitals, monasteries, boarding schools, and the like) whose homogeneity precludes their being communities. Too little homogeneity or too much size could also outreach a sense of community. Communities will differ by size and heterogeneity empirically; for example, an urban community is unlike a rural community.

Empirically, communities vary by the degree to which local institutions are present, just as the theories change by how much they emphasize institutions. Most theorists seem to agree on the functionalists' definition of institutions as organizations to meet collective needs, but while integrated local institutions are most important for functionalists, only selected institutions or parts of institutions are considered by other perspectives.

The heterogeneity, or differences among people, promotes some ranking of the differences, which vary as communities range empirically from egalitarian to hierarchical. While conflict theorists criticize stratification, it is also the most important part of communities to them, because it promotes contradictions and changes. Definitions, causes, and interpretations of stratification in relation to other community phenomena depend on particular theories.

Ideas about institutions and stratification are applied to more macro-level, large-scale social processes in communities, but people also interact. Community interactions are emphasized by some theorists, downplayed by others; nonetheless, each theorist has some idea about community interactions, which are defined as mutual influence of persons. For example, social psychologists see interactions as the crucial building blocks of communities. A gamut of interactions are found in communities, but which interactions are seen as community interactions is a theoretical question.

Space

Space is central for many ideas of community. In fact, many definitions of community emphasize that it is the combination of people and space that distinguishes community. More than 70 percent of the definitions Hillery found in 1955 included a physical area as essential to community. Localism is important in that many activities go on in or are at least oriented to a given space. Further, this space is confined, so that the issue of boundaries is tied directly to a concern with space. Territory and boundaries comprise the subdimensions of the spatial dimension.

Hillery refers to localization as "the quality of being located in only one place outside of which the system has no identity" (1968, p. 65). Community as a concept is distinct from other concepts, except perhaps that of nation-state, in that it is difficult to think of a community as the same if it is moved to another location. For example, Erickson describes how the Puritans in Massachusetts became decidedly different from the Puritans of England (1966).

At one end of the spatial pole are communities in which space is central and boundaries are fixed and defined. An example is the medieval walled city. Sjoberg analyzes the preindustrial city as distinct from the modern city in its spatial layout — particularly in the walled boundaries (1960). While the walled city has the most defined boundaries, Hillery (1968) cites both cities and villages as having vague boundaries, and Suttles notes that many rural areas stretch out indefinitely with almost nonexistent boundaries (1972, p. 29).

In the other direction of the spatial pole, some authors such as Webber (1963) and Tilly (1974) argue that people do not need to live near one another to form close ties. The concept of network is used to liberate interpersonal ties from proximity, as will be discussed in Chapter 7.

Time

Time is less often considered as a specific component of communities. There are no time references in Hillery's compilation of definitions (1955). He also points out that his theory of the village is ahistorical (1968). In community texts, history and other time dimensions such as process are less often mentioned. Nevertheless, time is implicit in what communities are: communities last. How long they last and the minimal time requirement of a community are empirical questions. Some communities (like Pueblo villages) have lasted longer than nations and most usually last longer than collective movements. Some of the communes of the 1960s, however, were short-lived (a few years), but were nevertheless communities.

Most community studies include some history. History can be considered in many ways — as evolutionary states, as cycles, or as dialectical processes. In addition to these broad historical changes, one can also look at time on a shorter span and analyze people's routine, day-to-day activities. The subdimensions of time include history and process.

Communities vary from long-lived to short-lived. People may live in a place all their lives, even for generations, or people may be geographically mobile out of communities. Communities seem to be able to last indefinitely when generation after generation of the same families live in the same place, but community fades off in the short-lived direction to concepts of collective behavior when people are together for only a short period, such as crowds.

Community theories with comparable dimensions form the main focus of this book, but as indicated in the above discussion, communities vary not only theoretically but also empirically. To enliven as well as apply the theories, I conducted two community case studies that illustrate the theories.

COMPARATIVE CASE STUDIES

Two particular U.S. communities were studied to illustrate and ground the theories: one a small agricultural area on the Wisconsin-Illinois border, called Zenda,* and the other a cosmopolitan urban

---

*Throughout the book, the term Zenda is used to refer both to the village and the surrounding farms.

neighborhood, Lincoln Park, in the heart of the nation's second largest city, Chicago. Representative of types rather than a statistical sampling, these two communities were selected purposely in order to address theoretical issues about the characteristics of communities in modern America. The two communities represent extremes within a single metropolitan area and also reflect the extremes of the polar concepts of community described by the classical theorists.

The communities are located in the Midwest — the place of the geographical and population centers of the United States — and in the Chicago metropolitan area, the seat of many community studies. The University of Chicago school of community studies originally designated Lincoln Park as a community, along with 74 other communities in Chicago, based on the criteria that it had its own history, name, and distinctive boundaries (Wirth and Bernet 1949). The further benefit of studying both a rural and an urban community in the same area is that their connection and interpenetration are visible and metropolitan changes can be examined in both communities. The aspect of interdependence becomes more important to some theories than others.

A further rationale for the choice of these two communities is that each place illustrates changes that characterize communities of the 1980s. The rural area, Zenda, is experiencing an influx of new, formerly urban residents who reside year around. Increase in non-farming rural populations is one of the most rapidly growing areas, according to recent census takers. The urban area, Lincoln Park, exhibits gentrification, a process whereby wealthier residents move into former slum areas to restore historic buildings and replace poorer populations.

Rural and urban communities also represent distinctive problems related to the polar types suggested by classical theorists. Rural communities like the preindustrial medieval cities seem to be out of date, on the periphery of modern life, and threatened to extinction by the forces of industrialization and urbanization. In Zenda empty stores and abandoned buildings abound.

On the other hand, it is questionable whether the large size and heterogeneity in urban settings permits a sense of belonging, a way of knowing neighbors, a community at all. In Lincoln Park such a variety of activities with so many people coming and going makes community questionable.

Lincoln Park and Zenda show us different people and different space at similar times, though with varying histories and processes. A comparison and contrast of these two can highlight many questions about communities, framed in theoretical perspectives, which in addition to increasing knowledge about these concrete cases, will allow generalizations to other communities and to the abstract concept of community. The combination of two important aspects of sociology — theoretical development and empirical research — provides an extensive exploration of the topic of community.

BOOK PLAN

Chapter 2 gives a background of the setting of the two empirical case studies. Using the format of most community studies, which gives a description and history, I describe the physical settings as they may appear to an outsider and present histories from local books and oral reports. This chapter provides a background for examples used in subsequent chapters. Some of the examples are elaborations of descriptions from Chapter 2 and others are new, but assume a knowledge of the background material.*

Chapters 3-7 detail the five major theories introduced in this chapter. The order in which the theories are arranged is based on both chronology and a progression from larger to smaller units. In most respects, human ecology is the older approach to U.S. communities, while network analysis represents the vanguard of current and future studies in relation to communities. The chapters proceed from the subsocial, almost biologic study of communities by human ecologists to the macro processes discussed by functionalists and conflict theorists, ending with the more individual person-based studies conducted by social psychologists and network-exchange analysts.

Chapter 8 addresses issues of comparison and synthesis among the theories and concludes by considering how the theories are applicable to practitioners in applied community fields.

---

*Some readers may not need the background information and can skip Chapter 2, or refer back to Chapter 2, only in connection with reading the examples.

2

The Rural and Urban Case Studies

This chapter offers a tour of Zenda and Lincoln Park in a naive, nonsociological way with no need for note taking. The travelogues and histories give initial impressions — primarily visual — of the two places. Later references to Zenda and Lincoln Park assume a knowledge of the details presented in this chapter. Like travelers visiting a place for the first time, readers will make use of maps and notice roads, buildings, and land use. Meeting natives and getting to know local inhabitants takes longer, so descriptions of people have been kept to a minimum. Like dramatic settings, the portrayals of the localities present what is seen and set the background against which community actions play the scenes according to different theories.

The descriptions and histories are raw data, some of them necessary for understanding the examples used in subsequent chapters. Other raw data are given in the tables in Appendix A. Just as Chapter 1 argued for theory use instead of definitions, this chapter more subtly argues the need for theories. The rest of the book indicates how to make sense of the two places, how to probe deeper and piece the parts together sociologically.

ZENDA

Lincoln Park and Zenda are located in the midwestern states of Illinois and Wisconsin, with Lincoln Park, a part of the city of Chicago on Lake Michigan, about 80 miles southeast of the rural area of Zenda (Figure 2.1). Zenda is an unincorporated village in Linn Township, Walworth County, Wisconsin, less than one mile north of the Illinois-Wisconsin border (Figure 2.2). The community of the village and surrounding farms is an area about seven miles wide and four miles long. Approximately five families just south of the state line in Illinois (McHenry County) and another five families east and west of the township consider themselves part of the Zenda community. Though Linn Township extends farther north, the northern boundary of the community ends almost at Lake Geneva, an oblong glacial lake extending east and west seven miles (Figure 2.3). Urbanites from Chicago have summer homes there; the denser housing of the lake area distinguishes the Zenda community. Figure 2.4 indicates the locations and populations of nearby towns frequented by Zenda residents.

Travelers in the Zenda area use Route 47 in Illinois from the south and Route 120 in Wisconsin from the north. Travelers and Sunday drivers viewing the lake scarcely notice the existence of the little village a few miles east of the major highway and south of the lake; little evidence shows a passerby that the farms form a community.

The Zenda area appears as a pastoral setting that rolls along gently sloped hills and gradually drops to Lake Geneva to the north. Oaks and maples cling to fence lines and lawns, and occasionally whole woods have been left surrounded by extensive fields. Vistas spread to far horizons, and for miles open fields, trees, and houses can be seen in the blue distance. The land, black and water-soaked in the spring, with some of the most fertile soil in the nation, is soon green with alfalfa, oats, soybeans, and corn, which quiltlike become distinguished textures and colors of gold, green, and brown into the summer and fall. In winter the high snowdrifts and stinging winds desolate and homogenize the entire landscape.

The sounds of Zenda — mooing cows, noisy tractors and machinery, a whistling train passing through — interrupt the peace otherwise punctuated only with breezes, bird calls, and the loud, cracking thunder of summer storms. Daily sirens in Hebron and Zenda announce noon. The sweet smell of clover, garden flowers,

FIGURE 2.1
Location of Study Area

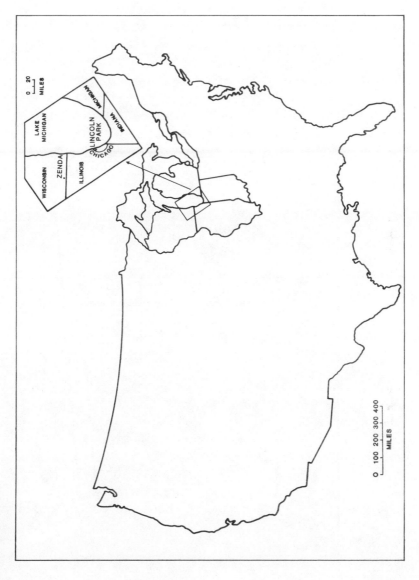

27

FIGURE 2.2
The Village of Zenda

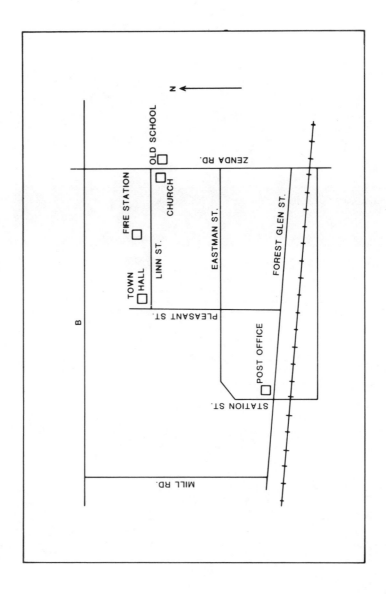

28

FIGURE 2.3
Linn Township

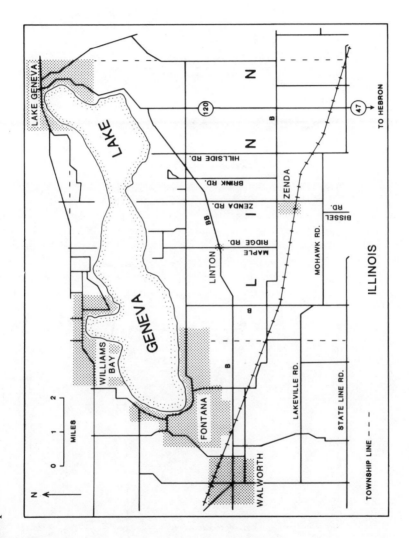

29

FIGURE 2.4
Zenda and Vicinity

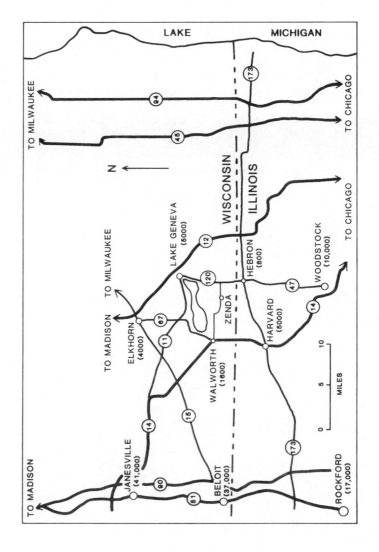

newly mowed grass and hay, and the refreshment of an overnight rain fill the spring and summer months, in contrast to the manure spread on the fields and the fermenting silage in the fall. The boat factory in Zenda discharges a pungent, gluelike smell of fiberglass, and occasionally the slaughterhouse in Hebron emits its odor of rotting meat.

Farms average 200 acres and neighbors are about three-fourths of a mile apart. Here and there the black and white of grazing Holstein cows accent the setting and, more rarely, pigs and sheep and an occasional horse may also be seen. The mammoth pillars of silos dwarf the barns, sheds, and garages of white or red that stand near the stately two-story white frame houses of the nineteenth century, some with one or even a series of additions. Often a new, single-story, ranch-style house stands among the well-tended lawns and gardens. Even more of the new houses are appearing in the wooded areas, and near the lake they dominate the land use.

Often ornately carved doors and woodwork adorn the insides of the houses, which are now carpeted and filled with stuffed chairs and antiques that have been passed down through the generations — an occasional old carved bedstead or a victorian table. Albums, old photographs, dishes, silverware, and knickknacks constitute cherished family heirlooms.

To the south, on a hill surrounded by farms, stands a cemetery with a wrought-iron gate and low, unassuming gravestones, many dating back to the early 1800s. Toward the back of the lawn, the remains of the old foundation of the church poke out of the grassless pockets. In the summer some of the graves bloom with carefully tended flowers, others with artificial bouquets and wreaths. The cemetery population is gradually spreading forward to the gate.

Local persons traveling over the tarred roads by tractor, truck, or slowly moving cars, see everything familiar and can tell something about the current status and history of each of the farms as a result of living there all their lives, going to school with each other, and occasionally seeing each other at the store or community organization meetings. In addition, many of the people are related to one another.

Wandering around the roads that connect people who have known each other all their lives eventually leads to an unincorporated village along Zenda Road, which runs north and south, with the Milwaukee Road Railroad running east and west. An old white church stands in the center, simple in its low, uncrossed steeple, and across the street an old red-brick school house forms the foreground for a small concentration of houses, old and new. Signs and emptiness reveal that these no longer function as a church and school and that other buildings in the village are unused or used for something other than their original purpose. A boat company and another factory have taken over.

A bumpy entrance over the railroad greets the traveler approaching the village from the south. A field, a tavern, the boat company, and the red-brick, three-room school house line the eastern edge of Zenda Road, which is backed by fields.

Next to the railroad to the west in an old, now empty store, the owners since the 1940s still live upstairs. Part of the boat company operates out of the former gas station. A lumber company, grain storage bins, and a cement-block factory whose products have created the tavern and another building, also flank the railway. At the farthest western end (three blocks from Zenda Road), along the railway, is a feed mill that used to be the dairy. The post office is located across the street from the railroad in the front room of the postmistress's house; her husband keeps chickens in the back.

Two streets lined with houses parallel Zenda Road to the west. The westernmost north-south street was constructed most recently (1960s) for houses owned by relatives of Zenda residents, all of whom came in the last few years from Chicago suburbs and bought the implement garage to the north of the village to establish a shutter factory.

The road between Mill Road and Zenda Road also consists primarily of houses, although the grocery store, still thriving until 1981, is found on this street, as well as a deserted garage and a blacksmith shop, an in-use bowling alley, and the town hall. The 40 houses in the village of Zenda cover three-fourths of a square mile. Right in the village there are farms and the farmland soon takes over the scene beyond.

History

Anecdotes and stories abound about the history of Zenda — Native Americans, early settlers, and origination of organizations. These data will later illustrate theoretical points.

The territory around Zenda opened to settlers as a result of the Blackhawk War, when soldiers removed Chief Big Foot and his 500 Pottawatamie Indians who had succeeded the Mound Dwellers around Lake Geneva (see the chronology shown in Table 2.1). Tearfully they went to Kansas, even though they had not fought in the war. The Pottawatamies' settlement was actually on the lake, but remainders of their arrowheads and trails on farms indicate that the Zenda area was also a home for them. Some Zenda area residents mentioned that their ancestors had Indians work for them. The last Indian in Linn, a graduate of Carlysle School in Pennsylvania, came to Linn as a blacksmith, but he took to drink and shot himself.

Soldiers and explorers publicized the fertility and beauty of the Zenda area. Juliette Kinzie, one of the first pioneers of Chicago, passed Lake Geneva with her husband in the fall of 1832 on their way to a northern fort. She left an account of the journey in her story entitled "Waubun," in which she described the scenery about Lake Geneva. She was probably the first white woman who ever visited the area and her party was the first of the white race known to have viewed the land.

Early Settlers

Subsequently, white settlers came from eastern United States, England, and Germany by wagons or through the Great Lakes, looking for a place to farm. The very first settlers came in 1836 and settled at Lake Geneva. Those who followed also looked for water and found it in springs. Like true pioneers, the early settlers arrived in covered wagons, or in boats on Lake Michigan from which they walked, carrying all they could. They usually came as families, whose first tasks were providing a place to live and clearing the land. Some early settlers fought over land claims, but many also helped one another because of the scarcity of facilities. The early records of Linn show that there were disputes over putting up fences between farms and also over the business of putting in roads and negotiating for land.

Sarah McBride, who came with her family in a covered wagon from Ohio, accompanied by a cow, described her feelings:

> We came through Chicago which was but a small village and very swampy all around it so we moved on til we came to what is now

Zenda Area Farm with
Lake in Distance

Northeast View toward
the Village of Zenda

Zenda Train Stop and
Lumber Company

Looking North down Zenda Road: Tavern and Boat Company

Linn-Hebron Cemetery: Original Site of Church

Grocery Store in Zenda (now closed)

TABLE 2.1
Chronology of Zenda Area

Dates	Events
1832	Explorers — Kinzie party
1832-34	Blackhawk War — removal of Pottawatamies
1836	First settlers
1838	Walworth County established
1844	Linn Township established
1844	Presbyterian church started
1861	Founding of Hebron
1867	Presbyterian church built at cemetery
1870-1920	Chicago entrepreneurs building along lake
1874	Yacht Club founded
1895	Country Club founded
1901	Railroad and beginning of Zenda village
1906	Gravel pit opened
1908-10	Town band
1910	Zenda School built
1911	Thimble Club and Neighborly Club organized
1913	Farmers' Club organized
1914	First fair
1914	Town Hall built
1916	4-H officially chartered
1922	Church building moved to village
1934	Feed mill established
1937	Garden Club organized
1945	Boat company founded
1946	Homemakers organized
1947	Bridge Club organized
1948	Fire
1950	Volunteer Fire Fighters organized
1950	Bowling alley built and leagues started
1965	Zenda school closed, bought by boat company
1966	Firehouse built
1967	Shutters factory started
1977	Presbyterian church moved to new building
1981	Grocery store closed
1982	Bowling alley closed

the town of Linn, Wisconsin, where we arrived June 4, 1836. Father said he was going to stop where he found good water and there he found excellent springs. (from Sarah McBride's essay 1890)

The McBrides, who were probably typical of the early settlers, first built a shanty out of bark peeled from trees until they could get their tools, which had been shipped to Milwaukee. After living in the shanty one month, they asked people as far as ten miles away to help them build their log cabin. Sarah describes the building:

Father made the shingles and floor and the door out of split logs, hewn with a broad ax, and we had no furniture, not even a chair, so he made some stools and a table, and bored auger holes in the side of the house and inserted poles for the sides and ends of a bedstead, and we thought it quite an improvement over the shanty (1980).

Sarah McBride further describes their troubles with mosquitoes and wolves. Later settlers stayed with established farmers while they built houses and cleared fields.

People depended on Chicago and other port cities for importing goods, for mail, and for items they could not make themselves. Much of the lumber for the first frame houses was pulled by ox teams from eastern United States.

In the 1840s and 1850s many more settlers came from eastern United States, England, Germany, and Ireland, many of whose families have remained on the land today. Soon, every few miles a creamery, a post office, and a blacksmith shop served local neighbors. The only one of these small commercial centers that remains, Linton, with a restaurant and about five houses, one mile northwest of Zenda village, got its nickname of Slopville from the creamery there, which drained the whey into a low place. Several one-room schools came into existence at this time also, though none of them were attached to commercial areas.

The earliest organization to form, the Presbyterian church, brought people together. Before a church building could be erected, parishioners met in homes and often in a school house. In those days the church served as a court for misdemeanors, with excommunication the punishment. According to one local historian (Thatcher n.d.), "At that time, this discipline was quite effective as the church was at the head of social life, and if a person was left out of that, they were isolated." The church building was first located at the

Linn-Hebron cemetery in Hebron Township, Illinois. Many people had been buried there before settlers came, as early travelers passed along an old territorial highway near there.

Lake Area

Several decades after these earliest settlements in Zenda, the Chicago fire occurred. This historic event affected Zenda because many entrepreneurs gained wealth in Chicago after the fire and decided to build summer homes along Lake Geneva. Before their homes were built, they often stayed at Kaye's Park. Located where a military academy now is, it was one of the best resorts in the Midwest from 1873 to 1901, and famous for its maple sugar and ice cream. During the period from 1870 to 1920 great estates were built along the lake, and a yacht club and a country club were established.

The country club has the second oldest golf course in the Midwest, with an exclusive 200-person membership descended from the original Chicago summer residents. The wealthy Chicagoans used to sail their yachts to catch the train known as the "Millionaire Special" from Fontana, a lakeside village at the western end of the lake. On the way home they would wager on whose yacht would reach the country club first. A 90-year-old former Zenda resident remembered working for one of the estates, which owned a great many horses and employed almost 20 servants.

Village Founding

By 1900 the farms of Zenda had all been established, the land cleared, and the people well settled. As mentioned, there were little, scattered commercial centers, with bigger ones in Hebron and Lake Geneva because of their railroad connections; in addition, people were socializing in the Presbyterian church. A big change occurred in 1901 with the coming of the railroad. The Palmer family, who had a farm and creamery in Zenda, petitioned the railroad to make a permanent stop. Everybody contributed money to help build the depot. They planned to name the village Golf, but discovered that a Golf, Wisconsin, already existed. The railroad president's daughter was reading *A Prisoner of Zenda*, and she named the village Zenda.

Some say a few houses were already in the village before the railroad came, the oldest of which was rumored to be a hunter's cabin, but the big boom came with the railroad. An enterprising young man from a neighboring county, who had promised his father he would help him farm only until he was 21 years old, started the first store in the village. According to his 90-year-old widow, the store had "everything from a needle to a thrashing machine." His wife, father, and sister joined him, and the post office became a part of that store.

Another entrepreneur from Hebron started a grocery store in Zenda and also bought the lumber from some of the old creameries to build houses there. This son later built the barber shop and tavern.

The railway acted as a magnet to attract the small commercial centers. A large creamery built at the railroad led to the closing of the other creameries and their small commercial centers, some of which literally moved to the village. The blacksmith from Bissel, one of the commercial centers, moved to Zenda, and the store owner at Bissel built a garage in the village. A lumberyard, mill, implement store, and hardware store all quickly opened. Later the first store owner built a drug store and recruited a doctor, but the doctor left in World War I, and the village had its first abandoned building, which, except for the upstairs apartment, stood empty until 1972.

In 1910 a three-room school in the village consolidated two other districts and closed down the one-room school houses. Some women had started a Sunday School in the village and they became active in raising funds to physically move the church from the cemetery to the village. The church building was hauled on logs pulled by horses. The ministers of the church were seminary students from Chicago.

Organizations

Residents organized a number of voluntary associations. These began with women instituting ways of overcoming their isolation with socializing and sewing. Inspired by women, children formed a 4-H club and men the Farmers' Club. The Farmers' Club, in turn, built a town hall in the village, which centralized activities of the organizations and the town government and also provided entertainment for the area. An annual fair was and continues to be the prime such activity. Chautauqua (programs of lectures and concerts) visited the town hall regularly. A village band played in the hall between 1908 and 1910, and the YMCA met there and played basketball. In addition, the town hall was used for dances, private parties, and weddings. In another form of early entertainment farmers held dances in their unfinished barns and thereby earned money to complete the barns. During this time the village seemed to serve all the needs of everyone around, and in any case it was difficult to go very far away. The merchants resided in the village, where they could sell to the farmers and also take the farmers' products and ship them to Chicago.

The Zenda Feed Company located in the old Zenda creamery. The owning family had a feed company in a nearby town and the local people of Zenda asked the feed mill to locate there in 1934. All six employees in 1976 were from Zenda and they supplied people within about 25 miles. The feed company will also buy and/ or ship local grain by rail.

The police department of Linn Township started in the 1940s at the request of the lake-shore people for property protection. Originally a one-person department operating out of the chief's home in Lake Geneva for 25 years, it is now housed in the village with three full-time police officers and three part-timers. In 1976 the police chief indicated that the wealth of the area, the sparse population, and few taverns with teenage hang-outs minimize the problems in the Zenda area.

Changes in the Village

While the railroad brought a focus and consolidation around the village, the post-World War II improvement in cars and roads and the influx of supermarkets and other chain stores contributed a change. Starting in the late 1940s and early 1950s, a different trend appeared. The major highways did not pass through the village and the chain stores located in the larger towns like Lake Geneva. Instead of coalescing because of the railroad, the improved transportation led to a dispersal. The blacksmith shop had become a lawn-mower and repair shop and then moved to a busy highway. Farmers no longer shipped milk by train — trucks picked up milk at individual farms. The hardware store, implement store, and general store all gradually went out of business. A combination ice cream parlor and pool hall burned and was not rebuilt.

In 1948 a huge fire in Zenda and the delay of the truck from Lake Geneva (maintained there by the township since 1937) resulted in much property damage. The people who lost their property in the fire and others decided that local equipment and people were needed to prevent such damage in the future, so they formed a volunteer fire-fighting unit and petitioned the town board to provide the equipment. A local historian (Kromwall n.d.) described subsequent additions:

> In February 1950 the department took delivery of its first truck which served as the only piece of equipment until 1965 when the department again received a new truck, a 500 gallon per minute tanker. In 1968 through efforts of some private citizens and especially the Farmers' Club, another water tanker was added. The first house was erected in 1966, the first year after receiving the new pumper. This building has enough space to house four trucks. In 1972, feeling the need for more water at large fires, a new 2,200 gallon tank truck was purchased.

The 25 volunteer fire fighters meet twice a month to practice drills and hold business meetings. They recently acquired plectrons (radio signals), so that they are alerted directly to fires instead of waiting to hear the whistles.

In 1965 the three-room school house closed and students were bused to one of two expanded rural schools near the lake — Reek and Traver — which had a teacher for each grade. These two elementary schools, which were formerly one-room schools, now serve the entire township. One is located two miles northeast of the village and the other two miles northwest. Their location near the lake reflects the growing population in that area.

Non-Presbyterian Protestants left the church to seek out their own sects and people went farther away to shop and sell. People who worked elsewhere began to live in Zenda. Some who live in the area may have no reason to go to the village. Many businesses have closed down or moved out.

A boat company was founded in the village in 1945 and was the first (and now the largest) light industry to locate there. It took over some abandoned garages and other vacated buildings. The boat company employed 55 people in 1976 and had its own fiberglass and sails divisions. While they sold only about 10 boats on Lake Geneva yearly, they sold 250 nationwide and their sails were sold internationally. The present owner, who lives by the lake and is the son of the founder, attained international fame sailing in the Olympics.

Other factories lasting only a couple of years have come and gone in Zenda; there was once a pickle factory, another that made hula hoops, and a bird-feeder factory. A shutters and aluminum-siding company was started in 1967 by a family who preferred to live in their summer home the whole year. The business had been located in the suburb, but seeing the old abandoned buildings in the village encouraged them to locate there. They brought several relatives with them, who built a row of houses on the west side of the village. Of their 11 employees, only 2 are from Zenda and sales are not local.

The post-World War II change in the village was also a time for more organizations to be formed. A bowling alley was built and suddenly everyone was involved with leagues, although few had bowled before. A garden club, a homemakers' club, and a three-table bridge club also started then, all of which were continuing to flourish in 1982.

In 1976 the Presbyterian church built a new edifice on a highway, greatly expanding its base for attracting parishioners, since it is the only Presbyterian church in the county. An independent Congregational group of people from Lake Geneva met in an old rural school house.

The number of trains passing through Zenda has greatly diminished, though in 1982 a daily commuter still traveled to Chicago. Since train services in Hebron and Lake Geneva terminated, the Zenda train attracted a few people who live by the lake and work in Chicago.

Not only did the village once serve most of the needs of the local people, it also served only those people, in a way shutting them off from others. Today Zenda no longer serves many needs, and in fact there are people who live in Zenda, but use none of the remaining facilities. Everyone has to use other towns (and which towns are used depends on the person and the circumstances). In addition, many strangers are in Zenda every day, as more people move into the area.

In 1976 slight economic and population shifts were apparent. A significant number of farmers were selling their dairy herds and going into cash crops. Reasons cited for this included the lucrative return on cash crops without the need for daily attention to dairy cows. With cash crops and big investments in machinery, fewer people can do more farming, and an examination of plat books (maps indicating ownership of farms) over the years shows more land owned by fewer families. Occasionally, abandoned barns and houses are seen, but more often, new houses are on farms because of a growing influx of people living in the country but not farming.

The history of Zenda, then, has been one of decentralization, centralization, decentralization. The original settlers were scattered, with no focus, while the railroad and village served as a magnet to commercial interests. Improved transportation and chain stores then led to a change in the village, from serving locals to being a tiny industrial-residential area. In spite of these changes a core of central families (about 40), whose ancestors go back to the mid 1800s in Zenda, stabilizes the place.

LINCOLN PARK

The commuter train from Zenda leaves a little after seven A.M. By then, farmers have been at work for a couple of hours and are just finishing milking or getting their tractors ready to go to the fields. Many cars are parked at the boat company in the village, indicating that work has started there also. In contrast, a small group of cars huddle at the railroad tracks across from the post office, and inside them business women and men sip coffee as they try to wake up. The train comes, barely stops, and is quickly racing along to the city, picking up more commuters who read newspapers, play cards, or doze. The train passes through fields, past bushes, marshes, and near lakes. Soon more houses and subdivisions appear and the open spaces diminish. More people get on at each stop closer to the city. It does not take long for the city life to appear, with car lots, back doors of factories and stores, and lumberyards in sight of the train. After an hour and a half, the train briefly goes underground to arrive in the city. The passengers exit through a damp, basement-like corridor, like a pack of rats rushing through the sewers of Chicago.

Outside Union Station, buses and sidewalks lead to the Loop which is the center of the city, but which is also the name of the curve of the elevated train track. Skyscrapers like the Sears Tower — the tallest of them — the flared bottom of the Harris Bank building, the ornate facade of Carson, Pirie, Scott, help form the multi-architectural city. Chicagoans walk down into the bowels of the city from

State Street or climb up to the elevated trains at LaSalle Street. From either a north-bound train leads to Lincoln Park.

The Chicago el (elevated) trains are predominantly old contraptions with worn, dark green seats and chrome handles, much graffiti on the walls, and the sweat and dirt of thousands of people. Loud and noisy, they bump and rock passengers above or beneath the city.

Lincoln Park occupies an area of approximately two square miles (Figure 2.5), with its southern boundary, North Avenue, 1,600 blocks (two miles) from the central business district, and its northern boundary, Diversey Parkway, three and one-half miles (2,800 blocks) north of the center of the city. Fullerton and Armitage are the other major east-west streets. The Lincoln Park district is almost trapezoidal in shape, narrower on the southern side — about one and one-third miles wide on the south and two miles wide on the north. In general, Lakewood and Clybourne Avenues near the industrial areas by the Chicago River form the western boundary and Lake Michigan the eastern. Halstead is the major north-south street. The streets have a grid pattern, with the exception of two major diagonal streets — Clark and Lincoln — which form a few wedge-shaped blocks (Figure 2.6). Seven named neighborhoods comprise Lincoln Park (Figure 2.7).

The major el stop for Lincoln Park at Fullerton Avenue is in some ways the center of Lincoln Park. The panorama from the Fullerton el station, above the convergence of Lincoln Avenue and Fullerton and Halstead Streets, gives an overview: the mansions of three-story ornate Queen-Anne-style houses, a run-down wooden frame Chicago cottage, DePaul University, Children's Memorial Hospital, the Aetna Bank, Lincoln Park Library, and, a few blocks toward Lake Michigan, the office of the Lincoln Park Conservation Association. White-uniformed hospital workers exit from the el trains on their way to work. Across the street is an A&P store and a factory being converted to condominiums.

The initial impression of Lincoln Park (in 1981) is the bustle of building activity, not so much creating new buildings as remodeling old ones. In almost every block sand blasting, landscaping, or gutting of buildings changes them into upper middle class houses or condominiums. Even the hospitals are being painted and remodeled, and DePaul University workers add new entryways and sidewalks. Dominant in all this activity is the "condominium touch," which

FIGURE 2.5
Chicago and Lincoln Park in Chicago

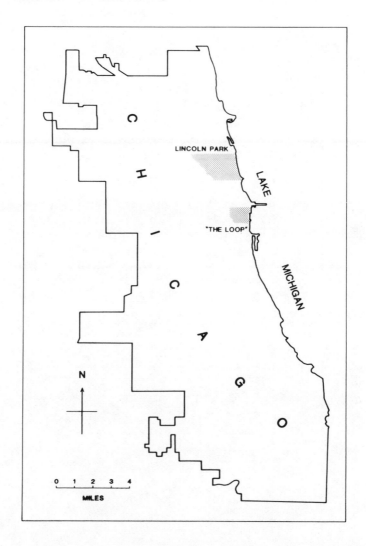

FIGURE 2.6
Lincoln Park

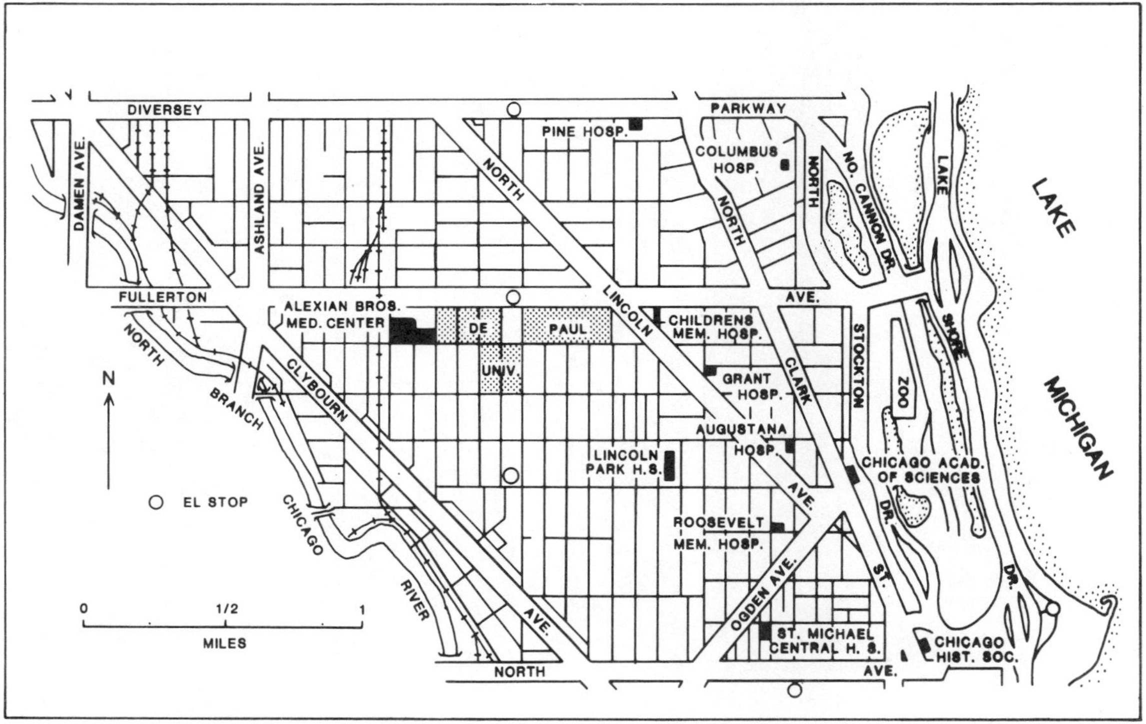

FIGURE 2.7
Lincoln Park Neighborhoods

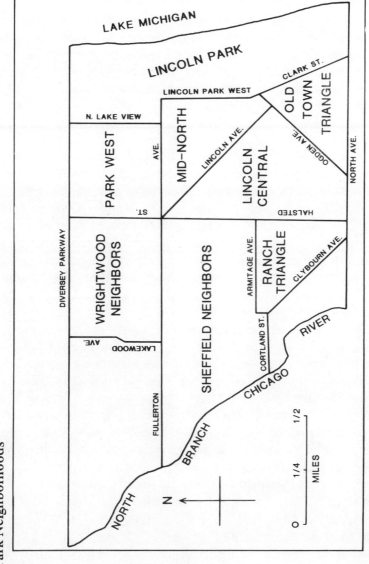

Source: Lincoln Park Conservation Association (n.d.).

seems to turn all buildings, not just apartment buildings but old factories and warehouses, even a building from the McCormack Theological Seminary, into private dwelling places. All have signs advertising the contractors and sales.

So much of Lincoln Park looks new and cleaned up: cleaned bricks, new doors and gates, new iron fences, sidewalks replaced, well-laid-out formal gardens. Lincoln Park is flat. No rises give vistas of the lake, although on southern Lincoln Avenue, and at the lake itself, a clear day gives glimpses of the Chicago skyline. Many of the streets are tree-lined and, with the buildings, the streets seem to shade off into distant triangles.

The houses make the Lincoln Park streets interesting because each one is so different, so many different colors and shades of brick and stone, some vine-covered. Most of the houses are adjoining, with no space between them. Some have party walls, which means that two houses share the same wall. Many buildings have little yards in front or back, blooming with flowers in summer and fall. Some yards have iron fences and gates outside the yard, others have an iron fence at the front door — all curlicuing and spiraling in different designs. Most of the houses are three-story, some with many stairs and a main entrance at the second story, but there are also cottages and apartment houses.

The new residents tastefully decorate the interiors of their homes, sometimes with modern furniture; but more often, antiques grace the walls and floors of Lincoln Park homes, many of them purchased at antique stores and art galleries that have invaded Lincoln Park in the last ten years.

A few Chicago cottages with wooden frames — some with gray or pastel shingling — and peaked roofs remain in Lincoln Park. They rise one to one and a half stories, many with a high entrance up several steps. Near the lake, high-rises tower above like a series of overgrown forts shielding the area from the park and lake.

The park itself occupies the eastern edge of the area. It does not belong only to the Lincoln Park community, but attracts visitors from all over the city and from farther away. Lake Shore Drive forms the eastern boundary of the park, though east of it are sandy beaches with summer swimming. Inlets from the lake form the lagoons of Lincoln Park, many of which dock boats. Lincoln Park has the largest stretch of grass and trees in the area. The zoo with its newly (1971) designed buildings occupies a large portion of the park and includes a huge red barn, which allows city children to see farm animals. Botanical gardens and formal gardens also add color and life. The Chicago Historical Society borders the southern edge of the park and the Academy of Sciences is in the park.

Other parks also leave open spaces. Around the high school are grassy areas and playgrounds, and farther south on Lincoln Avenue is another park. Smaller playgrounds dot the area. The parks seem to attract organized groups — a day-care group with children two-by-two, a high-school summer program, senior citizen outings.

DePaul University stands in another grassy area, where old vine-covered buildings mix with a high-rise building of classrooms, a cafeteria, a field house, a chapel, and a dormitory. DePaul is a Catholic university that attracts primarily working-class students from all parts of the city. In the summer of 1981 many signs were posted on campus saying that classes would not be suspended if the Chicago Transit Authority shut down.

Lincoln Avenue, Armitage, Halstead, and Clark are the major commercial streets, with Lincoln Avenue setting the trends for much of the city. People from all over come to the Biograph Theater, which shows the latest and best in foreign films. Next door is the Chicago Repertory Dance Theater. South a block or two is the Body Politic Theater and to the north, the Apollo Theater, both of which introduce Chicago-authored plays. Many restaurants and night-life entertainment places thrive on Lincoln Avenue. Lincoln Park always manages to have whatever is the latest fad or fashion. A western bar with a mechanical bull springs up near a punk rock bar. Tantalizing aromas from the newest restaurants waft out onto the street — perhaps vegetarian delights or seafood. Although the onion-grease smell of MacDonalds has been kept out of Lincoln Park, almost every block has its Red Hot (hot dog) stand. In Sheffield a few Italian restaurants remain and Mexican restaurants are found throughout the community.

The large, multistoried edifices of the hospitals with their parking garages create still another contrast in the area. Children's Memorial, Grant, Augustana, and Roosevelt Hospitals are near Lincoln Avenue. Columbus Hospital is north, near the park, and the Alexian Clinic is in the western section.

Grime and dirt cling to sticky, sweaty bodies in the summer and the muddy moisture penetrates in other months. The heavy, muggy air of summer contrasts with the piercing cold of winter. Almost always at least some breeze or actual gusts blow down east-west streets off the lake. Sometimes little eddies form, swirling and blowing newspapers, leaves, and dirt into a gyre. The loud zoom of buses, the clacking of the trains, and the staccatos of sidewalk drilling and sandblasting drown the constant roar of traffic.

Signs posted on trees and telephone poles announce sales or lost animals. Another sign warns of the $200 fine for animal litter. People crowd the streets near the el station, and it is impossible to distinguish residents from visitors, since so many outsiders need to use the facilities of Lincoln Park. All varieties of people are here, though English-speaking whites and Spanish-speaking browns seem more common. Young Latino men gather near the Armitage el stop, drinking soda out of bottles.

On the west side of Lincoln Park, near the river, stand several factories that appear as a series of cone-topped chimneys belching out different colors of smoke. North-south strings of railroad tracks and chain-link fences separate the factories and warehouses from the residential areas. The factories are not really part of the community. No representatives from them serve in the community organizations and few Lincoln Park residents work in the factories. Many residents further east hardly notice the existence of the factories.

The southwest side of Lincoln Park in the shadows of the factories seems blackened and blighted. Here homes are run-down and the poorer ethnic groups — blacks and Puerto Ricans — crowd together. A few of the houses are being bought and remodeled, predicting the future of this area.

On October 20, 1981 the *Chicago Tribune* chronicled the story of one of the Halstead Street houses in the southwest neighborhood of Lincoln Park, which was bought by an accountant who evicted three tenement families. One was an extended black family with a grandmother, mother, uncle, son, two daughters, and their children. The building was dirty, falling apart, bug- and rat-infested, but the $125 rent was reasonable for the family, who were forced to move to the public housing project of Cabrini Green just south of Lincoln Park. The other tenants, a hospital worker whose son had been killed in the neighborhood and an elderly woman, found housing in other tenements. Meanwhile, the accountant turned the building into a work of grandeur with paneled library, fireplace, and Tiffany lamps, renovated the apartments, and rented them to new, wealthier tenants. The replacement of poor people by the wealthy is just one of a long series of changes Lincoln Park has experienced throughout its history.

The typical Lincoln Park residents of the 1980s have arrived within the last five years from other parts of Chicago and may have moved a few times within Lincoln Park itself. They are professionals, active for a few years in the Lincoln Park Conservation Association, serving on committees and possibly boards. Lincoln Park residents have small families, if any, with other relatives living in other parts of the city. They spend several hours at work in another part of the city and visit friends in other parts of Chicago. Their hobbies include decorating their houses and belonging to a tennis club or some other recreational organization. Many have summer homes in rural Wisconsin, Michigan, or Illinois.

History

In Zenda historical anecdotes abounded, but since most Lincoln Park residents are new and have no family roots there, its history had to be gleaned from various documents — records of organizations, hospitals, and schools, and history books on Chicago (especially Mayer and Wade 1969). Lincoln Park began much like Zenda, but Zenda remained a farming area, as it began, and Lincoln Park underwent many changes. In less than a century, Lincoln Park evolved from a wilderness to a farming area to a suburb to a city neighborhood (see Table 2.2).

Early Settlement

Native Americans first inhabited Lincoln Park. Like the permanent settlement of Big Foot's Pottawatamie enclave just north of Zenda on Lake Geneva, a Pottawatamie village occupied the heart of Lincoln Park, which is now the intersection of Fullerton and Halstead Streets and Lincoln Avenue. The village land was the highest ground between the lake and the river (Sheffield Neighborhood Association 1981). Pottawatamies and other natives, such as the Sacs and the Fox, made trails through Lincoln Park on sandbar formations left by glaciers, the only well-drained ground above the swampy sands. Lincoln Avenue (formerly Green Bay Road), Clark Street (Little Fort Road), and Southport were all originally Indian trails. Presumably some of the same Indians traveled to both Lincoln Park and Lake Geneva.

Scene on Fullerton Avenue, Showing Chicago Cottage, Brick Row House, and Three-Flat

Lincoln Park Avenue at Fullerton with High Rises Near the Lake in Background

Lincoln Avenue

Fullerton Street El Stop with Factories in Back

Queen Anne Stone Houses

Old McCormick Seminary Building Turning into Condominiums

TABLE 2.2
Chronology of Lincoln Park Area

Dates	Events
	Indian Trails
	Pottawatamie village
1673-1763	French exploration and rule
1770	Dusable trading post in Chicago
1795	Treaty of Greenville
1803-12; 1815-57	Fort Dearborn
1818	Illinois statehood
1824	Army post and trading center at Clybourne and Armitage Streets
1829	Clybourne slaughterhouse
1832	Improvement of Green Bay Road
1832	Cholera victims buried at Lincoln Park
1833	Lumber mill
1833	Town of Chicago organized
1834	Smallpox hospital and cemetery at Lincoln Park
1835	Auction
1835	Town of Chicago incorporated
1837	City of Chicago incorporated
1845	Sheffield truck farming
1850	Horse-drawn omnibus
1851	Southeast corner of Lincon Park incorporated into Chicago
1851	Bridges built across Chicago River
1853	Lincoln Park incorporated up to Fullerton Avenue
1854-90	Lake View Hotel
1856	Chicago Historical Society founded
1857	Chicago Academy of Sciences built
1860	McCormick Theological Seminary built
1864	Park improved
1865	Park named Lincoln Park
1869	Part of park annexed to city of Chicago
1869	German Lutherans built St. James Church
1871	Streetcars
1871	Chicago fire
1872-95	Building boom
1874	Last graves removed from park
1875	St. Vincent's Church
1880s	Heavier industry including John Deere Factory
1882	Julia Porter Hospital

TABLE 2.2, continued

Dates	Events
1883	German Hospital
1883	St. Josaphat's Church
1884	Augustana Hospital
1884	Fresh Air Tuberculosis Hospital
1888	Police precinct in Lincoln Park
1889	City of Lake View incorporated into Chicago
1889	St. Vincent's College
1896	Nursing school added to German Hospital
1897	Elevated trains reach Lincoln Park
1897	Alexian Brothers Hospital
1900	Parker School
1904	Porter Hospital incorporated as Children's Memorial Hospital
1906	Chicago Plan
1907	St. Vincent's College becomes DePaul University
1917	German Hospital becomes Grant Hospital
1920	Luxury cooperative apartments built
1921	Carriage lanes of park converted to auto drives
1926	Queen Maria of Romania visits Romanian Greek Orthodox Church
1938	Lathrop Homes built
1940	Zen Center started in Lincoln Park
1948	Old Triangle Association formed
1950	Mid-Horth Association formed
1950	Old Town Art Fairs began
1954	Lincoln Park Conservation Association
1955	Park West Association formed
1956	General neighborhood renewal plan
1957	Lincoln Central Association formed
1957	New zoning ordinance
1960	Sheffield Neighborhood Association formed
1962	Wrightwood Neighbors Conservation Association formed
1966	Concerned Citizens Survival Front formed
1968	Democratic national convention in Chicago
1969	Protests and demonstrations
1970	Urban renewal approved
1976	McCormick Theological Seminary relocates

Near Lake Michigan, standing water rose among the sandbars with the rains and snowy winters and fell to a scummy film with the humid winds of summer. In a few places prairie grass filled in the sand and, closer to the Chicago River, many species of trees, especially pines and oak, forested the land. The mosquitoes outnumbered bear, deer, numerous bird species, and other wildlife. The gathering and hunting Indians took advantage of Lincoln Park's many resources as well as the lake and river waterways.

The waterways also brought the French explorers, Marquette and Joliet, who claimed the territory for France. In 1674 Marquette wintered at the mouth of the Chicago River. Soon other explorers, hunters, and traders were following the waterways and Indian trails for new lands and new sources of wealth. In 1763 Britain won the region from France for a 20-year rule. Other than the Indians, no one lived there until 1770, when Dusable, whose father was a merchant in Quebec and whose mother was a black slave, established the first permanent settlement. He built a trading center around the site of Marquette's camp.

Indian relations influenced further settlement of the Chicago area. Through the Treaty of Greenville of 1795, Indians ceded six square miles, which became the center of Chicago. The establishment of Fort Dearborn in 1803 created a frontier outpost and a stopping place for pioneers traveling westward.

Beginning in 1804, John Kinzie traded with the Indians around Chicago. He and his wife Juliette were also among the first non-Indians to explore the Zenda area around Lake Geneva on their travels to a northern fort.

With the War of 1812 and with Indian attacks, the Chicago area was abandoned from 1812 to 1816, when the Sacs and Fox ceded a large block of land. Then many settlers came, primarily from New York and the northeastern states. The opening of the Erie Canal in 1825 facilitated even greater westward advancement.

Indians and army together formed a trading post at Clybourne and Armitage Avenues in the Lincoln Park area around 1824. A few years later Archibald Clybourne, whose family was among the first in Lincoln Park, built a slaughterhouse, Chicago's first meat-packing plant, on the north branch of the Chicago River in the Lincoln Park area, to feed the army and traders. The Clybourne home still stands at 2111 North Seminary. In the 1830s, with the defeat of Chief Black Hawk, the government began to pay more attention to the area and in 1832 improved Green Bay Road and in 1834 auctioned off the land. Henry and Horatio Cleveland bought the largest section of land for $200 and a week later sold the land for over three times that (Sheffield Neighborhood Association 1981). An 1830 map designates the land along the lake as canal land; the rest was entirely wooded. In addition to the Clevelands, John Ludby and William Bennett owned blocks of land.

In those early days most Chicagoans considered the area undesirable and sent their sick and dead there. The land that became the park was originally an Indian burial ground, and a cholera epidemic among soldiers in 1832 added whites to the cemetery (Anderson 1971). The city also established a smallpox hospital at the burial site.

Farming Suburb

In 1845 a nurseryman from Connecticut bought land southwest of Fullerton and Halstead to the river and started truck farming. Soon more land was cleared and German immigrants provided the labor for more farming, which helped feed the growing population of Chicago. With wooden frame houses and neat rows of vegetables, Lake Park (as it was called then) changed from a wilderness to an important farming area. Horse-drawn wagons now clattered over old Indian trails, carrying vegetables to downtown Chicago and returning with tools and other necessities. The area around North Avenue was known as the Cabbage Patch, where Germans grew celery and potatoes in addition to cabbage and kept chickens and cows (Commission on Chicago Historical and Architectural Landmarks 1981, p. 10).

The Lake Park vicinity was also a resort area for picturesque drives outside of the city. The northern part was originally part of the town of Lake View, which harbored a fancy hotel. The Lake View Hotel served as a resort getaway for the wealthier Chicagoans and as a refuge from the cholera epidemic of 1854 (Sheffield Neighborhood Association 1981).

By 1850 public transportation arrived in the form of horse-drawn omnibuses, and bridges across the Chicago river made the area more accessible; streetcars came in 1871. People started commuting to work in the city, land values rose, and Lake Park became a suburb, though it was quickly incorporated into the city. In 1851 Chicago annexed the southeast corner, which was called North Town, and in 1853 Fullerton Avenue became the northern boundary of Chicago.

This new part of the city developed some important institutions, including the Chicago Historical Society and the Chicago Academy of Sciences, the oldest museum in Chicago. The Academy was built as a memorial to Matthew Laflin, who built stockyards and bus lines in Chicago and wanted to be buried in Lake Park.

McCormick Theological Seminary was established in 1860, attracting Scotch and Irish immigrants who added to the labor force of truck farmers. Cyrus McCormick, inventor of the reaper, donated most of the money and land to move the seminary from Indiana. He funded the denomination to dissuade it from taking a stand against slavery in the Civil War.

In 1864 there was a movement to make parks a part of the city. Since Lake Park was accessible by horsecar and locals wanted to preserve the beach area, graves were removed and the sandy, weedy cemetery became an elegant park with a lagoon, well-tended lawns, and ornamentation. In 1865 the park was renamed Lincoln Park in honor of the recently assassinated Abraham Lincoln. Soon afterwards, part of the park was annexed by the city.

Urbanization of Lincoln Park

In the dry, windy autumn of 1871, the great Chicago fire spread north as far as Fullerton. It entered Lincoln Park between Larabee and Clark and destroyed the German farmers' wooden houses. Some took their children to outlying communities; others stayed to bury valuable possessions, including an organ. Open fields slowed the blaze until it was a flame rushing down Clark Street. The fire, which lasted three days, did not touch many buildings north and west of Lincoln and Larabee but nevertheless left widespread rubble and ashes elsewhere.

Gardeners returned to divide their land into lots as a way to help the homeless. Some temporary shacks remained. The west side of Lincoln Park attracted many workers, since the housing ordinance prohibiting wooden, flammable housing did not apply to Lincoln Park. Also, there was little rubble and the land was already cleared. The last remaining wooded area was between Magnolia and Lakewood. The Fire Relief Association provided free lumber and help with building for those who had lots before the fire. The frame houses became known as "Chicago cottages."

Before the fire there had been plans, which were implemented after the fire, to raise the level of the roads. Consequently, some homeowners built entrances on the second floor. A few houses appear to have sunken since the street is above their entrances. Soon row houses and apartment houses replaced most of the cottages.

On the east side, near the lake, the wealthier and middle classes, including many German brewers, shopkeepers, and clerks, built Queen-Anne-style brick and stone houses. Rather than destroying Lincoln Park, the fire only accelerated its growth. Many of the buildings were built just after the fire. The north side of Chicago doubled in population in the decade after the fire. Light industry, especially in furniture and wood, began at this time, followed later by heavier industry, including a John Deere factory. Many breweries were also built in Lincoln Park and just south of it. The city of Lake View, just north of Lincoln Park, developed single-dwelling houses around the streetcar lines for an emerging German, Swedish, and Irish middle class. Lake View was incorporated into Chicago in 1889, and the more populated south side of it became associated with Lincoln Park.

The fire did not destroy the ethnicity of the community, but brought more foreign-born and the institutions they founded. Poles, Slavs, Romanians, and Hungarians scattered west of Clark Street. By 1890 over half of the city of Chicago was foreign-born, and most of these were Germans, who built the German Hospital and churches in Lincoln Park. German groups held money-making affairs for the hospital and some German benefactors bequeathed money to the church. The Irish built St. Vincent's Church and College, later to become DePaul University.

Other hospitals, churches (including the Polish St. Josaphat's), and schools were founded in this postfire period. Later, Queen Maria of Romania would visit the Romanian church in Lincoln Park. Children's Memorial Hospital began as the Maurice Porter Memorial Hospital, founded by Julia Porter in 1883 — at first just a cottage with eight beds for poor children. A floating tuberculosis sanitarium located in the park lagoon. A small group of Swedish immigrants had formed a part of the north side community, but a cholera epidemic killed them. During this epidemic, a Swedish doctor and Lutheran pastors helped in an effort that initiated the Augustana Hospital of Lincoln Park.

The early 1900s brought name changes and reorganization of institutions, as they went beyond their founding mothers and fathers to become corporations with boards of trustees. The German Hospital became Grant Hospital, in part because of the distrust of Germans brought about by World War I. According to Ducey (1977), Germans were afraid to continue their conversation sessions in the park and some wealthy Germans moved out. The Irish also began to move out and Italians moved in near terra cotta works (Kitagawa 1963). In the 1920s, a small enclave of blacks moved in because deteriorated housing became affordable to them.

Speculators built luxury cooperative apartments near the lake during the 1920s, but rooming houses started to appear in the older buildings. The Chicago plan of 1906 included lake landfill and the creation of Lake Shore Drive. Further road improvements came in 1921, when the carriage lanes of the park were converted to automobile drives. Lincoln Park became polarized, with the wealthy residents near the lake and the workers near the river, although not to such extremes as farther south in the Gold Coast and the slums (Zorbaugh 1929), and none of the race riots of this period affected Lincoln Park. The year 1938 brought Lincoln Park its first public housing with the construction of the Lathrop Homes on the site of the John Deere plant. Both industrial and population growth continued.

After 1940 many buildings aged and deteriorated when families moved rather than repair them. Cheap housing in the west side of Lincoln Park attracted blacks, Appalachian white immigrants, and Spanish-speaking people from Mexico, Puerto Rico, and the southwest United States. Japanese established Zen centers. The city built a huge housing project, Cabrini Green, just south of Lincoln Park. Overcrowded dwellings were prevalent in Lincoln Park by 1940, housing derelicts, misfits, and others. Dillinger, a Chicago gangster, lived in Lincoln Park for a while and was killed where the Biograph Theater now stands. The St. Valentine's Day Massacre, a mass mobster killing, occurred in a garage in Lincoln Park.

One Lincoln Park resident who moved there in the 1940s said that it was impossible to get a bank loan on any building west of Lincoln Avenue because of the area's instability. Others described strange neighbors who urinated out of the windows and a woman who lived in a basement with 24 birds. A resident near the lake in the 1940s said she would not travel west of Clark Street because it was run-down and unsafe. Rats multiplied and garbage accumulated.

A decrease in property values, combined with cultural interests in the universities, museums, and hospitals, attracted bohemians, artists, and intellectuals to Lincoln Park in the 1950s. They first congregated on Wells Street in Old Town, and started theaters and the Old Town School of Folk Music, but with the Sandburg Village housing development just to the south, Old Town became commercialized and the radicals moved just north of Fullerton on Lincoln Avenue. According to Ducey (1977), this area of Lincoln Park was a counter-culture center in the 1960s, with psychedelic stores and underground newspapers.

Renewal

The response by some residents to deterioration was to preserve and refurbish the neighborhoods in a movement by local organizations that began in Old Town in 1948, moved north to the Mid-North Association, and culminated in the Lincoln Park Conservation Association (LPCA) in 1954. The LPCA gave the neighborhood associations a broader base and, in turn, fostered the development of other neighborhood associations: Park West (1955), Lincoln Central (1957), Sheffield (1960), and Wrightwood (1962). The seventh area, Ranch Triangle, remained deteriorated until the 1980s. According to its brochure, the LPCA "and its seven affiliated neighborhood associations offer residents, businesses, and institutions in the area opportunity to actively participate in the preservation of an important community: Lincoln Park."

These communal organizations formed to clear the area of slums and also to preserve the old buildings. The major institutions of the community — DePaul University, McCormick Theological Seminary, the Aetna Bank, the churches, and the hospitals were instrumental in the formation of LPCA and continued to be the associations' primary financial support.

The early efforts of the LPCA concentrated on recruiting members and raising money. One issue was open membership. When the association found one of their members involved in violating building codes, membership provisions were revised to include only those who would follow the goals of the association.

LPCA also established liaisons with other groups such as church councils, realtors, and especially the government of Chicago and its conservation board. Eventually LPCA also sought federal government involvement and applied for urban renewal funds. The LPCA used the tool of building codes to get rid of run-down buildings and over-crowding. With the help of the realty board, the organization sponsored a contest for the best neighborhood. The city further assisted in 1957 with a new zoning code that included even more stringent physical and spatial requirements. The LPCA moved to remove abandoned cars and some unsanitary horse barns, as well as to organize social events to promote neighborhood unity. In 1950 Old Town started a tradition of money-making affairs with the Old Town Art Fair, the oldest juried art fair in the United States.

Civic classes at Waller High School became interested in LPCA and a youth component was added. From the beginning the association has been interested in school issues and works with the Board of Education to improve the schools. For example, it advised the board on the relocation of a school so that it would not destroy a residential area.

Waller High School was becoming all black, in part because white families with high school students either left the community or used private schools. Since the 1960s, the improvement of Waller High has been a project of the LPCA, and by the 1980s the school was remodeled, changed to a magnet school — Lincoln Park High — with specializations in science, arts, and foreign languages.

The 1960s brought federal help to Lincoln Park through the War on Poverty, Model Cities, and Vista. LPCA members fought to keep the park green and clean up the lagoon. Into the 1980s the organization continues to preserve clean neighborhoods, fight crime, help senior citizens, and carry out the money-making traditions of garden walks, antique sales, and carnivals.

In 1976 the McCormick Theological Seminary relocated in Hyde Park as part of the University of Chicago. The LPCA sought to preserve the seminary buildings, many of which became part of DePaul University. DePaul also acquired the Goodman School of Drama and gained a national reputation for its basketball team. The LPCA led a petition drive for a library branch in the community and instituted a whistle stop-crime prevention program. Another project was seeking landmark preservation, which Old Town and Mid-North received, and Sheffield is on the national registry of historic places.

In the summer of 1981 everyone was talking about the rising costs of transportation. Bus and elevated train rates were raised to one dollar, and commuter train fares were raised proportionately even more, as the companies threatened bankruptcy and going out of business. The fare rises kept the poor even more immobile and suburban residents considered more seriously moving into places like Lincoln Park to be closer to work.

Lincoln Park has been home for almost every type of person. It grew from a wilderness and farming area to become part of the city of Chicago through population growth and ethnic diversification. The population growth and deterioration of housing were reversed by concerned citizens who conflicted over helping the poor or making Lincoln Park more upper-middle-class. A trend toward more upper-middle-class residents continued in the 1980s.

Readers who waded through the vast array of facts and details in this chapter are probably asking themselves, What is the point? What does this all mean? What should I be getting out of it? The answers to these questions are found in subsequent chapters, where theories make sense of these raw materials. The rural community, Zenda, shares basic similarities and differences with urban Lincoln Park. How the comparisons of these two are interpreted depends on the organizing principles of the particular theory involved. A major argument of this book is that the two communities will appear in a different light with each theory.

3

Human Ecology:
Community as Competition

In the early 1970s the word "ecology" exploded in the news media, as a social movement emerged. The movement members, concerned about such changes and destruction in the environment as overpopulation, pollution of water, air, and land, preservatives in food, and depletion of natural resources, agitated for social change. Proponents of the movement believed that people's relationship to the environment was incongruent; unlike American Indians, modern Americans no longer harmonized with the land.

The phrase "human ecology" is much older than the recent ecology movement, but both share some of the same concerns. Human ecology as a theoretical research approach emphasizes the distribution of aggregates in relation to space and material resources in the study of community. Dynamically, within communities, diverse aggregates compete for sustenance in a scarcity of space as populations shift and reorganize to achieve a balanced capacity for subsistence. Some human ecologists, as ecological determinists, believe that the physical environment causes human groupings and behavior.

Human ecology, as a branch of sociology that specializes in demographics, population statistics, and migration, also has a very old tradition of examining human communities. This is not only one of the oldest approaches to communities, but is also subsocial in that nonsocial forces such as biology, geology, and physics are held to regulate human communities in the same way they regulate plant and animal communities.

Because of the emphasis on aggregates and the environment, human ecology makes it possible to consider various designs of cities, suburbs, towns, and rural areas, and especially how these connect in a single environment. A community such as an ethnic enclave appears as the smallest unit of similar aggregates in this system. Different kinds of communities develop, depending on their location near the center of a city or the periphery of a metropolitan area. Thus human ecology is well suited to examine Lincoln Park and Zenda, not only individually but also as connected in an ecosystem of subsistence and competition. The importance of space and cyclical change in communities has grown out of a series of ideas developed theoretically by human ecologists over the past century.

The human ecology approach to community supplies the elements for this study's model of communities, based on metaphor, methods, and the people-space-time dimensions. We can use these elements to compare and contrast Zenda and Lincoln Park. These issues will be discussed after a consideration of the development of the human ecology framework.

HISTORICAL DEVELOPMENT

Unlike the other four paradigms, which build upon the work of European classical founders of sociology, human ecology is basically an American theory. Exceptions to the American founding of human ecology are found in tangential references to Darwin, Spencer,*

Darwin and Spencer contributed to both human ecology and structural-functional ideas of historical change. In his travels around the world, British naturalist Charles Darwin observed unique plants and animals adapted to their environments. He theorized that evolution from a few species of plants and animals, by their adaptation to new places, brought about a multiplex of varieties. Evolution occurs gradually with the dying out of species that are not suited to particular environments and the introduction of new species that are strong (1859). Another Englishman, Herbert Spencer, introduced the concept of survival of the fittest, meaning that organisms with superior intelligence and groups better adapted to their environment continue and multiply, whereas and Durkheim. Human ecology started with rural studies, but became well known through studies in Chicago led by Robert Park. Later, Amos Hawley revised human ecology in the neo-orthodox school. Social-area analysis and sociocultural studies led to contemporary human ecology studies (Theodorson 1961).

Early Rural Studies

In a classical early rural study of Walworth County, Wisconsin, where Zenda is located, Galpin (1915) delineated rural communities in terms of services from villages to farms. Galpin not only analyzed wagon tracks from farms, but also surveyed banks, newspapers, stores, and schools to determine their clientele. He contributed a major human ecology tool, that of map drawing, as a way to indicate spatial organizations of communities.

Galpin surveyed 12 towns and villages in Walworth County from 1911 to 1913, not including Zenda, in order to examine the interrelationship between farms and villages, and the extent of community services. He found that community extension varies with different services. From this study Galpin developed a concept of the agricultural community as a circle with the village in the center, with the edges of the circle overlapping with other communities, and with the radius of the circle somewhat longer than half the distance between any two communities (p. 19).

Sanderson (1939) used Galpin's method in upstate New York, where he found a congruence of school, church, and shopping areas. He defined a rural community as "that form of association maintained between people and between their institutions, in a local order in which they live on dispersed farmsteads and in a village which is the center of their common activities" (p. 50).

---

weaker species die out. Unlike human ecologists' impersonal view of change, Spencer believed that differentiation evolved because of rational decisions to maximize happiness (1898/1967). (See Chapter 4 for more information on Spencer.)

*According to Schnore (1958), Durkheim's concept of social morphology was an original ecological conception inspired by the work of E. Haecklel who used the word "ecology" for plants. Social morphology consists of the examination of the environmental basis of social organization and of population phenomena.

Chicago School

Robert Park coined the phrase "human ecology" in 1921 and led many studies of Chicago under the auspices of the University of Chicago, which had the first sociology department in the United States.* In the spirit of midwestern progressivism, the university fostered the study of the social problems so evident in the city, rather than the religious orientations that had been the previous academic fare. The traditional human-ecology school is perhaps best represented by Robert Park, Ernest Burgess, Roderick McKenzie, and Louis Wirth, who in their research explored the spatial organization and urban settlements of the city of Chicago.

W. I. Thomas (see Chapter 6) recruited news reporter Robert Park to Chicago from Alabama, where he had worked for Booker T. Washington. Park laid the conceptual foundation of human ecology,† drawing on the problems of his students who studied Chicago and his own experiences to explain the ecological functioning of the city.

Park (1952, p. 14) defines human ecology as a description of two types of forces (biotic and social) that bring about orderly groupings of populations and institutions. Subsocial forces influence biotic levels of communities; that is, struggles for existence and competition for scarce resources determine the organization and spatial distribution of persons, animals, and plants. All living beings in the same habitat share impersonal and subsocial forces such as climatic changes. Park (p. 148) describes the community thus:

> The essential characteristics of a community . . . are those of: (1)
> a population, territorially organized, (2) more or less completely

---

*Both human ecology and symbolic interaction originated at the University of Chicago and their community studies are both called the Chicago School. The symbolic interactionists study one community group and their interaction patterns (see Chapter 6), while the human-ecology approach considers several communities in their relation to the city.

†Park remained true to both sides of the Chicago School and also considered individuals in his examination of racial issues, marginality, social distance, and social control.

rooted in the soil it occupies, (3) its individual units living in a relation-ship of mutual interdependence that is symbiotic rather than societal.

He designates as communal the interdependence of living things that arises out of competition.

In addition to the biotic level, the social level, which is unique to humans, also organizes communities:

> The community, then, is the name that we give to this larger and most inclusive social milieu, outside of ourselves, our family, and our imme-diate neighborhood, in which the individual maintains not merely his existence as an individual, but his life as a person. (Park 1952, p. 57)

Human communities are more than aggregates; they are also col-lections of institutions. The sublevels of society — cultural-moral, technological, and communication, can be viewed as a superorganism resting upon the biotic level. Biotic levels of subsistence must be fulfilled before cultural levels are possible. Park also developed ideas about competition, evolution, and adaptation, which will be discussed in the section on time.

Park further collaborated with two students, McKenzie and Burgess. Burgess remained a student of urban communities through-out his career at the University of Chicago, which began with his graduate work in 1908 and ended in 1957. Emphasizing the human ecologists' concern with the effects of space and time on human aggregates, Burgess led the specialization in space with his concen-tric-zone theory, and McKenzie concentrated on the time dimension, laying out a series of stages through which communities succeed one another. Burgess defines communities as "societies and social groups . . . considered from the point of view of the geographical distribution of individuals and institutions" (Park and Burgess 1921, p. 163). McKenzie discusses the inception of human com-munities in the "traits of human nature and needs of human beings" such as shelter, food, and water (1968, p. 5). For him, the com-munity was the most elementary form of social organization. Mc-Kenzie's collaboration with Park was cut short by his early death.

Louis Wirth shared the teaching of the community courses with Burgess at the University of Chicago and they also started the Chicago Community Inventory to collect community studies. Wirth himself studied a Chicago Jewish ghetto (1928). Unlike the other three founders of human ecology, however, he held a pessimistic view of the city. In his famous essay, "Urbanism as a Way of Life" (1938), Wirth strictly followed the human ecology idea that the environment influences behavior and groups. He delineates three aspects of the city − large size, density, and heterogeneity− which contribute negatively to people's relationships.

Neo-Orthodox Human Ecologists

Several years after the original human ecologists, and with increased criticisms of the biotic levels and the spatial emphasis, neo-orthodox human ecologists revised the paradigm to emphasize the organization of subsistence activities. Hawley leads this faction of human ecology, along with Quinn and Duncan.

Hawley equates human ecology with the study of human communities, which he describes as "structures of relationships through which a localized population provides its daily requirements" (1950, p. 180). He defines human ecology as the techniques of adjustment by which a population maintains itself in its habitat (p. 68). Thus, subsistence is the key issue for human ecology; populations must adapt to sustain themselves. Well-organized divisions of labor rather than subsocial forces provide adaptation. Hawley (1968) lists four phases of human ecology: seeing the organization arise out of the interaction between population and environment; emphasizing the organization of populations; defining organization as a self-sustaining whole based on the differentiation of parts; and assuming equilibrium.

Hawley further uses the concepts of commensalism and symbiosis in explaining the interdependence that organizes equilibrium. Human organisms coact with others who are similar commensally and with others who are different symbiotically. Commensalism is based on supplementary similarities and symbiosis on complementary differences.

Quinn, like Hawley, characterizes ecological structure as the division of labor and the spatial organization of the city, with an economic emphasis on minimizing losses and maximizing profits. He defines human ecology as the study of community, but for him, the subsocial aspects of the structure, which change relevant to scarce supplies in the environment, are the most important parts of community (Quinn 1950). Quinn contributed the ecological concept of interaction which will be discussed extensively later.

Duncan adds technology to the other variables, previously introduced by other human ecologists, of population, organization, and environment. Technology can be considered a kind of organization that conditions adjustments of populations to the environment. For example, factory systems and transportation systems made changes in the spatial organization of cities. Each of the four variables has its own effects on each of the others, resulting in a mutually explanatory balance of forces. Duncan calls this interdependence the "ecosystem," which is a community in which like species are intradependent as well as dependent on other species and on the environment; the species exchange materials, energy, and information (1964).

In addition to Hawley's revival and revision of human ecology, social-area analysis and sociocultural ecology have made contributions to the subject.

Social-Area Analysis

Shevky and Williams (1949) and Shevky and Bell (1955) developed social-area analysis as a research tool. Social-area analysis, also called factoral ecology, identified homogeneity within census tracts in a parsimonious way. Thus, it follows human ecology in relating characteristics of populations to space — in this case, their location in a census tract. By measuring economic status (by occupation, education, and rent), family status (by fertility, women in the labor force, and number of single-family dwellings), and ethnic status (by isolation and group segregation ratios), social-area analysts find a tendency for similar populations to be segregated from others. A social area, then, is a unique configuration of these variables.

Shevky and Bell (1955) used social-area analysis to show changes in the San Francisco Bay area from 1940 to 1950, and also to correlate social-area indexes with such activities as participation in voluntary associations and neighboring. Social-area analysis also benefits by comparing distributions of social areas between cities or identifying social areas for fieldwork.

Hunter (1971), Abu-Lughod (1971), and Berry and Kasarda (1977) make more recent applications of social-area analysis.

Hunter's application of social-area analysis to Chicago from 1930 to 1960 indicates fairly persistent ecological structuring, with increased differentiation. He finds economic status the primary factor in residential segregation. Janet Abu-Lughod studied the interrelationship of ecological factors in Cairo, Egypt, using the factors of life-style, settlements of unattached males, and social pathology, which explained over half the statistical variation in the census tracts. From this analysis she was able to map 13 subcities of Cairo. Berry and Kasarda relate new social-area variables to residential determination. Income, state of the life cycle, life-style preference, and attitude toward journey to work influence where people live.

Sociocultural Ecology

In addition to social-area analysis, some have argued that sociocultural variable must be added to human ecology. Fiery (1945) led the criticisms of human ecology, based on his study of Boston, that location and characteristics of aggregates were not the sole determinants of land use. Instead, sentiments attached to historical places, such as the Boston Common or the Old North Church, prevented their being torn down for more economical use of the land. Also people made choices about where to live, such as Beacon Hill or the North End, rather than blindly being distributed by ecological forces. Fiery has been included in the chapter on social psychology because his interest in individuals, choices, and feelings is closer to social-psychological approaches and contradicts the human ecology emphasis of macro-level approaches.

Human Ecology Studies in the 1980s

Human ecologists continue to study communities emphasizing the shifting of populations over time. They explain movements to suburbs (Frey 1979; Marshall 1979; Marshall and Stahura 1979 a, b; Logan and Sterns 1981), movements to rural areas (Sly 1972; Sly and Tayman 1977, 1980; Frisbie and Poston 1975, 1978a, b; Heaton, Clifford, and Fuguitt 1981), and movements back to the city (Laska and Spain 1980) with continuing processes of segregation (Roof and Spain 1977; Pampel and Choldin 1978; Clay 1979; McGee and Boone 1977; Fly and Reinhart 1980).

To summarize, Durkheim's idea of morphology and early American rural studies inspired some of human ecology. Park, Burgess, and McKenzie laid a firm foundation for the study of biotic communities and spatial dimensions of cities. The neoclassical human ecologists emphasized sustenance organization, and the most recent continuation of human ecology lies in migration and segregation studies. It is now time to consider the basic elements of human ecology and their applications to Lincoln Park and Zenda. Human ecology provides unique people, time, and space dimensions to community (Table 3.1).

TABLE 3.1
Human Ecology Community Dimensions

Dimension	Description
Metaphor	Plant and animal communities
Methodology	Surveys, census data, maps; statistical analysis to test relations among populations, organizations, environment, and technology
People	
Institutions	Organizations of subsistence activities; adaptations to space and specific populations
Stratification	Dominance
Interaction	Mediated through environment
Time	
History	Evolution and expansion; succession cycles
Process	Shifts in populations; related to subsistence activities
Space	
Territory	Zones, natural areas, a resource
Boundaries	Physical; extent of symbiosis

METAPHOR

In using biological metaphors for human ecology, Lincoln Park and Zenda are photographed from a plane that hovers high over their territories. Looking down, we cannot see individuals, only crawling movements of transportation systems and factories, and the patchwork of land use, much as in looking down on an ant or bee colony.

Human ecologists borrow from a branch of biology to see that human communities are like plant and animal communities. The ecology of humans compares to the ecology of all living beings, plants and animals alike. In fact, some ecologists do not see plant and animal ecology as a metaphor, but analyze how humans, plants, and animals form a united interrelated community. For example, Thompson (1949) relates the climate and soil of the Fiji Islands to the interdependence of yams, breadfruit, bananas, pigs, and people. The islands had achieved an ecology that the arrival of people upset. Subsequently, a new balance developed out of the cultural patterns relating to the conditions of the natural setting. Human ecologists use the life-science terms of econiche or habitat, chain of life, predators, dominance, symbiosis, competition, and evolution.

The habitat or econiche is the environment of the plant and animal community, consisting of air, water, land, and other natural resources. Environmental factors such as weather, soil, and terrain determine the varied habitats of desert, ocean, pond, meadow, forest, swamp, and so on. Within each of these habitats coexists a unique configuration of plants and animals that have adapted to that particular environment. It is now their native land.

Within each econiche plants and animals depend on one another in a delicate balance called the chain of life, in which plants, and especially animals, prey on one another. Rather than creating warlike chaos, however, a harmony ensues in which population growth is controlled. A transference of energy is made possible, so that the largest animals are able to survive because the lower animals can transform chlorophyll into protein. An example of the chain of life begins with single-celled beings such as algae or plankton, which get eaten by small fish. Larger fish eat the small fish; larger animals eat the bigger fish and so on. Sometimes species link in symbiotic relationships and no longer compete because of different demands on the environment. For example, the giraffes who eat leaves from tall trees do not compete with the other hooved animals who eat the grass on the ground. The varied populations tend to stabilize in a balance of nature and equilibrium.

Park calls the interrelation among plant and animal populations, "the web of life in which all living organisms, plants and animals alike, are bound together in a vast system in interlinked and interdependent lives" (1952, p. 145). Webs often consist of concentric circles, Burgess's vision of the spatial structure of cities. Park gives the example of clover, which is dependent on bees, whose population is diminished by mice, which in turn are controlled by cats, who are pets of humans; hence, clover seems to do best near towns. Some are prey, others predators, as in the relationship between elk and wolves.

One species may use more of the resources and influence other species in a pattern called dominance. Hawley (1950) compared dominance of a population to large evergreens in a forest, which spread out in the air and sunlight, utilizing them to such a great extent that some shorter plants are unable to live there. Evergreen roots and dropped needles also usurp the ground, preventing many kinds of grasses from growing there. Other plants, like moss, ferns, and lichen, thrive in the protection of the tall trees.

The balance with several interdependent species or one dominant one can be upset abruptly or gradually. Changes in the atmosphere, disease, human-made products like insecticides, or new predators may destroy an econiche literally over night. One or more of the populations may become unchecked and may expand out of control, as in a pond that has an overabundance of algae, or crops destroyed by boll weevils, locusts, medflies, and the like. If one of the species lower in the chain is destroyed, those higher may starve. For example, the panda population in China is decreasing because of lack of bamboo. If a dominant population succumbs to disease, other populations that were protected by the dominant may die or the place of the dominant may be usurped by the predator.

Gradual change occurs with evolution and adaptation to new conditions. Eventually specialists arrive at unique functional niches. For example, some plants may gain a place in a rock crevice in which soil has blown, and attract other plants and animals. Over time, the rocky mountain breaks down and the species of plants and animals convert to forms better suited to the new environment. This process could take several thousands of years.

In sum, human ecologists argue that aggregates of people are like plant and animal communities with varied land use, with both interdependence and competition to stay alive, and sometimes with one group dominating. Human communities also experience cycles of changes and evolution.

METHODOLOGY

Given that human ecologists view human communities as similar to and sometimes even part of plant and animal communities, what questions does the metaphor present? First, human ecology forces researchers to look at collective, aggregate units and not individuals or single species. Second, human ecologists ask about natural resources, the physical and spatial attributes of communities, because of the importance of resources in shaping the nature of dynamic relationships among units and subunits. Third, human ecologists focus on competition and symbiosis as these are linked in adaptation and survival.

Methodologically, human ecologists proceed deductively and descriptively, using aggregate data to test hypotheses about the interrelationships among populations, organizations, the environment, and technology. For example, Duncan (1961) relates smog in Los Angeles, concentration of people, bowl-shaped setting, technology of cars, and industry to local groups that attempt to combat smog. Hawley (1941) gives nonspatial ecological correlations between sizes and types of populations and the number and variety of institutions and services available. Park (1952, p. 177) suggests that it is only because populations occupy different space and territory that statistics can be used at all.

Governmental census data furnish human ecologists their major source of information about such statistics as population size, income, occupation, and education. These data are given by census tract (the smallest unit), by Standard Metropolitan Statistical Areas (the most common unit), by states, and for the nation as a whole. Human ecologists extract such statistics as population sizes, migration rates, and racial composition from the census and statistically manipulate the data, using correlations and regressions.* For example, Logan and Sterns (1981) explain changes in racial composition of suburbs by the initial proportion of black populations and the presence of white ethnics. Social-area analysis uses factor analysis to determine which census variables best explain the homogeneity in a census tract.

In addition to census data, other statistics gathered from such government documents as income tax records, police records, and sales volumes are useful, and human ecologists also use national surveys such as those at the University of Michigan or the University of Chicago (National Opinion Research). Occasionally, they will collect firsthand data, in which case the random sampling survey of a community is the technique employed.

Many human ecologists (such as Burgess) also use maps to develop conceptualizations of communities or more frequently, to analyze distributions — that is, differences in rates by location. It may be desirable to map the extent of communities according to criteria such as sustenance organizations, transportation, or use of facilities. The combination of aggregate data with mapping illustrates human ecologists' attempt to explain varying rates by location.

In sum, human ecologists collect numbers on populations. They hover about spatial areas, not seeing individuals as individuals, but counting them to obtain information on group aggregates. Human ecologists analyze the data with sophisticated statistical tests to make conclusions and attempt to explain differences among populations.†

PEOPLE

Human ecologists define communities in terms of large aggregates of people. Institutions as subsistence organizations adapt to the

---

*Explaining complex statistics and how they are computer-processed are beyond the scope of this book. The same is true of factor analysis and sampling procedures. Students are advised to consult such books as Blalock (1972) and the *Statistical Package for the Social Sciences* manual.

†While census and other aggregate data were collected on Zenda and Lincoln Park, no hypotheses were tested nor was a social-area analysis attempted. The Census of 1980 was not available at this time.

environment over time. Dominance by one group's better adaptation to the environment or by its centralized location provides community stratification. Groups interact indirectly by their relationship to the environment and their competition for subsistence.

Institutions

Organization of Subsistence

Hawley defines institutions as agencies established for the needs of the general population, and suggests that a community's structure is a particular combination of institutions (1950). A more appropriate human ecological definition of institutions is the organization of subsistence activities. That is, human ecologists regard institutions as patterned ways in which aggregates maintain themselves. McKenzie (1968) suggests that institutions have become the basic unit of symbiotic activity. For Park, institutions are part of the cultural level of organization imposed on the biotic level, since plant and animal communities do not have institutions. He discusses economic organization as the flow of goods, services, and the division of labor, and political organizations as laws, customs, artifacts, and beliefs that restrain competition (1952).

Looking at Zenda and Lincoln Park with subsistence activities organized by occupations and stores, we find more primary, direct activities of food production in Zenda, and a greater variety of occupations and services in Lincoln Park. Within the communities we find symbiotic groupings, as well as symbiotic relationships between Zenda and Lincoln Park. Symbiosis refers to dissimilar groups living together with advantages to both.

While food products are created in the gardens, orchards, barns, and fields of Zenda, just as a few vegetable gardens in Lincoln Park backyards produce food, most of these products in Zenda are not consumed locally but flow to other locations, particularly to the Chicago area. Symbiotically, Zenda residents depend on merchants who will sell them goods. Formerly the merchants were located in the village, but now larger towns serve Zenda, and sometimes residents go as far away as Chicago or Lincoln Park to get services.

A greater divison of labor exists in Lincoln Park, with a greater number and variety of local stores, than in Zenda. People in Lincoln Park also go beyond the local community to meet a variety of subsistence needs. In Zenda most people are farmers; in Lincoln Park most people are professional bureaucrats with a wide range of specializations. Zenda farmers are less specialized and each does the whole range of planting and harvesting. In both places, income is used for sustenance, but in Lincoln Park income is acquired in a more heterogeneous way. In Zenda some subsistence is acquired directly from each person's own labor without the mediation of income.

Lincoln Park specializes not in one (as in Zenda), but in several activities: industry, manufacturing, higher education, medical services, and retailing. Whereas Zenda can no longer support even a grocery store, Lincoln Park has many cleaners, antique shops, and one-of-a-kind places such as a high-quality foreign film theater, a folk-singing school, and the like. The retail diversity of Lincoln Park contrasts with the almost nonexistence of retailing in Zenda, with the exception of tavern, feed store, and lumber shop. For example, walking down Armitage Street, a pedestrian passes in just one block a restaurant specializing in Italian lemonade, a women's and children's bookstore, a hardware store, a western shop, the Old Town School of Folk Music, a sanitary fuel company, and a second-hand dress shop, while in Zenda the village consists of only a few square blocks and a pedestrian passes houses, empty stores, and then open fields.

At another level, Lincoln Park and Zenda are part of the same community, since they interact symbiotically to supply sustenance to one another. The milk products and grain from Zenda supply food for Lincoln Park and Lincoln Park supplies products and services for Zenda. A John Deere tractor plant was at one time located in Lincoln Park. Now Lincoln Park residents engage in activities that help provide indirectly to Zenda such services as insurance, finances, and media. The raw materials from Zenda flow into Chicago to help feed the people in Lincoln Park, while other services flow from Chicago and help sustain residents of Zenda. Zenda is considered the outpost or milkshed of the Chicago metropolitan area, since it is one of the most remote points that still has as its center the Chicago market and grain exchange.

Differentiation

In the past Lincoln Park and Zenda, both producing food, were similar, but now, as we have just seen, they have different specializations that complement each other. According to McKenzie (1968), community institutions begin few in number, relatively simply, multipurpose, and geographically restricted. On the other hand, Park (1952, p. 162) believes that institutions, like social movements, arise to meet specific needs and then become localized and identified with a specific place. Human ecologists explain the differences in Zenda and Lincoln Park and what happens beyond the initiation of communities by the concept of differentiation. Differentiation refers to a gradual change by which living things acquire more specialized parts in the course of development.

Table 3.2 shows a variety of human ecology explanations of differentiation. Population growth and changes in technology are the major causes of greater specialization.

According to McKenzie (1968), with improvement in transportation and communication technology and with population growth and concentration, institutions of industry and commerce expand, while other institutions of local services remain relatively unchanged. With the advent of automobiles, the telephone, and the

TABLE 3.2
Differentiation in Institutions

Author	*Cause*	*Outcome*
McKenzie (1968)	Technology, transportation, communication Population growth and concentration	Increase in specialization; expansion of spatial scope
Wirth (1938)	Population growth, density, heterogeneity	Formalized, bureaucratized institutions with experts
LaGory and Nelson (1978); LaGory (1979)	Population growth	Specialization in transportation and management
Hawley (1941)	Population growth	Institution sales growth; fewer institutions
Reiss (1951); Kass (1977)	Specialization in community institutions	Population characteristics

radio, institutions have expanded their spatial range and become more specialized, larger, and fewer in number. Four patterns of institutions evolve: small service units, department stores, local chain stores, and federated systems (such as national franchises). LaGory (1979) and LaGory and Nelson (1978) add managerial activities to McKenzie's transportation as the major correlates of population growth from 1900 to 1940. In addition to specialization, institutions became more formalized and bureaucratized with experts, according to Wirth (1938).

Hawley (1941) finds that the average institution size, in terms of sales, increases with the size of the city and that the size of sales correlates inversely with the number of institutions; that is, the larger the institutions, the fewer they are. He also relates mean per capita sales to population characteristics. If a population increases, the increase in sales depends on the type of institution. For example, food stores show little change in sales with increase in population. The largest cities have the smallest variation in sales volumes among different institutions. In addition to population size, the income of a community explains institutional volume. Older populations lead to a higher sales volume, especially in smaller cities. A higher percentage of foreign-born consumers produces less volume, except in food stores and eating places. With less manufacturing, institutional structures are more highly developed.

The nature of specializations in communities influences population characteristics, according to Reiss (1951) and Kass (1977). Communities that specialize in retail and trade are distinguished from those in wholesale trade, maintenance trade, and nontrade centers by somewhat older populations, smaller households, more women working, higher socioeconomic levels, and more males employed in tourism, leisure-related, and private-household occupations. Manufacturing-specialized communities have the largest proportion of males employed. On the opposite end, communities specializing in finance, insurance, and/or real estate have an excess of older population and a high proportion of women in the labor force. College communities, public administration centers, transportation centers, military communities, entertainment centers, recreation centers, and medical centers show less pronounced population differences. Reiss concludes that functional specialization does have an effect on social morphology.

Kass's more recent study modified that by Reiss. He demonstrates that educational, financial, and public-administration specializations in communities promote a higher proportion of males than other communities. Further, fewer females are found in the labor force in communities that specialize in the manufacture of durable goods, but a higher proportion of women work in communities specializing in the manufacture of nondurable goods.

Applying these studies to Zenda and Lincoln Park helps us understand that the distinctions in populations — 1,910 people in Linn Township versus 67,793 people in a smaller area in Lincoln Park — influence the differences in subsistence organization. What about technology?

While the rich land of the Zenda area and the location of Lincoln Park in Chicago, as well as the population size differences, influence their current specializations, the way they labor has been influenced by technology. Although Zenda has maintained farming as the primary subsistence activity, changes in transportation and commerce have influenced farming technology, with fewer people needed to work, with shipping carried by trucks, and with a few farmers shifting to grain and vegetable production. Zenda has also seen the recent introduction of light manufacturing in the village. Transportation in Lincoln Park today, with its proximity to an international airport, means that its residents can work for multinational corporations whose current technological revolution involves computers.

Thus for human ecologists the organization of subsistence activities constitutes institutions. Differentiation, population sizes, and technology help one understand the greater specialization of subsistence activities in Lincoln Park. Differentiation leads to inequality and ranking of groups.

Stratification

Dominance

Power, class, and status issues do not inform human ecologists' position on stratification, although they do consider the distribution of status groups in communities. Hawley (1950, p. 233) suggests that while inequality is an inevitable component of differentiation, in American society classes are almost indistinct. Instead, dominance — a concept from biological ecology — constitutes the way human ecologists view stratification.

Dominance implies superior adaptation and some sort of control over others. Alihan (1938, p. 44) summarizes human ecologists' definitions of dominance as "ascendancy to a more controlling position among one or more elements among competing units." Bogue (1949) suggests that dominant groups control life conditions of others. According to Park (1952), the control is not by coercion or wish, but is simply the natural, symbiotic outcome of competition. Bogue (1949) points out that metropolitan centers dominate without coercion or legal authority. Dominant groups adapt best to the particular environment in which they are located (Quinn 1950), and they occupy the most important niche. Dominance attaches to the unit that controls the conditions necessary to the functioning of other units, controlling the flow of subsistence, the allocation of space, employment, funding, and information (Hawley 1981). McKenzie believes that transportation and communication contribute to dominance (1927).

According to Park, dominance has a number of functions and does a variety of things for a community. It determines the ecological pattern and the interrelation among niches, stabilizes communities, regulates numbers, limits competition, and distributes groups on the land and in subsistence activities. Different levels in communities — economic, political-military, and cultural-moral — all have their own kinds of dominance. To Hawley, dominance serves a regulating function (1981), while Quinn (1950) and McKenzie (1927) see that dominance also integrates the parts of a community.

Duncan and Duncan (1955) consider spatial aspects in the study of urban stratification — specifically, the distribution of occupations by location. Their findings indicate that ecology explains more about the distribution of occupations than socioeconomic data. Dissimilarity in residential distributions associates with dissimilarity in occupation; those of highest and lowest socioeconomic status are more segregated from other groups than those of middle socioeconomic status.

In both Zenda and Lincoln Park some groups dominate the subsistence activities more than others. Zenda farmers have dominated in the use of resources and sustenance activities. In Lincoln Park the large institutions of hospitals and schools seem to win the competition over land use. Changes are coming in Zenda with the influx of outsiders, of urban residents, and the farmers' dominance may not continue.

Location and space can also dominate. A central location seems to determine other positions in a city. Spatial dominance is important to Burgess (1927) in that the central business district dominates and has the choicest location (to be discussed further under the section on spatial dimension). Further distance from the central business district produces less dominance. For Park (1956) the area of highest land values, usually places of shopping or banking, dominate communities.

Lincoln Park and Zenda do not have clearly defined centers. In the past the village was the center of Zenda, although the land values were never higher there. Now other nearby small towns are the centers of shopping and banking and there is no single center. The intersection of Fullerton, Lincoln, and Halstead Streets constitutes something of a center for Lincoln Park, since DePaul University and many hospitals, stores, and the main bank are all located there. Clark and Fullerton Streets, and Halstead and Armitage Streets are also central shopping areas for Lincoln Park, but as in Zenda, it is less clear that these centers exert control over the rest of Lincoln Park. Instead both Lincoln Park and Zenda look to the metropolitan center of Chicago.

Types of Metropolitan Dominance

The metropolis dominates its society as well as all the lesser-sized communities surrounding it. Hawley explains metropolitan dominance as

> the exercise of influence from a central point over the activities distributed in the surrounding region by virtue of the concentration of the administrative market, and other organizations that control access to information, credit, and other exchanges within and beyond the region. (1981, p. 364)

Hawley (1950), Bogue (1949), and Duncan et al. (1960) classify cities by types of dominance and amount of influence. According to Bogue, cities that specialize and produce more are those that control less specialized, less productive communities.

Bogue delineates four kinds of dominance relations found within any one area: dominants, which are the metropolitan centers, such as Chicago; subdominants, which are hinterland cities such as Chicago suburbs; influents, which are rural nonfarm towns, perhaps like Lake Geneva, Wisconsin; and subinfluents, which are rural areas like Zenda. Thus, Bogue would believe that Lincoln Park is far more dominant than Zenda, which exercises no influence.

Going to wider units, various metropolitan centers are classified by their sphere of influence; what Hawley (1950) terms primary, secondary, and tertiary correspond with the domination types (Duncan, *Resources for the Future*, 1960). Primary influence consists of daily movements between the center and periphery, including commuting and shopping. Duncan's diversified industrial centers, specialized industrial centers, and particular types of cities exercise primary influence, which is confined to a single metropolitan area. Here we see a small percentage of Zenda residents who commute to work or regularly shop in Chicago, under the primary influence of Chicago; most Lincoln Park residents fall under primary influence.

Secondary influence refers to daily, indirect contact such as phone calls, radio, and newspaper circulation. Duncan calls these regional and submetropolitan regional capitals whose administrative and economic functions are exercised over a surrounding territory. Chicago certainly has secondary and regional influence over Zenda, as evidenced in the widespread reading of the *Chicago Tribune* and the wide audience of Chicago radio stations (especially WLS) and television stations.

Tertiary influence (Hawley 1950) or national metropolitan centers (Duncan, *Resources for the Future*, 1960) exercise vast — even worldwide — influence, particularly in financial, administrative, and information activities. For example, Paris dominates the fashion industry and New York's Wall Street the financial world.

To summarize, human ecologists stratify communities by the dominance of subsistence groups and by the location of groups in relation to the centers of cities. In turn, types of communities and cities can be ranked according to the extent of their influence.

Interaction

While the other four schools of community all include at least some micro element of interaction, human ecologists focus most exclusively at the macro and even subsocial level. Neither Quinn (1934) nor Hawley (1950) regards motivations and attitudes as the proper focus of human ecology.

According to Quinn, subsocial interaction involves the utilization of limited resources or limited space. The process of subsocial interaction distributes units spatially in accordance with the principle of minimum cost. Quinn defines ecological interaction as "mutual modification of living creatures through the medium of a limited source or supply upon which they are each dependent" (1934, p. 567). Each population or organism needs sufficient resources to survive and reproduce. Quinn gives as an example of ecological interaction two organisms locked in an airtight container and each using oxygen. The units of interaction may be single organisms, groups, or institutions. Types of ecological interaction include mutual reinforcement, adjustment, and competition. Competition does not encompass all ecological interactions, since living creatures may benefit each other by increasing resources. Aggregates do not confront each other, but impersonally and indirectly influence each other through the environment and the utilization of space or some scarce type of resource. For example, Zipf (1949) measured the interaction rate among cities by the volume of telephone calls, trips, household moves, freight shipments, and newsletter circulation. He found interaction related to the size of the population and the distance between cities.

When a Zenda farmer tries to buy land that a Lincoln Park resident wants for a summer home, they are interacting ecologically, as are a Zenda resident and a Lincoln Park resident applying for the same job. In Zenda the use of chemicals and other treatment of the land (draining, cutting trees) indirectly changes the environment and affects other people. In Lincoln Park pollution from industries, dog nuisances, and noise are examples of ecological interaction. Lincoln Park and Zenda interact indirectly with one another. Lincoln Park residents use resources from Zenda, such as milk and land. Zenda experiences Lincoln Park ecologically through the crowds coming from the city into their territory and the airplanes from O'Hare Airport circling overhead. In both Lincoln Park and Zenda interaction occurs when people are engaged in any of the subsistence activities of working, shopping, or consuming.

On the other hand, Quinn qualifies his emphasis on ecological interaction by saying that for humans, social interaction, which includes mental awareness and use of symbols, is also necessary, since for humans ecological interactions occur in cultural contexts. Park and Burgess (1921) discuss interaction as the basic principle of society (but not community), with its natural levels of interactions of senses, interactions of emotions, and interactions of sentiments and ideas. Most human ecologists do not discuss interaction.

TIME

Long term is more important to human ecologists than short term, because the cycles of competition and succession that distinguish human ecology from other approaches to change occur in the long run, as do more gradual changes of evolution and adaptation. In the short term, populations shift throughout the different time periods of the day. Both long term and short term involve the shifting of aggregates through space.

History

In the long run, human ecologists view two interrelated but distinct processes of evolution and succession cycles. Even though the first is continuous and the second discrete, they both apply to communities.

Evolution

Over long periods of time communities change gradually, as populations grow and differentiate into increasingly specialized divisions of labor. Expansion and technological change contribute to the twin evolutionary processes of growth and differentiation.

Human ecologists relate evolution to changes in technology and new forms of sustenance organizations. Changes in technology produce new capacities for utilizing resources. Duncan et al. (1960), Hawley (1950), and McKenzie (1968) discuss the technological transitions from nomadic hunting and gathering societies, to horticulturalists, to agricultural and herding societies, to industrial orders. Duncan (1964) relates evolution to the accelerated use of new forms of energy, such as coal and gas. Gras (1922) proposes five states of evolution: collectional economy, cultural-nomadic economy, settled villages, towns, and metropolises. While Zenda seems less evolved at the village, agricultural stage than Lincoln Park at the industrial, metropolitan stage, both have experienced technological changes with improvements in machines and transportation.

Expansion

Like plant and animal communities, human communities grow with population increase and encompassment of more territory. Hawley (1950) defines expansion as "progressive absorption of more or less unrelated populations and land area into a single organization" (p. 348). A locus broadens its periphery of influence in either a centripetal way, drawing external populations inward, or in a centrifugal way, pushing from the center outward. Historically, cities have first expanded centripetally because of the attraction of populations to places of movement and crossroads.

The growth of Zenda and Lincoln Park both began centripetally as pioneers migrated in and as people from Chicago moved northward to Lincoln Park. Then Lincoln Park itself grew and expanded centrifugally and was absorbed by the city of Chicago; Lincoln Park reflects the outward growth of Chicago. Zenda, as a nonmetropolitan area, has experienced no centrifugal expansion. Lincoln Park's population size reached its peak in 1950, the same year Zenda started to grow more rapidly (see Table 3.3).

In the continued growth of cities, at the conflux of movement, improved technology advanced and markets developed. In turn, trade enlarged the subsistence base and broadened the cooperating populations. Populations flowed inward to staff growing functional units and native populations grew because of the increased subsistence

TABLE 3.3
Population of Linn Township and Lincoln Park, 1920-70

	Linn Township	Lincoln Park
1920	1,210	94,274
1930	1,220	97,873
1940	1,179	100,826
1950	1,455	102,996
1960	1,620	88,836
1970	1,910	67,793

base, resulting in more births and fewer deaths. The shift in population from technology changes resulted in the reorganization of the territory and a re-sorting of the population in functional units. Along with population growth and reorganization must come physical structures — buildings, roads, and so on. With continued growth, populations shift even more and may decrease at the center (Hawley 1950).

McKenzie (1927) opposes Hawley in believing that communities first expand at the periphery, uniformly and symmetrically, extending boundaries outward. With more sophisticated transportation and communication, populations expand in an axiated and differentiated way, sending out spokes from various points and lines on the boundary. For example, Lincoln Park grew rapidly along public transportation routes, and the railroad stop in Zenda caused the beginning and growth of the village.

According to Hawley, expansion of the city does not at first increase the scope of local communities. They remain compact and independent, because initial changes in transportation improve long-distance but not short-distance hauling. Not until the invention of automobiles and the building of highways did local communities significantly change. With the technological development of motorized vehicles and telephones, local services and stores shift, weakening the traditional support of local communities, as illustrated in Zenda. New categoric associations form in local communities, though the political organization becomes confused and dispersed, with only one unit. Cost, time, and competition with other communities and other metropolitan areas limit expansion.

Technology has brought changes in Zenda and Lincoln Park. The advent of the railroad produced a centralization in Zenda, although later improvements in automobiles and roads led farmers to ship milk by trucks. Lincoln Park was made possible by the building of bridges across the Chicago River, which opened up the North Side. Changes in public transportation, from horse carts to elevated trains, tied Lincoln Park more and more to the city of Chicago.

U.S. history also reflects this gradual expansion of the metropolis. When the first census was taken in 1790, 95 percent of the population was rural and 5 percent urban — defined as residency in a municipality of 2,500 people or more. The urban population gradually gained over the rural population, so that by 1920 the ratio was about even. In 1940 the Standard Metropolitan Statistical Area (an area with a population of 50,000 or more) was added to the census. By 1970 the reversal of the original census was almost complete, with more than 70 percent of the population urban and less than 30 percent rural.

In addition to rural-to-urban expansion, urban areas have continued to grow outward to suburbs and rural areas. Marshall explains white movement to suburbs by the availability of space for new housing (1979), while Ericksen (1979) says that the location of work opportunities, the economics of traveling to work, and the availability of housing contribute to suburban residential patterns.

Since the 1940s, after the Second World War, U.S. suburbs experienced the greatest increase in population, but the 1980s are witnessing the growth of nonmetropolitan areas, even though they constitute only a small proportion of the population. Change in sustenance organization forms the major explanatory variable, according to Frisbie and Poston (1975, 1978a,b). Heaton, Clifford, and Fuguitt (1981) agree, citing especially tourism and retirement as increasing industries of sustenance organization. Thus they explain the change in nonmetropolitan areas by recreation and leisure industries and the growth of retirement populations. Sly (1972) and Sly and Tayman (1977, 1980) link loss of population from central cities to the exodus of nonresidential activities that extend beyond the boundaries of metropolitan areas, a characteristic of the advanced stage of metropolitanization.

Cycles

In addition to the gradual evolution and expansion of communities and metropolitan areas, human ecologists envision more abrupt community changes that occur with succession cycles of different groups and different land usages. The cycles consist of alternating phases of equilibrium and competition. McKenzie defines ecological process as "the tendency in time toward special forms of spatial and sustenance groupings of the units of an ecological distribution" (1926, p. 144), and lists five such processes: concentration, centralization, segregation, invasion, and succession.

McKenzie's concentration and centralization overlap with Hawley's expansion and reorganization because they all denote the growth processes of communities. The processes of competition and succession, which show changes in land use, institutional services, and occupation type, began with a concentration of people. Concentration is "the tendency of an increasing number of persons to settle in a given area or region" (McKenzie 1926, p. 144), as measured by density. Where once concentration was dependent on food supplies and natural resources, strategic locations of concentration are now based more on commerce and industry, as exemplified in the beginning of Lincoln Park and Zenda by waterways, and the greater growth of Lincoln Park because of its proximity to industry and commerce. Concentration in one place often implies its opposite — dispersal — in another place. Institutions also tend to concentrate in places of large population size.

"Centralization is an effect of the tendency of human beings to come together at definite locations for the satisfaction of specific common interests such as work, play, business, education" (McKenzie 1926, p. 146). It is a stage after concentration and implies an organization with a middle and periphery. McKenzie equates it with community formation. The focal point of concentration is the marketplace. According to Quinn (1950), centralization functions to integrate surrounding areas. It further connotes an increase in functions, specialization, and a shift from agriculture to urban-area activity.

Competition and selection produce segregation, but segregation may also follow succession. Segregation territorially separates populations. Quinn (1950) posits that it exists when greater numbers of ecological units of a given type occur in one or more sections of a territory than in others. Segregation shifts and sorts people into homogeneous groupings. McKenzie believes that economic segregation is the basic form, but also may include language, culture, and race. Economic segregation is more homogeneous at the bottom of the economic scale.

Human ecologists would see many communities in Lincoln Park, since segregation prevents some ethnic groups from sharing with others, whereas in Zenda one group has maintained a strong hold on the environment through much of its history and no ethnic or racial differences exist. For example, according to the 1970 census, Lincoln Park had 1.5 percent blacks, whereas Linn Township had .1 percent; Lincoln Park had 20 percent Spanish-speaking, whereas Linn had .2 percent; Lincoln Park had 36 percent foreign-born and Linn 8 percent.

The process of succession involves invasion, competition, and segregation. Once populations have become concentrated and centralized, their order may be upset by the influx of a different population. "Invasion is a process of group displacement; it implies the encroachment of one area of segregation upon another" (McKenzie 1926, p. 140). According to Aldrich (1975), invasion may initially occur because a residential group no longer replaces itself. Invasion of a new group is readily seen in schools, but stores and churches may hold their patrons even though they move out of the territory. Zenda and Lincoln Park both began as invasions into the territory of native Americans and succeeded the Indians there. In turn, the invasion resulted from expansion, first from the growth of eastern U.S. communities and then from the migratory and trade routes through the waterways surrounding what became Chicago.

In competition, living beings struggle for existence and for location (Park 1952). Hawley defines competition as a kind of interaction in which "each individual affects the behavior of every other by its effect upon the common supply of sustenance materials" (1950, p. 39). It varies with the organism-to-resource ratio, the segregation of populations, and the degree of similarity among competitors. Hawley suggests that the stages of competition are, first, a demand on resources that exceeds the supply; second, homogeneity among competitors, calling for conditions of competition and uniform responses; third, the pressure of congestion, which eliminates the weakest; fourth, the resulting differentiation and reorganization, because the weaker either segregate into a different territory or adapt to the old community in a new way (1950, p. 202). Competition is a self-resolving relationship. Park (1952) distinguishes competition, which occurs at the community level, from conflict, such as war, which occurs at the societal level.

Zenda seems to compete with outsiders, primarily urbanites, and has continued to do so since the 1870s, when urbanites first built summer homes around the lake and converted farmland to residences. Now urbanites are invading the village and bringing industry. Lincoln Park also has land competition. Hospitals and schools have expanded their land use and taken over previously residential territory, proving the institutions more fit and better adapted to the territory while residential land use appears weaker. On the other hand, residential use has prevented commercial take-over and restricted some tendencies toward greater concentration of people.

In the process of succession, different groups are invading, competing for the resources and space in a given niche, and often a new dominant group arises. Succession is an orderly sequence of change (Park 1952, p. 152) that replaces one occupant or land use with another.

Duncan and Duncan (1955) suggest that the succeeding populations resemble the replaced populations because of the structure of the city in what they call situational and site variables. The situational factors refer to the function of each niche in relation to the whole city — for example, serving a residential purpose. Site factors refer to physical attributes such as building and landscaping, which are difficult to change.

Taeuber and Taeuber (1969) delineated a model of racial transition in ecological succession. As with other ethnic groups, blacks first settle near the center of the city and may, with economic improvement, move farther out. Although most central cities remain predominantly black, some studies in the 1970s and 1980s focus on black movement to suburbs. In three different articles Marshall and Stahura find that growth of black populations in suburbs depends on the characteristics of the suburb and also on the size of the central city (1979a,b).

Lincoln Park provides good examples of succession cycles. German truck farmers first invaded Lincoln Park. After the Chicago fire, with a demand for housing in Lincoln Park, residential land use took over farming, while industry located along the river. Swedish, Irish, Scotch, Polish, Slav, and Hungarian groups were part of this new invasion, though Germans continued to be dominant. Ethnic churches, hospitals, schools, and stores were built, which in the early 1900s became more secular. Italians came, too, and by 1920 a small enclave of blacks. In the 1940s Spanish-speaking people, Appalachian whites, and more blacks invaded the now dilapidated buildings of Lincoln Park — then Bohemians and artists — until the 1950s, when a reversal began that continues today with an influx of white upper-middle-class residents. The remnants of previous invasions remain in various parts of Lincoln Park, particularly in the Ranch Triangle, from which Spanish-speaking ethnic groups are naturally beginning to move farther west.

Succession is cyclical, as it is with plant communities, with one ethnic group replacing another or with industrial or commercial use replacing residential land use. Ethnic groups or other interest groups may compete for space use and services in an area until one succeeds another. Park and others note a climax stage in succession in which one group "matures" and maintains a stable hold on a particular location.

In sum, communities grow and differentiate through migration and technological changes. With segregation in communities, groups compete for space and resources and, as a result, change their locations through cycles of succession. The cycles show a great difference between the rural and the urban community, with Lincoln Park experiencing numerous cycles and Zenda only a very few.

Process

In the short term, populations shift places of concentration throughout the day. Foley (1954) finds historical, economic, and technological forces that help explain the spatial change of populations from night to day. During the day many people commute to central business districts and deplete residential areas because of the concentration of employment, shopping, and professional and cultural services in big cities. He contends that changes in spatial location from day to night have an ecological basis, since the movements link functional areas and integrate cities characterized by specialization and segregation. Historically, location of daytime populations has remained fairly stable, while residential areas have undergone dispersal; technological improvements in transportation facilitate the continued daily increase in central city populations.

O'Brien (1942) finds almost the opposite pattern for Beale Street in Memphis, Tennessee. The nighttime blues of Beale street attracted a greater population than the daytime commerce, but this also shifted historically. Before the popularity of the blues on Beale Street, nighttime populations diminished, as they do now that the music establishments are no longer so prominent.

Daily populations shift in Lincoln Park, as most residents leave the area for work, but many other non-Lincoln Park residents enter the area to work, use the hospitals, schools, and cultural facilities. Other populations come for the Lincoln Park night life. In Zenda very little daily shifting occurs; only a few people leave the area to work and a few enter to work in the village factories. No night life attracts populations.

Schwartz (1978) examines the ecology of time use in terms of waiting and delay in doctors' offices. He found a relationship of income and race to waiting time (p. 1203), "because concentrations of family doctors are centered in the most affluent section of the white community." At the center of these concentrations doctors compete for clients, while at the periphery clients compete for doctors.

In addition to daily movements of populations and waiting time of different groups, time has also influenced daily life in spreading production, which impacts on sustenance activities. The division of labor speeds time and specialization decreases time limitations (Hawley 1981).

Time does influence the subsistence activities of Lincoln Park and Zenda in different ways. Zenda residents depend more on seasons, while hours and days of the week do not determine harvesting or planting. The organisms of cows and crops impose natural cycles of milking and feeding. More tourists invade Zenda in the summer months. In Lincoln Park, bureaucratic time structures 8-to-5 jobs and weekdays, as distinct from weekends.

SPACE

Territory

Space as a dimension of community is far more important to human ecologists than to any other community theory. Space has been a part of every section of this chapter: the econiches and habitats of the metaphor; the spatial distributions and mappings of the methodology; the accommodations of institutions to space and increased specialization of institutions in relation to increased density of populations in particular locations; dominance by location; interaction as use of space that impinges on another group; expansion as increasingly larger territorial organization; cycles of succession within places and segregation by spatial distance; daily movement of populations in space. The word "ecology" has almost become synonymous with space use and distribution. This section emphasizes the structure or layout of space in communities and how this has changed, as well as how the spatial organization is variously interpreted. The words "space," location," "place," and "environment" have been used indiscriminately, but Hawley defines environments as "all external conditions which impinge on human behavior" (1950, p. 188), including populations, topography, climate, and sustenance materials.

The ecologist most associated with spatial structure is Burgess, who analyzed the structure of the city of Chicago, which showed a contrast to historically older cities. For example, Sjoberg (1960) describes the preindustrial city as a walled citadel that contains a center consisting of a cathedral and government offices or a palace surrounded by the residences of the wealthiest class. Farther out were the artisans' houses and the market; farming occurred beyond the walls.

Focusing on the territorial bases of communities, Burgess developed his concentric-zone hypothesis, which is an ideal typification of the physical layout of Chicago as well as of the way cities grow. From the center to ever-increasing distances from the center, land use and patterns of residency differ.

> Every community as it grows expands outward from its center. This radical extension from the downtown business district toward the outskirts of the city is due partly to business and industrial pressure and partly to residential pull. Business and light manufacturing, as they develop, push out from the center of the city and encroach upon residences. At the same time, families are always responding to the appeal of more attractive residential districts further and even further removed from the center of the city. (Burgess 1928, p. 106)

Burgess distinguished five distinct zones: the central business district, the zone of transition, the zone of working class homes, residential zones, and commuter zones (see Figure 3.1). Each zone has a center and boundaries based on physical-geographical features or land values.

The central business district, the Loop in Chicago, is the location of financial districts, shopping centers, theater districts, hotels, and skyscraper office buildings. It provides a significant proportion of jobs and restaurants. The central business district centralizes and dominates the rest of the city by being the most desirable zone with the highest property values.

Surrounding the downtown area, the zone in transition houses factories and an impermanent area for new immigrants, the poor, and derelicts. As the least desirable part of the city, the zone in transition is crowded with rooming houses, ethnic ghettoes, and criminals. The natural areas of the zone in transition have been studied more than any other zone.

People in the third zone have escaped the area of deterioration and are blue-collar residents. They live in apartment houses and

FIGURE 3.1
Burgess's Concentric Zones

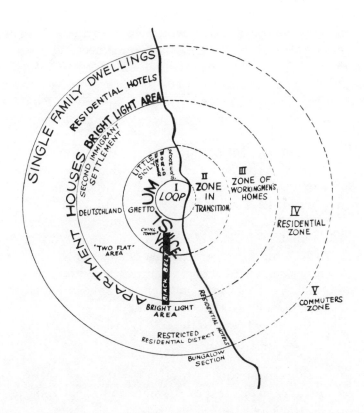

Source: Reprinted from E. Burgess, "The Growth of the City" in *The City* (Robert Park, Ernest Burgess, and Roderick McKenzie, eds.) 1925, p. 55. Copyright 1925 by The University of Chicago Press.

have not been able to move to better districts. In the fourth district are single-family homes of the white-collar families. Occasionally small service or entertainment centers of bright-light areas are found in these zones. The fifth zone consists of commuters from suburbs and satellites. Suburbs may taper off into even farther out communities that have their own concentric zones, depend less on the metropolis, and are called satellites.

Students of Park and Burgess applied the zones theory to show and explain how statistics varied, depending on the city area: rates of suicide (Cavan 1928), mental disorders (Faris and Dunham 1939), and crime (Reckless 1926). All of these rates tended to be higher near the center of the city and to decrease with progression away from the center.

The zones, transportation, and other topographical features break the city into small areas, which Zorbaugh (1929) calls natural areas — natural in the sense of being unplanned and a result of the city's growth. They are small spatial units, separated from other parts of the city, in which nestle homogeneous groups that are equivalent to communities. Zorbaugh, a student of Park, described the mix of such areas on the near north side of Chicago — the Gold Coast and the slum. Natural areas tend to coincide with cultural groups — for example, Little Italy, Harlem, Chinatown.

The spatial structure of Zenda is somewhat closer to the medieval pattern, with (formerly) a church and (still) the town hall in the center of the village surrounded by farms. Lincoln Park forms part of the concentric zones of Chicago. As these zones have changed over time, Lincoln Park has changed from an outlying farm district to a suburb to a middle-class area that changed into a zone in transition, and now has reverted to a wealthy residential area. Functions segregate Lincoln Park into residential zones, industrial parks, hospital and university districts, but these do not form concentric zones, since the area closest to the lake is the most desirable.

Criticisms of Burgess's concentric zones led to alternative theories of the physical structure of cities, because not all cities are laid out in concentric zones. Hoyt's (1939) sector theory envisions city structures as wedge-shaped divisions radiating from one center, often along transportation lines. Harris and Ullman (1945) saw that instead of one center, cities have several centers and proposed the multinuclei theory. Each center may specialize in a different function, such as financial, commercial, or wholesale. Specialized concentration promotes greater attraction to the services; for example, people will shop areas that have several shoe stores to get the best selections and buys.

Zenda has a northern sector of urbanites who live along the lake, just as Lincoln Park has industrial sectors, hospital sectors, and shopping sectors that stretch along some of the major streets. Zenda has almost no nucleus other than the village, although it could be argued that since most people bank in Hebron, use medical services in Lake Geneva, and shop in Walworth, these are also nuclei. Lincoln Park has several shopping centers besides the numerous ones of greater Chicago. Some communities have shopping centers in addition to those in the downtown area.

To human ecologists, space as well as location is a resource. As a resource, it produces something. Living beings compete for space as for air, water, and other natural resources. Lincoln Park has the locational advantage, but Zenda has the resource of space. Lincoln Park is closer to the central business district and its advantages of culture, specialized employment, and good medical care, but it is also closer to the zone in transition and its disadvantages. Zenda is located closer to natural resources.

Space as a resource is more apparent in Zenda, where fields of crops dominate the land use as the main sustenance activity in Zenda. In Lincoln Park land is a resource for buildings such as hospitals, which make their sustenance contribution to keeping people alive. Space becomes a scarce resource as populations and institutions grow. Zenda has an abundance of open space, whereas the density of Lincoln Park means open space is a scarcity.

With spatial resource differences, the weather, as part of the environment, becomes more important to Zenda than to Lincoln Park. For example, a storm, blight, or pest invasion in Zenda at a wrong time can ruin crops and, therefore, people's livelihood. In Lincoln Park work continues in bureaucracies regardless of weather conditions; only major crises and disasters such as the blizzards of 1979 and 1981 cripple the work activities. On the other hand, climate conditions that affect the crops in Zenda can influence the prices or scarcity of products in Lincoln Park.

Boundaries

Human ecologists pay particular attention to physical boundaries. Park defines boundaries in terms of barriers to communication and movement: "Geographical barriers and physical distance are significant for sociology only when and where they define the conditions under which communication and social life are actually maintained" (1952, p. 174). Physical barriers include natural features of the landscape — for example, bodies of water, mountains, deserts, and forests. People's use of land also creates boundaries — such as highways, industrial parks, railways, and buildings — that can hinder flows of people. Boundaries can be overcome by improved technology: bridges can span a river, airplanes fly over boundaries, and people can talk to one another via the telephone and citizen-band radios. Modern technology blurs boundaries, according to Hawley (1950, p. 255). Both Lincoln Park and Zenda have natural boundaries of lakes, the river in Chicago, and person-made boundaries of highways, streets, and industrial areas. Both also lack clearly defined boundaries that separate them from other communities, particularly to the north and south of Lincoln Park and the east and west of Zenda.

According to Barry and Plant (1978), metropolitan and non-metropolitan areas compete for land and extension of metropolitan boundaries. For the most part, metropolitan areas are winning, as urbanization generates idle land. Land-use controls are too costly and weak to prevent the continuation of metropolitan expansion.

In addition to physical barriers, human ecologists use extent of sustenance organization to determine boundaries: to the extent that populations depend on one another for their livelihood and are symbiotic, the community continues. For example, Galpin's (1915) examination of the extent of community services provides an index of community boundaries. Since each service yields a slightly different margin, boundaries tend to be imprecise. Park (1929) suggests that the extent of newspaper circulation may be the best indicator of community boundaries. The extent of dominance is another. Technology and metropolitanization have expanded communities to metropolitan areas and even to a worldwide interdependence (McKenzie 1968). According to Hawley, rural boundaries are more distinct: they "are formed where the territories of neighboring communities converge and overlap, where the integrating influences emanating from different centers meet in competition" (1950, p. 249). Boundaries become fixed by the maximum radius of movement to and from a center. The sustenance organizations link Zenda and Lincoln Park and make Zenda the outer boundary of the Chicago metropolitan area. It is one of the farthest points from Chicago that has a commuter train to Chicago. Zenda is also one of the most distant places to supply milk to the city.

SUMMARY

Since early in this century, human ecologists have been striving to develop a distinct way of studying communities along the lines of biological research. Rural and urban areas both received attention from early human ecologists who soon concentrated at the University of Chicago with Robert Park and his students to study space and subsocial forces. Later other University of Chicago personnel, under the leadership of Amos Hawley, transferred human ecology emphasis to the study of subsistence activities. Human ecologists continue to study communities in terms of large aggregates of populations that rearrange over space and time.

In organizing into subsistence activities for staying alive, populations compete with some groups and are symbiotic with others. One group may dominate others and control their livelihood and placement. With evolution, groups grow and expand until other groups take over in a series of succession cycles involving competition for space. Even over a day, populations transfer from one part of the city to another. Space is very important to human ecologists, involving the study of econiches, zones, centers, and sectors. Physical boundaries contain the extent of subsistence activities.

Human ecologists would see Lincoln Park and Zenda as different-sized aggregates adapted to their environments, with subsistence activities that link the rural and urban areas symbiotically. The central business district of Chicago dominates both places. Lincoln Park has experienced more succession cycles and has become more complexly differentiated. It has the advantage of a location closer to the central business district, while Zenda has the advantage of space as a resource, which produces subsistence.

Critics have disagreed with human ecologists who claim that human communities differ little from plant and animal communities. Functionalists, in examining less spatial, less changing aspects of community, attempt to present a more social view of communities and a more in-depth view of single communities.

4

Structural Functionalism: Community as Consensus

The preceding chapter identified the human-ecology focus on communities. Comparing human communities to plant and animal communities, human ecologists see competition and subsistence as the processes. Communities progress through shifting spatial distributions of people and changes in land use.

In contrast, functionalists emphasize the organization and integration within communities: stability rather than change and structure rather than process. While both human ecology and functionalism are related to biology, functionalists take a holistic view of a single, unified community rather than relations among communities.

The central question functionalists ask about communities is what holds them together. Part of the answer is consensus or agreement on norms and values. Social order is based on the interdependence of social units with shared values and norms. Another part of the answer is that each social structure is dependent on all the others, because each contributes a function necessary to the survival of all. The key concepts, then, are structure, function, and consensus.

Levy (1968, p. 31) defines function as "any state of a unit of the type under consideration in terms of a structure." A structure is "a pattern in terms of which action takes place." Looking at the purpose of the parts and how they work through order and harmony summarizes the answer to what holds a community together. For example, Lloyd Warner and Paul Lunt (1941, p. 12) define a community as "a working whole in which each part had definite functions which had to be performed or substitutes acquired if the whole society were to maintain itself." In other words, functionalists believe that every social structure must serve some end or it would not exist.

Further structural-functional definitions are in terms of the people who call themselves functionalists and the kinds of concepts they have developed. To apply structural functionalism to communities, we use the historical development of the paradigm, which shows the sources of the systems metaphor and the functionalist treatment of each of the three dimensions of community: people, place, and time. Functionalism focuses on the institutions, boundary maintenance, evolution, and roles of Zenda and Lincoln Park.

HISTORICAL DEVELOPMENT

The historical development of structural functionalism proceeds from its classical founding by French reactions to the revolutions and by British anthropologists, through American interpretations by Parsons (1937, 1949, 1951) and Merton (1949), ending with empirical applications of functionalism to communities. In reaction to the chaos wrought by the French and Industrial Revolutions, structural functionalists wanted to reinstate order. They looked to traditional communities as they had been before the great transformations, and developed theories that promoted the former, stable way of life. Durkheim leads this school of thought, although Comte and British anthropologists also made contributions.

The Classical View

Disturbed by the fall of the *ancien régime*, the French founder of sociology, Auguste Comte proposed a new ordering of institutions able to cope with the changes in the new society. Advocating an "organic attitude" (1896), he thought sociology could serve an integrative function to realize order; that is, principles could be developed for creating social consensus. Comte sought to discover laws that prescribe a plan for the reconstruction of society under the primacy of order, and proposed a vision of society as a holistic unity that was greater than the sum of its parts. Comte's functionalist concept was social statics through which he explained the co-existence and interrelation of social phenomena, including all institutions, morals, and beliefs.

While Comte named the discipline "sociology," Emile Durkheim (another Frenchman, born in 1858, the year after Comte died) was the first person to hold an academic position in sociology, and he initiated the first sociology journal, *L'Année Sociologique*. Durkheim worked hard to make sociology a distinct discipline, particularly with his concept of social fact defined as "every way of acting, fixed or not, capable of exercising on the individual an external constraint" (1950, p. 13). He argued that social facts were not reducible to biological or psychological phenomena but were the collective constraints uniting people.

Durkheim also preferred an ordered society. With his theories emphasizing solidarity and moral integration, he treated departures from order and equilibrium as pathological. In *The Division of Labor in Society* (1964), Durkheim explained in a functionalist way that the division of labor integrates society either by everyone working alike (mechanical solidarity) or by differences in work complementing one another (organic solidarity) (p. 10). He was also concerned with the chaos resulting from a breakdown of morals. In his study of religion, *Elementary Forms of Religious Life* (1965), he constructed religion's function as constraining people by rules and norms, which, in turn, express a sense of solidarity for people.

In addition to discussing solidarity in labor and religion, Durkheim's methods book, *The Rules of Sociological Method*, gives explicit functionalist prescriptions:

> The determination of function is . . . necessary for the complete explanation of the phenomena. . . . Consequently, to explain a social fact it is not enough to show the course on which it depends; we must also, at least in most cases, show its function in the establishment of the social order. (1950, pp. 96-97)

Inventions from the Industrial Revolution, particularly in navigation, and the need for resources and markets led to exploration and colonization of Africa, Asia, and America and the development of anthropology.* British anthropologists Radcliffe-Brown (1958) and Malinowski (1936) named the theory of structural functionalism and provided the first empirical works to support it. While not doing field work himself, Spencer's (1898) structural functionalist ideas were also influenced by British imperialism and knowledge of different peoples.

Spencer believed in the self-regulatory mechanism of society, based on individual pursuits, rather than the collective emphasis of Durkheim. He contributed to functionalist thought the adaptation and evolution concepts through a classification of societies based on the complexity of structure and how each part contributes to the whole:

> If organization consists in such a construction of the whole that its parts can carry on mutually dependent actions, then in proportion as organization is high there must go a dependence of each part upon the rest so great that separation is fatal; and conversely. This truth is equally well shown in the individual organism and in the social organism. (1966, p. 473)

According to Spencer, societies proceed through gradual differentiation in complexity and functions, which bring superior adaptations to the environment. Reduction of disharmony is a quality of superior survival.

Radcliffe-Brown (1958) changed social anthropology from a preoccupation with historical development and psychological extrapolation to a comparative study of how societies persist and function. He believed that solidarity was necessary for survival, and therefore consistency among parts of a community was important. Finding that societies exhibit basic structural consistencies, he then asked: How does each structure contribute to the maintenance of the whole? He defined structural functionalism as analyzing

---

*Imperialism made possible the study of tribal and peasant peoples. Gough (1968) calls anthropology "the child of imperialism," because anthropologists' knowledge was useful in exploiting people and resources. As Caulfield (1969) suggests, "a definition of problems in anthropology has been shaped by the need to explain the relation of dominated to dominating people" (p. 182).

the "continuing arrangement of persons in relationships defined or controlled by institutions with socially established norms or patterns of behavior" (p. 77).

Malinowski (1936)* defines structural functionalism as "the principle that in every type of civilization, every custom, material object, idea and belief, fulfills some vital function, has some task to accomplish, represents an indispensable part within a working whole" (p. 132). He delineates basic needs, such as food, shelter, reproduction, and how these are met by structures in societies. All cultural parts meet some need.

The American Interpretation

The American interpretation of functionalism emerged in a historical period in which disorder and the decay of free enterprise appeared imminent. An economic depression and the foreboding of a second world war were major social forces influencing intellectual thought. In the 1930s Talcott Parsons formed a broad, modern theory of order based on the classical theories. In so doing, Parsons became America's best known sociologist. While believing that science could preserve Western values, Parsons removed himself from social problems, in the name of detachment, and viewed the larger total system. He was further sheltered by Harvard University which only wealthy elites entered (Gouldner 1970). Friedrichs (1970, p. 17) points out that Parsons's later works developed in an era of conformity and commitment to the status quo.

Parsons's theories consist of systems and subsystems within systems, which interrelate, yet also have their own integrative problems. The three main systems are personality, cultural, and social. The personality system is based on the social system, because actors are oriented to a consensus of values, norms, and beliefs (the cultural system) that derive from the social system. Parsons defines the social system as "a mode of organization of action elements relative to the persistence or ordered processes of change of the interactive

---

*Malinowski, known through his diaries as a racist as well as an imperialist studied Melanesians and others for the British (Willis 1969).

patterns of a plurality of individual actors" (1951, p. 24). The orientations of the three systems are directed to integration and stability.

> The problem of order, and thus of the nature of the integration of stable systems of social interaction, that is, of social structure . . . focuses on the integration of the motivation of actors within the normative cultural standards which integrate the action system, in our context interpersonally. These standards . . . are patterns of value orientation. (Parsons 1951, p. 36)

A further link between the social system and the personality action system is in the convergence of roles and institutions. The actor participates in social systems through only a part of the action, which is a role. Parsons points out that "social structure is a system of patterned relationships of actors in their capacity as playing roles relative to one another" (1949, p. 230). Actions that are patterned and repeated become institutions. Institutions meet needs of actors and social systems combined.

What do systems need in order to survive? Parsons defines the requisites as "the functional needs of social integration and the conditions necessary for the functioning of a plurality of actors as a unit system sufficiently well integrated to exist" (1949, p. 22). He proposes four needs or prerequisites that all social systems function to fill, commonly referred to as AGIL: adaptation, goal attainment, integration, and latent pattern maintenance. A system relates to the environment and secures resources for the system through adaptation. Goal attainment is a political function, determining and executing priorities. Integration is the most important because it links the parts of the system. Latency pattern maintenance consists of systems of socialization and tension management. A final part of Parsons's systems is their gradual change through evolution. AGIL slowly become differentiated and subsystems form, from a simple system to a more complex system (Parsons 1966).

In an essay on community, Parsons (1960) refers to the community as a social system or a part of a social system that has a territorial referent and from which specific role categories develop. The four categories of community are residence, work, jurisdiction (such as government and church), and communication complex (including common culture, technology, and monetary exchange).

A community is organized about a complex network of relations between place of residence, employment of adults, and schooling of children. These relations are regulated by jurisdiction and connected by communication complexes.

Robert Merton, a student of Parsons, elaborated Parsons's functional systems through the concepts of manifest and latent functions, role sets, status sets, and status sequences. He argued that the concept of function has many implications and is not only what people intend or recognize. Some functions are manifest, others latent:

> Manifest functions are those objective consequences contributing to the adjustment or adaptation of the system which are intended and recognized by participants in the system. Latent functions, correlatively, being those which are neither intended nor recognized. (Merton 1967, p. 105)

In addition, there may be functional alternatives — one structure may have many functions and some functions may be filled in many ways. This means that a system such as a community can survive without all local subsystems or institutions.

One example Merton gives of functional analysis applies to community. His analysis of political machines can relate to community because he views political machines as part of a community, filling functions unmet by other parts of the community: namely, to personalize provision of goods and services to deprived classes and to provide political partiality to businesses and mobility to some people. Political machines further organize, centralize, and maintain the scattered fragments of power. Merton's political-machine analysis reveals his advocation of middle-range theories, which derive from grand theories but provide a closer tie to empirical realities. Another set of his middle-range theories is on roles and statuses.

According to Merton, each status or position in a social system involves an array of roles or orientations to various people. For example, a community leader (status) has a variety of roles relating to outsiders, other leaders, and constituents. Merton labels these various roles for a single status as role sets. On the other hand, a status set refers to all the statuses of a particular individual. A community leader may also be a parent, have an occupation, be a church member, and so on. Status sequence refers to the change in statuses of one person over time. According to Merton, these three — role sets, status sets, and status sequences — also require a kind of consensus or consistency: "Operating social structures must somehow manage to organize these sets and sequences of statuses and roles so that an appreciable degree of social order obtains" (Merton 1949, p. 424). Role sets, status sets, and status sequences are integrated into systems.

Empirical Analysis

While Parsons and Merton both made contributions to the study of community, they are primarily theorists, whereas the authors discussed in this section on empirical analysis are more explicitly community analysts. Sanders (1958) and Warren (1978) are theorists and have written community textbooks. The remaining authors discussed in this section have carried out empirical studies.

Sanders and Warren (and earlier, Mercer 1956) have made the widest application of functionalism to communities. As the major community textbook writer in the 1950s and early 1960s, Sanders (1958) emphasizes the community as a system and addresses issues of equilibrium, community institutions, requirements (or operations), and adaptation. The main body of the text covers the five basic parts of community systems: economy, religion, government, family, and education. Each of these contains subsystems, social groupings, and role relations. Among these systems are processes of interaction, change, and control.

Roland Warren, another textbook writer, defines community as "that combination of social units and systems that perform the major social functions having locality relevance" (1978, p. 9). He analyzes five major functions with reference to locality: production-distribution-consumption, socialization, social control, social participation, and mutual support. Like Sanders, Warren primarily writes about community institutions and their independence as systems, but he adds some new conceptualizations relating to community. His major contribution is the development of the idea that communities have vertical and horizontal axes.

According to Warren (1978, p. 13) the horizontal pattern is "the structural and functional relation of the various local units to each other." He addresses problems with local units, such as autonomy, fiscal crises, and transiency. Instead of dismissing the whole idea of community because of contemporary problems, Warren denotes how communities attach to other social systems through a vertical pattern: "the structural and functional relation of its various social units and subsystems to extra-community systems" (p. 163). The vertical pattern is how community institutions relate to other institutions and organizations outside the community. Many churches, lodges, and business establishments that have local branches are parts of national or international organizations.

The empirical study of communities in the United States was first carried out by anthropologists who were emulating studies of tribal and peasant communities. The classic American community studies that relate to functionalism are the Lynds' study of Middletown and Warner's Yankee City series.

The Lynds set the guidelines for future community studies by moving into a midwestern town and spending 18 months observing and learning about the community. Although they began with a study of religion in Muncie, Indiana, they found it difficult to study one isolated institution; a picture of the total community and the interrelations of institutions was needed. Thus, they studied earning a living, making a home, training the young, using leisure, engaging in religious practices, and engaging in community practices, all chapter subjects of *Middletown* (1929). Their approach is institutional and holistic.

Lloyd Warner, who had studied Australian aborigines, chose an American community that had a "social organization which had developed over a long period of time under the domination of a single group with a coherent tradition" (Warner and Lunt 1941, p. 4). Warner studied the community with the "analogy of the organism" (p. 12). He found consensus on Yankee City in that the residents had common interests and a common organization. In the five volumes written on Yankee City (Warner and Lunt 1941, 1942; Warner and Srole 1945; Warner and Low 1947; Warner 1959) the focus is on its class system, addressed from the functionalist viewpoint of what holds the classes together. Warner's community class system will be discussed in the section on stratification.

Terry Clark (1968) makes a direct application of Parsons's AGIL to communities. He discusses communal economic institutions that meet adaptation needs, communal political institutions that deal with goal attainment, and political parties and voluntary associations that serve the integrative function. Educational, religious, and other cultural institutions function to maintain patterns.

Communes

Other functional applications to communities have been studies of communes. Communes in the United States are relatively small, isolated, alternative communities, intentionally formed by people who react against societal norms. When many communes were formed by counterculture movements in the 1970s, sociologists began to study the phenomenon. Rosabeth Kanter, the most prominent commune researcher, defines communes as "voluntary, value-based, communal social orders" (1972, p. 2).

As a Harvard doctoral student, Kanter researched historical communes from a functionalist viewpoint. The three functions she considered necessary for a social system were continuance, cohesion, and control. Each of these functions is filled by a concomitant part of the personality system that Parsons had previously developed. All people orient themselves to a social system instrumentally, affectively, and morally.

Kanter's central concept is commitment, by which the personality system and social system are mutually benefited. She defines commitment as the "willingness of people to do what will help maintain the group because it provides what they need" (1972, p. 66). Her thesis is that increasing levels of commitment will lead to more successful communes (defined as long-lasting). Using historical documents of communes that flourished between 1780 and 1860, she finds that 21 communes lasted less than 16 years, and 9 lasted longer than 33 years. Kanter proves her thesis by showing that a greater number of commitment mechanisms are found in long-lasting communes than in short-lived communes.

The personality and social system needs that are filled by commitment mechanisms are summed in Table 4.1. Instrumental commitment implies a weighing of costs and profits and relates to continuance. Affective or cathectic commitment is the emotional part of a person. Affectivity joins persons into cohesion or solidarity. Obedience to norms and values is an evaluative, moral commitment that provides social control. For each of the three types of commitment, a person gives up something, especially in relation to previous community life, and gives to the new community, the commune.

TABLE 4.1
Kanter's Commitment Mechanisms in Relation to the Social and Personality Systems

Social System	Personality System	Commitment Mechanisms		
		Giving Up	*Giving To*	

Cohesion	Instrumental	Sacrifice:
		  Abstinence
		  Austerity
			Investment:
			  Physical participation
			  Financial contribution
			  Irreversibility of contribution	

Continuance	Affective	Renunciation:
		  Insulation
		  Cross-boundary control
		  Renunciation of couple
		  Renunciation of family
			Communion:
			  Homogeneity
			  Sharing
			  Labor
			  Regularized group contact	

Control	Evaluative	Mortification:
		  Confession and mutual
		    criticism
		  Sanctions
		  Spiritual differentiation
		  Deindividuation
			Transcendence:
			  Ideological awe
			  Awe to power and authority
			  Guidance
			  Ideological conversion
			  Tradition	

A few other studies on communes relate to functionalism. Stoneall's (1974) case study of a western commune utilized Parsons's concept of integration to show how the parts of the communal system work together. Gardner's (1978) examination of 13 contemporary communes indicates that, of Kanter's commitment mechanisms, only sacrifice and renunciation distinguish success.

More Recent Studies

A perusal of *Sociological Abstracts* from 1977 to 1981 reveals a minority of U.S. communities studied from a functionalist perspective. One major thrust of most recent functionalist approaches to community has been comparison cross-sectionally or historically of differentiation and functional specialization in communities. Donald Warren (1978) discusses differentiation of urban neighborhoods by function. Guest (1978) examines functional differentiation in employment.

Another area of concern for current functionalist approaches to community is the ways in which various functions are met. Dye and Garcia (1978) compare functions of city governments. Stahura (1978) questions what influences the functions of suburbs as well as what causes the evolution of statuses of suburbs (1979). Vickerman (1979) decided that urban systems best fill the function of adaptation, rather than equilibrium. Sale (1978) tries to calculate the community size that allows for optimum functioning with fewest problems.

Still other community functionalists consider the decline of functions. According to Guest (1977), employment and housing functions have declined in major metropolitan areas, due to the aging process of communities. Sternlieb discusses the declining autonomy of small cities (1978).

Throughout the history of structural functionalism, from its appearance shortly after the French and Industrial Revolutions to more recent applications to community, a concern with consensus, order, and purpose have continued to dominate functionalist thought. The history of functionalism lays the foundation for the theoretical elements of community — metaphor, method, and the three dimensions of community: people, time, and space — that are specific to functionalism (Table 4.2). These theoretical elements are illustrated with comparisons and contrasts of the rural and urban communities of Zenda and Lincoln Park, from a functionalist viewpoint.

METAPHOR

The metaphor of a perspective can provide a *Gestalt* or overview of what a community looks like. The functionalist metaphor of a system shows an arrangement of parts meshing together in unity and stability. Communities as systems (Bates and Bacon 1972) can be seen as organic or mechanical.

Organic

Biology furnishes one image to functionalists of the organismic metaphor. Biologists have determined the relationship of each organ

TABLE 4.2
Functionalist Community Dimensions

Dimension	*Description*
Metaphor	Organic and mechanic systems
Methodology	Participant observation; data on values and institutions; comparative analysis; demonstration of institutional integration and latent patterns
People	
Institutions	Integrated, based on consensus to hold communities together
Stratification	Reward systems
Interaction	Roles
Time	
History	Evolution, adaptation
Process	Equilibrium
Space	
Territory	Localization of systems
Boundaries	Boundary maintenance

to the body. These organs and their functions are analogous to the structure and functions of a community. The parts of a community are different, just as the liver and heart are different, yet these organs interact to keep the organism alive; similarly, the institutions of a community are integrated to maintain the community with special sustaining, distributive, and regulating systems. The arteries of commerce are like the circulatory system of an organism. The nervous system of an organism is analogous to governmental systems in that both serve regulating functions (Spencer 1989).

An organism is a living being that has a complexity of structures and functions. It may be as small as a single cell having a nucleus, amniotic fluid, and membrane, all of which form a primitive system. A community, as an organism, is more likely seen as a large animal or human body that has specialized tissues adapted to specific functions and consists of several subsystems. Many of the classical functionalists used the word "organic" in their theorizing — Comte's organic attitude, Durkheim's organic solidarity, and Spencer's social organism.

The comparison of a community to a body provides a vocabulary of living or dead, weak or strong, healthy or sick, growing or aging. Like the one-celled organism, communities may begin as single units. Such a simple community has a minimal number of parts that must meet all the local needs. As communities grow, the parts gradually differentiate and become specialized. Communities may also grow old and die.

When the parts all work well, the system is alive and healthy. Something can go wrong (such as community conflict) and this is seen as a danger, a threat to the system, a sickness. Communities with less consensus or less commitment are weak. Coser (1956, pp. 16-22) points out that early American sociologists viewed conflict as a disease. For example, Parsons sees nonconformity and class conflict as diseases, and suggests that a propaganda specialist is like a doctor who treats the diseases (1949, p. 182).

When communities cease to exist, they have died. Cottrell (1951) writes of death by dieselization — a change in technology "killed" the community of Caliente. Kanter (1972) suggests that even if they contain commitment mechanisms, most communes eventually die. Prosperity, lack of adaptation, aging, and lack of ideal attainment "kill" communes. Some may survive but lose their vitality and become sterile. Perhaps, to remain viable, communities need to reproduce in some way.

According to Kanter, a community system may also become too healthy. We can imagine a Charles Atlas type with overdeveloped muscles, whose bulging body has become grotesque and, in some ways, dysfunctional; or "health food nuts" overly concerned about eating habits and proper foods, to the detriment of their health. Kanter is referring to communities that have too much commitment. Too much commitment may become dysfunctional because it is oppressive and threatens personal autonomy. In such cases, the relationship between personality and social systems is out of balance. For example, Kanter questions whether Synanon (a California commune having as its purpose the elimination of addiction) may be too strong because personal identity is diminished (1972).

Mechanical

In addition to resembling an organism, a social system may have factors in common with a machine. In the machine analogy, the parts are cogs, gears, and levers that connect by pulleys and wires into systems. Durkheim had envisioned both organic solidarity and mechanical solidarity. Some functionalists use the language of homeostasis, equilibrium, feedback, and inputs and outputs. The homeostasis (steady-state) idea implies a thermostatic balance within communities.

Balance is not only internal; it also relates inputs and outputs. The inputs and outputs of a system — such as the raw materials put in and the manufactured products coming out — harmonize in an orderly procession. According to Parsons, systems synchronize and integrate through input and output exchanges. Some systems produce goods and services that become resources for other systems (1966).

Inputs and outputs are not only in goods and services but also in information. Information feeds back in an orderly flow through a kind of cybernetic system. Cybernetics is a science dealing with the comparative study of complex electronic calculating machines and the human nervous system. Kanter discusses feedback of information through permeable boundaries in retreat communes, which creates a greater connection between these communes and the "outside."

As with living organisms, machines may break down due to age or radical change. They may become too complex and thus remain unused, or they may fail to synchronize with the environment and other systems. When the community machine fails, community no longer exists.

METHODOLOGY

Imagining a community as a mechanical or organic system leads functionalists to ask certain questions. As has already been seen, the central question is: What holds the community together? The system metaphor provides additional related questions asking: What are the subunits of the community? How do the parts interrelate? How do the parts contribute to the maintenance of the community? In Zenda and Lincoln Park, the functionalist imperative is to consider institutions and their interaction.

Merton's protocol (1967) lists the order and method in which answering these questions should proceed. A functionalist should begin with a careful description of the parts of the system, including the activities and groups involved. Second are the excluded alternatives or patterns that "provide direct clues to the structural context of the pattern, and by suggesting pertinent comparative materials, point toward the validation of the functional analysis" (p. 111). Observation and abstract reasoning are used to give descriptions of the parts and of the excluded alternatives.

Third, motives are elicited. Why do people say they participate in the pattern? Fourth is the whole array of motives, the distinction between the motivations for participating in the pattern and the objective behavior involved in the pattern (1967, p. 114). The third and fourth steps reveal the manifest functions, usually through the researcher's interviewing of residents.

The fifth item of the protocol is to ascertain the latent functions, unintended and unrecognized by the participants. Since the residents do not see the latent functions, researchers must observe them or reason their existence.

Functionalists have used many data-gathering techniques. In order to ascertain their commitment mechanisms, Kanter (1972) primarily examined documents of historical communes. Warner (1963) and the Lynds (1929) used participant observation and interviews. All these methods were used in the studies of Zenda and Lincoln Park.

The analysis of data is predominantly an abstract and holistic description of how a community works. Each part of the community is seen as being directed toward specific goals; all the goals are then seen as contributing to both the order and survival of the community. Some functionalists also compare community systems (for example, Dean 1967). The end product of a functionalist study is a book like *Middletown* (Lynd and Lynd 1929), which discusses each of the institutions as well as their interrelationships. Thus, inquiries into the nature of the parts, as both singular and component elements upholding the community, are answered by observation, interviewing, and/or analysis of documents. These data are used to produce an abstract demonstration of institutional integration.

PEOPLE

People are organized into systems, such as communities, designed to work well through institutionalization, rewards of statuses, and roles. To functionalists, institutions are the most important part or subsystem of communities. They keep working, in part because of statuses people accrue through their work and associations with institutions. Within institutions, people relate to one another through roles, which are standards of behavior established through institutionalization.

Institutions

Institutions constitute the fundamental units of communities structured to meet local needs. Functionalists equate institutionalization with the existence of a system and discuss institutions by each need and function as well as by the connection among them, both vertically and horizontally. The heterogeneous ways in which community needs are met in Lincoln Park contrast with the homogeneity in Zenda. In both communities, institutions consist of systems within systems.

Kingsley Davis, a student of Parsons, considers the normative order necessary to the existence of society. Institutions are segments of the normative order and provide an orderly relation among norms. Davis (1949, p. 71) defines institutions as "a set of interwoven folkways, mores, and laws built around one or more functions. It is a part of the structure, set off by the closeness of its organization and by the distinctiveness of its function." Each institution is organized around distinct functions. Davis considers the main institutions to be economic, political, educational, religious, familial, and recreational. Unlike some other theories, structural functionalism considers each institution important for communities. The interdependencies of these constitute the most salient features of the social organization of communities.

Economic Institutions

Economic institutions primarily fulfill the adaptation function, which relates internal systems to external systems and provides economic means to keep systems in operation. Most communities are part of larger economic systems. Zenda, with an agricultural adaptation, may be contrasted with Lincoln Park and its service adaptations.

Zenda has adapted to its fertile land by producing surpluses of milk products for export. Recently there has been a new adaptation, as economic conditions in the larger system have shifted. Several farmers have sold their dairy herds and now raise only cash crops, because of favorable market conditions.

Lincoln Park has adapted to the increase in middle-class populations, related to increasing costs of commuting and the location of white-collar occupational positions in the Chicago Loop. Lincoln Park's proximity to the large corporations of Chicago precludes an adaptation of white-collar positions. Within the community, a diversity of specialized stores have adapted to the needs of the local population for such items as antiques, furnishings, clothing, and specialty food. Merchants sometimes form an organized system such as the Sheffield area business association.

Governmental Institutions

Governmental institutions serve the regulatory function of a community, including social control. Parsons's functional requisite of goal attainment is met by political institutions.

Local governmental agencies and police operate differently in Zenda and in Lincoln Park. The governmental agency for most of the Zenda area is the Town Board of Linn, which meets bimonthly to regulate roads, to license liquor establishments, to announce Boy Scout breakfasts, to consider requests from the fire department, and the like. The township board, which meets in the village, sets and executes some goals for the community, but other goals are part of the larger societal system. For example, the Linn Town Board also seeks federal funding for pollution control of the lake and local revenue sharing, which form part of a larger, noncommunal system. The other town governmental body is the three-person police department.

Lincoln Park also is a goal-attainment system within a system — part of the city of Chicago. As the 43rd ward, it has representatives on the city council. Given its class composition, however, it is one of the more independent wards in the city and does not work directly within the political machine. Consequently, it is often impossible for the alderman to deliver ward services because of his independent status. A committee representative of the political machine, however, runs a service office for the 43rd-ward residents, doling out patronage jobs and solving ward problems. Some state and federal congressional representatives also have offices in Lincoln Park. In addition, the 18th and 19th police districts are in Lincoln Park, with their own local offices. The police, courts, welfare agencies, and other parts of the city of Chicago do not belong only to Lincoln Park. Consequently much of their goal setting is tangential to Lincoln Park.

As a result, a local regulatory system, the LPCA — which has no legal sanctions — sets just for Lincoln Park the goals of retaining historic buildings, crime protection, helping people, and so forth. It regulates in cooperation with the larger system by controlling building-code violations, illegally parked cars, graffiti on walls, and the like.

Parsons's latency pattern maintenance is usually carried out by schools, families, and churches, which function to socialize new members and restrain tension.

Educational Institutions

Schools socialize children and provide them with the norms and values they need in order to function in the local community and to become fully functioning adults. Neither Zenda nor Lincoln Park has its own school system, although Zenda did in the past. Most Zenda children go to one of two rural grade schools in Wisconsin, as required by state law. Grade-school children are assigned according to state-determined boundaries and are bused to Reek and Traver schools, two county schools near the lake. High-school youths go to

Walworth or Lake Geneva. Children in Illinois are bused to the grade school and high school in Hebron. No Zenda-area children attend preschool or private schools.

The public schools in Lincoln Park are an outpost of the Chicago school system, with a high school and nine grade schools, some of which specialize in subjects such as foreign languages, arts, or sciences, and serve as magnet schools open to application to anyone in the entire city. In Lincoln Park, the existence of Catholic, Lutheran, and academically excellent private schools further complicates the educational structure of the community. Twenty-eight percent of Lincoln Park's grade-school children and 46 percent of Lincoln Park's adolescents attend private schools (1970 census) and most children attend nursery school. In addition, Lincoln Park has DePaul University, McCormick Theological Seminary (until recently), technical schools like the Coyne Refrigeration school, and specialized art and music schools.

Religious Institutions

Durkheim discussed the function of religion as providing a collective identity and shared values and norms. Religion may be integrative for a community, but competition among religions may create divisions, as in the community of Pine Grove (Turbeville 1949).

For over one hundred years, the Presbyterian church has dominated Zenda. Until five years ago, when a Congregational group occupied an old schoolhouse, the Presbyterian church was the only church in Linn Township. All Protestants participated in the church until improved transportation made it feasible for those of other denominations to travel to other communities to attend services. In 1976 the village church building was abandoned and a new edifice was erected near the lake to attract Presbyterians from far and wide, since it is the only Presbyterian church in Walworth County.

Lincoln Park has no such religious focus, but maintains a diversity in religious functions. Over 23 Lincoln Park churches meet the religious needs of Catholics, Protestants, Buddhists, Greek Orthodox, and Romanians. Until 1974, the McCormick Seminary educated ministers for Presbyterian churches nationwide.

Recreational Institutions

Recreational systems fill leisure-time activity and integrate by promoting solidarity among locals. Zenda has no specific recreation program; rather, this function is met in a number of ways, especially by voluntary associations. Women's organizations hold potlucks and desserts, with speakers and other entertainment activities for their members, as well as Christmas, Easter, and other holiday parties for the entire community. Bowling leagues exist for all ages at a bowling alley in the village. Children participate in recreation primarily in schools, but a few also belong to the Boy Scouts or 4-H.

Lincoln Park is part of the institutionalized recreation program of the city of Chicago, which maintains the park with its zoo and other facilities. Private recreation is found in clubs and specialized voluntary associations, ranging from the Lincoln Park Gun Club to the Lincoln Park Art Studio. Many residents belong to organizations outside of Lincoln Park, including professional organizations, and many outsiders use recreational facilities in Lincoln Park. For example, there are many specialized entertainment places for films, theater, dance, and many night clubs and restaurants. The most popular organizations among Lincoln Park residents relate to health and sports (Taub 1979).

Family

Families serve reproduction, socialization, child-care, and other social functions. They are not a subsystem of a community; rather, each family is a system. Families are especially integrative for Zenda, because the key families have lived in the community for several generations. In addition, three generations of many of the families all live in Zenda. A greater range of family types exists in Lincoln Park, with a higher percentage of single persons and fewer people with children than in Zenda. According to Richard Taub's (a University of Chicago sociologist) 1979 telephone survey of 400 randomly chosen Lincoln Park residents, only 14 percent are married with children, and 25 percent are married without children, whereas 70 percent of Linn Township residents are married (1970 census).

Integration of Institutions

All of AGIL has now been covered, except I (integration). What integrates institutions? As Roland Warren (1978) conceptualized, institutions are integrated both vertically and horizontally (see pp. 110-11 of this book).

Shared values integrate or hold together the disparate institutions in the horizontal axis. The dominant shared value for both Lincoln

Park and Zenda is the desire to maintain the community. Differences in degrees of consensus in the two help explain why Lincoln Park meets needs in such heterogeneous, diverse ways, while in Zenda most people meet their needs through the same institutions. Zenda residents share values to a greater extent than Lincoln Park residents, both because a greater proportion of Zenda residents agree and because a greater number of values are agreed upon among them. For a functionalist, the degree of consensus corresponds to the degree of community. In this sense, Zenda is more a community than Lincoln Park. Overlapping membership in several voluntary associations by Zenda residents helps integrate, whereas Lincoln Park residents specialize in particular voluntary associations. The structure of umbrella organizations, like LPCA or merchant associations in Lincoln Park, develop to integrate institutions and compensate for more direct integration.

Most communities are open systems with vertical axes to connect community institutions with outside systems of greater scope. For example, Zenda is tied to the international organization of Presbyterians just as are the three Lincoln Park Presbyterian churches and the McCormick Seminary, but Lincoln Park also has ties to numerous other worldwide religious organizations. It has connections with more outside systems because of the heterogeneity of its institutions, and the extent of these vertical ties also calls into question how local the Lincoln Park system is. Zenda has lost some local institutions altogether, such as its grocery store, and its dependence on extracommunity systems entirely (like supermarkets) for some functions also weakens its claim to being a community, which is somewhat counteracted by the strong consensus.

Thus varied institutions integrate to form local systems of communities. Greater variety among institutions, as in Lincoln Park, reflects less consensus as well as more ties with extracommunity systems. Strong consensus and overlapping participation in local institutions integrate Zenda, but its loss of some local functions forces some dependence on extralocal systems. Ranking systems also integrate and maintain communities.

Stratification

Functionalists stratify communities in terms of orderly rankings of status groups, which serve the purpose of motivating people to do necessary tasks. Davis and Moore (1945) argue that motivating people to do the work needed to keep society functioning can become a problem, especially when extensive training and sacrifice are required to be able to do the jobs. In order to motivate people to undertake the difficult discipline and complete the work, such people are given higher status. Thus, stratification functions to provide a reward system. Davis and Moore also cite evidence that status ranking exists in every known society.

We can see in Zenda and Lincoln Park rewards that fill status functions. Farmers have needed help and have obtained it from their children, usually a younger son who is rewarded by inheriting the family farm. This further integrates the community by retaining farms in the same families and perpetuating similar values. In turn, such families receive higher status in the community than newly arrived or transient families. Lincoln Park also rewards its professionals, such as doctors and lawyers who go through so much schooling and training, and business persons willing to take risks are rewarded with higher status and income.

Warner's functional approach is often used as the model for community stratification. In Yankee City (Warner and Lunt 1941, 1942), Jonesville (Warner et al. 1949), and Old City (Davis, Gardner, and Gardner 1944) Warner and his associates identified six classes: upper upper, lower upper, upper middle, lower middle, upper lower, and lower lower. In the South (Old City) separate ranking for blacks and whites existed. Warner based status characteristics on occupation, source of income, house type, and dwelling area. August Hollingshead (1949) also delineated status groupings for Elmtown, based on subcultures, traits, and ways of participating in community activities. Warner asked how the community was held together and what integrated the classes, rather than what caused them, and found that voluntary associations, conflict with an outside enemy, an ideology of egalitarianism and democracy, and especially collective rituals were integrative factors. Warner is especially known for his analysis of Memorial Day as an American secular ritual and symbol of collective representation (1959).

Using Warner's criteria of community status groupings for Zenda, we can see a few housing and occupational differences. The well-kept old farmhouses and new dwellings contrast with houses rented out on some farms and in the village, which tend to be older and less well kept. The self-employed, like farmers and village merchants and factory owners, contrast with those who work for others. Only upper-middle and lower-middle classes can be found in Zenda; rarely, upper-lower class people periodically appear in Zenda, unable to get jobs and pay rents. Going to church together, participating in voluntary associations such as volunteer fire fighters or women's organizations, resenting "Lake" people, and the annual fair and other traditions unite status groups.

All six of Warner's classes are found in Lincoln Park, with a wide variety of occupations, sources of income, house types, and dwelling areas, ranging from the very wealthy who live in mansions down to lower lowers who live in subsidized housing or deteriorated buildings. Activities of the LPCA and neighborhood fund-raising projects are unifying functions, but the far fewer community rituals in Lincoln Park make classes less united than in Zenda.

Interaction

For functionalists interaction occurs in terms of roles and statuses, with roles forming the smallest unit of systems. Roles as actions belong to particular statuses and refer to how a person acts in orientation to another's roles and statuses. (Review Merton, p. 109, for definitions of role sets, status sets, and status sequences). Community roles are subsets of community institutions. The contrast between Lincoln Park and Zenda lies in the fact that in Lincoln Park roles are more fragmented. In Zenda most people have a similar status sequence — going to the same schools, getting married, working for parents, taking over the family business, and passing it down to offspring. In addition, Zenda residents have overlapping role sets and status sets. When Zenda residents interact, they are relating to each other in terms of a number of roles and statuses. For example, two people relating to each other at voluntary association meetings also share roles as neighbors, churchgoers, previous fellow students, shoppers, and in many cases, as kin.

In contrast, people in Lincoln Park tend to relate to one another in one role only — as members of the Lincoln Park Conservation Association, or as coworkers or neighbors, but these rarely overlap. When people know each other in terms of multiple statuses and bundles of roles, they tend to see each other as individuals; in Lincoln Park the status role is all people know, since they do not see a person's other facets.

Not only are there more roles and a greater variety of roles in Lincoln Park, but each role is quite specialized and distinct from other roles, whereas the overlap of institutions in Zenda makes for fewer distinctions among roles. For example, only five people specialize in government in Zenda, but all these people are also farmers or small business owners, whereas in Lincoln Park many persons' entire occupation is with the government, with specialists just for that community. The city of Chicago, the state of Illinois, and the federal government employ thousands of people, many of whom live in Lincoln Park. The director of the LPCA is a full-time paid employee.

TIME

Functionalists deprecate change, which sometimes is viewed as something wrong with a system. A long-term, gradual change through evolution and adaptation seems to work best. In the short term, after change, systems must be restored to order and balance.

History

The functionalist idea of societal evolution parallels Darwin's ideas on biological evolution. According to him, mutability of species and natural selection created the diversity of species and species variation by place (1859). Only the strongest or the fittest survived the struggle for existence, because they were better adapted to their environment. By analogy, the diversity of communities may be explained by their growth and changing adaptation to their environment. Communities are moving toward being more fit.

Social systems are sometimes defined as enduring through time (Roland Warren 1978, p. 138). Functionalists have been criticized for omitting the factor of change. With respect to communities, however, functionalists do envision a gradual change occurring through the processes of growth, development, differentiation of parts, and increased functional specialization. A community may start out small and homogeneous; then, over time, more parts and subsystems develop, which are distinguished from one another. Each serves unique purposes, but all become needed by the larger community system. Each form develops from an earlier form. Through these changes, the adaptation to the environment shifts, thus promoting better adaptation. Functionalists, then, see history as progress.

Parsons borrows from Spencer in that both discuss evolution as increasing differentiation, new mechanisms of integration, and increasing capacity for survival in relation to the environment. For example, Lincoln Park has evolved to a greater division of labor, a greater degree of specialization, than Zenda, in part because it has grown larger. Zenda has evolved in that it has adapted new technologies to the system's farm production. More voluntary associations have also been added over the years. These gradual changes in both Zenda and Lincoln Park create more efficient systems.

Another aspect of evolution is that structures that are no longer needed may drop out, producing a "loss of community." Communities such as Lincoln Park and Zenda are becoming less functionally complete because the subsystem of community in some aspects is succumbing to the larger social system. Zenda's history has been a rise and fall of commercial units. Between 1900 and 1950, the community was functionally complete in that all the needs of the residents were met locally. Since then, many stores have gone out of business, and church and school have moved out of the village.

Just as animals grow from a tiny cell to increasingly complex and differentiated beings, so communities begin simply and become more complex. A community as an organism may go through the stages of youth, maturity, and decline. Thus, functionalists see long term as a natural growth or a need for better adaptation.

Process

While evolution and adaption seem beneficial, functionalists deplore sudden and abrupt change to the point of calling it pathological. Rapid change puts a community out of balance and, in order to be healed, the community needs to reestablish its original state. Communities as self-regulating mechanisms return themselves to stability. For example, Parsons says, "At any given time, a relative equilibrating balance in a pluralistic society is maintained so that conflicts and divisive tendencies are controlled and more or less fully resolved" (1951, p. 482). Conflict and change may threaten the survival and continuity of a community.

Deviants, such as criminals in Lincoln Park or outsiders in Zenda, threaten these community systems. The two communities have different ways to deal with such threats. More formal, institution-alized patterns of police control exist in Lincoln Park, while Zenda works more informally through talking about outsiders and dis-associating from them. A few years ago in Zenda, after 50 continuous years, the annual Farmer's Fair was not held, and many residents feared that this meant the downfall of the community. The next year people did organize a fair, and the community was returned to its previous state. To the functionalist, punishing criminals and repudiating outsiders restore order and the original values of the community.

On the other hand, Roland Warren suggests that communities may not return to their original state of balance, but to a new balance. It is the frequent readjustments of the system to an outside impact that create adaptation and evolution.

> Thus, equilibrium is not the status quo, for as the system operates through time making adaptive changes to the impacts upon it, the equilibrium that is sustained or restored is seldom precisely the equi-librium that existed before the impacts. (Warren 1978, p. 146)

Equilibrium is also necessary in order to maintain integration. A change in one subsystem affects all the other subsystems. For example, the abandonment of the school and church in Zenda meant that fewer people were in the village on a daily basis, and this influ-enced the amount of revenue generated by the local grocery store, which, indeed, is now out of business.

SPACE

Territory

In comparison to the other paradigms presented in this book, space is the least important to functionalists. On the other hand, space is there, a necessary backdrop for institutions and shared values. In his essay on communities, Parsons subordinates the physical dimension as being necessary but inadequate: "A society is not a physical object, but these action systems are 'rooted in' the organism and its physical environment" (1960, p. 276).

Roland Warren (1978) views the territorial aspect of communities as service areas where the local functions coincide in the same place.

As with Parsons, the space is a background on which the institutions are united and local, or dispersed. Space localizes systems.

Effrat (1974) developed a typology that shows the diversity of communities according to whether functional unity overlaps with the territorial unit. She calls the complete overlap of territory and local functions "the compleat territorial community," and uses the example of villages. Society is more complicated than mere villages, and three other kinds of communities relate to space and functions. The community of limited liability (taken from Janowitz; see Chapter 6) specializes in only a few functions in one place, such as small-scale neighborhoods and urban subareas. Community as society (minorities and occupational groups) and networks are kinds of communities having minimal spatial referents, although the former may be more complete functionally.

While both Zenda and Lincoln Park have spatial territory, functionalists would be more interested in what kinds of institutional integration and consensus occur within such space. Zenda used to fit the ideal type of village and provide all services to local people, but many of its functions have subsequently been relocated outside the village. Lincoln Park has more complete functions locally, although its subordination to the city of Chicago also forces many functions beyond the local region. Parts of Lincoln Park may be seen as communities of limited liability — for example, the great specialization in medical care.

Another functionalist way to regard the spatial aspect of communities is the manner in which spatial segregation may promote distinct values. Values cluster in space and form a common culture. To the extent that Zenda and Lincoln Park are isolated and spatially distinct from other units, they will have more distinct values. Lincoln Park, in the heart of Chicago, cannot be as isolated as Zenda. A variety of life-styles are found in Lincoln Park, including students, white-collar workers, and the wealthy; Zenda has less diversity and all share the hard-working farm ethic.

Radical changes in the spatial environment can have an impact on values, as shown by Kai Erickson's study of the flood at Buffalo Creek, West Virginia. When he discusses the destruction of community there, he means less the physical destruction than the moral destruction, the change of values. With fewer survivors than victims and such a loss of close relations, values changed — people were less collectively oriented, crime rose, and adolescents were harder to control. "It would seem that the boundaries of moral space began to collapse as the walls of physical space were washed down the creek" (Erickson 1976, p. 205).

Boundaries

As with territory, for functionalists, boundaries are less physical and more related to values. As Parsons points out in his essay on community:

> Physical boundaries and the jurisdictional authority which orients to them, are not simple reflections of the physical factors or exigencies influencing behavior, but are points of articulation between these physical exigencies and the nonphysical aspects of the social system. The sociocultural meaning of a physical boundary is never statable in geographical terms as such (1960, p. 278).

The key concept is boundary maintenance.

Boundary maintenance relates to equilibrium in preserving a steady state, a consensus of values, autonomy, and identity. Parsons suggests that boundary maintenance has two aspects — compatibility of components and maintenance of the distinctiveness of the system over against its environment (1951, p. 36). Boundary maintenance is needed to distinguish groups from one another and from the environment. The existence of other systems reinforces internal bonds.

Kai Erickson's study of the Puritans concentrates on deviance, but he is also writing about the communities Puritans occupied. One of his key concepts is boundary maintenance. According to him, a "community is boundary maintaining in the sense that it takes over a particular niche in what might be called cultural space and develops its own ethos or way within that compass" (1966, p. 10). Boundary maintenance limits activity and fluctuation.

According to Kanter (1972), physical separation facilitates boundary maintenance. Modern service communes work best because their boundaries are based on affirming values, and they keep out people who do not share these values by exclusion across boundaries and strictness within boundaries. In contrast, retreat communes subscribe to protesting values (being against something in American society) and negative boundaries. They are open in that they include everyone and are permissive within the boundaries (a wide range of values are tolerated). These retreat communes are weak and not conducive to building commitment (see Table 4.3).

In Zenda a lake to the north is a physical barrier that somewhat bounds the community, but more important than the lake itself is the fact that urbanites live along it and their values differ from Zenda values. By repudiating the urbanites, Zenda residents reaffirm their values and maintain their boundaries.

Lincoln Park faces internal differences in values chiefly from criminals who do not follow the rules. The community is also threatened by outsiders, wealthy people seeking to live near the lake. Its residents see the old neighborhoods as having changed due to the gentrification process. In short, community territory and boundaries are maintained by a consensus of values.

SUMMARY

Functionalists have a long history, going back to the beginnings of sociology, which was influenced by the French and Industrial Revolutions. The classical sociologists and anthropologists, Comte, Durkheim, Spencer, Radcliffe-Brown, and Malinowski all contributed concepts that centered on order, solidarity, and functioning of systems. Since functionalism has dominated American sociology under the aegis of Talcott Parsons, it is not surprising that many studies of American communities, from villages to communes to urban areas, have applied functionalism.

The functionalist perspective has made it necessary to view a community as an interdependent system that may be likened to an organism or machine. The central parts of the community are institutions that meet collective needs. The community is held together by consensus, an agreement on norms and values.

TABLE 4.3
Boundaries in Service and Retreat Communes

	Service	Retreat
Definition of boundaries	Affirmation	Negation
Across the boundaries	Exclusion	Inclusion
Within the boundaries	Strictness	Permissiveness

Communities change slowly through evolution and, in so doing, attempt to maintain an equilibrium. Equilibrium is facilitated by boundary maintenance through which people with different values are not easily welcomed in the community. Finally, interaction occurs through roles that are governed by norms. Order, stability, harmony, and integration of parts reign in the functionalist perspective.

Zenda and Lincoln Park have been seen as systems that are parts of other systems and, in turn, contain subsystems within them. Both have institutions that are integrated. The two communities have evolved and attempt to maintain a steady state. Both have been threatened by outsiders, but have withstood the challenge.

Functionalism also focuses on differences between the rural and urban communities. Zenda appears to be less differentiated and not as highly evolved as Lincoln Park, but Zenda exhibits greater consensus, more conviction among residents of shared values. While Lincoln Park has greater institutional complexity and a greater array of roles, Zenda is more intricate in the overlap of roles in interaction.

Critical of functionalism for failing to deal with rapid change and conflict in communities, Marxist theory has been applied to communities and focuses on class, power, and confrontations. The next chapter will show how conflict theorists account for contradictions and absence of consensus in communities.

5

Conflict Theory: Community as Contradictions

The next three chapters, each in its own way, are reactions to and criticisms of the functionalist position. Conflict theorists criticize the functional emphasis on order and stability as well as consensus. Functionalists see communities as smoothly running systems that have gradually adapted and differentiated. With well-defined normative rules, values, and roles that community members internalize, communities develop their own integrated institutions to keep themselves alive.

Conflict theorists view communities as divided and with internal conflict and abrupt change. Sometimes called critical sociology, conflict theory condemns the class relations of communities that exploit and discriminate against certain groups of people. Conflict theorists criticize the political economies of cities, the power structure of communities, and racial and gender discrimination in jobs and housing. While both conflict theory and functionalism emphasize the macroscopic level of society, in other respects they are polar opposites.

Conflict approaches to community are distinguished from other approaches by the particular aspects of the community they emphasize. A conflict theorist studying a community would ask

135

such questions as: What are the divisive elements of the community? What is conflictual, contradictory, antagonistic? Thus the conflict approach emphasizes discord, power groups, oppression, and resource allocation. The opposition of power and interest groups leads to change. Randall Collins defines conflict sociology as the study of people pursuing interests (1975, p. 21) and suggests that social class is the single most important variable, followed by power struggles.

For conflict theorists, change is endemic, arising out of a juxtaposition of opposites. Every part of a community contributes to its disintegration; coercion is the only means by which communities are held together. The critical perspective further advocates change toward a more equitable society and toward a realization of people's potential.

Conflict theory developed out of analyzing the conditions created by the rise of capitalism, but conflict perspectives experienced a strong revival in the 1960s, when functionalism was unable to explain the racial riots and other conflict issues that riddled American communities. Images of wars and battles in communities provide the martial metaphor of conflict theorists, which colors their version of people, time, and space in communities. Their emphasis is on community class and power, as elites gain control of time and space in communities. Lincoln Park and Zenda are both subject to power differentials and to control by outside forces. After examining the historical ascent of conflict theory, I shall apply the concepts to the rural and urban examples.

HISTORICAL DEVELOPMENT

Just as functionalism developed in reaction to the great changes in society of the French and Industrial Revolutions, so conflict theory also originated in response to the upheavals. Rather than deploring the changes and hoping for a return to the previous, seemingly less changing condition, however, conflict theorists spurred on the changes, demanding ever greater perfection, while at the same time criticizing the new forms of exploitation that the factory and industrial system created.

Strasser describes the radical conflict approach as "emancipatory," springing from the "idea of liberation . . . from the social system constraints" (1976, p. 21). He equates social emancipatory interests with progressive interests that are critical of society. Progressive thinking is directed toward change and future possibilities. Social emancipationists recognize the creation of society (and of sociological thought) as an extension of people rather than a thing unto itself. Being concerned with "the materialization of theory, not with its confirmation" (1976, p. 11), they seek to release individuals from social ties and traditions by critically examining society. Conflict theorists look to Marx and Weber for ideas.

From his early undergraduate education in Germany, Marx was interested in social problems and in philosophical theories, particularly those of Hegel. Banned from Germany and France as a radical, Marx migrated to England where he joined with Engels, an English factory owner, to write denunciations of industrial capitalism in the *Communist Manifesto* (1848). Engel's study of the working class in England (1844) conceptualizes a structure of the city similar to that of Burgess, yet Engels criticizes the spatial structure as benefiting the moneyed aristocracy and preventing them from perceiving the misery of the working classes.

Marx and Engels indict the existing order through an alignment of theory with action or praxis. They propose a materialistic version of people in society by which production and the conditions of labor not only produce varying forms of class relations throughout history, but also impose a consciousness and alienation on workers in the industrial era. Dialectical changes in stages of history with an emphasis on class struggles form the Marxist approach.

Marx, as the major founder of conflict theory, conceptualizes communities as divided into classes based on the work world of those who own the means of production and those who must sell their labor. The dichotomous capitalistic classes of the bourgeoisie (owners) and the proletariat (workers) is facilitated by the scarce resource of power monopolized by the owners, and this unequal distribution of power creates a conflict of interest. The built-in contradiction between these two groups inevitably raises revolutionary class conflict.

Such a revolution can occur when the exploited class recognizes its condition and becomes a class for itself. The ideology of the dominant class blinds the oppressed class to its true conditions, but false consciousness changes by expression of dissatisfaction and by struggle, especially in concert with other workers. This point is relevant to the discussion of community, because consciousness raising among exploited workers is more likely when they are concentrated in space together — that is, when many workers are part of the same community.

The intellectual history of conflict theory proceeds in a dialectical fashion with one theorist after another criticizing the previous one and modifying the theory. Max Weber reacts to Marx's dichotomy of classes by delineating three ways to stratify society. He equates status groupings with communities. Weber felt that Marx's unicausal explanation of relating everything to economics, specifically to the mode of production, was an oversimplification. While Weber borrowed Marx's historical method, he was more liberal than radical and emphasized the political more than the economic. He saw history as a movement toward increasing rationalization, which he related to the Protestant ethic of hard work, capitalism, and bureaucratization. His definitions of the state and the city are often cited.

Weber distinguishes the nation state as having a monopoly on violence. According to him, "Ultimately, one can define the modern state sociologically only in terms of the specific means peculiar to it, as to every political association, namely, the use of physical force" (Gerth and Mills 1958, p. 79). Weber contends that the state can legitimately monopolize violence within a given territory. We may ask to what extent a community is a state.

Weber defines the city of the past by its military components of fortifications and armed forces. The other major component of cities, both past and present, consists of economic factors — in particular, a market with its courts, associations, and autonomy (Weber 1962, p. 88). He describes cities as settlements based on versatile and permanent trades. His method was to study cities historically and typify their economic relations. The urban community is a specific kind of city with a special politico-administrative structure found only in the West, contrasting with Asian cities administered by the state.

Practical applications of Marxism did not always work as Marx predicted, necessitating further revisions. Lenin (1917) added imperialism to conflict theory to show how the conquering by industrialized powers of nonindustrialized areas of the world exploits people's resources and may prevent revolution in industrial countries by benefiting lower classes and separating classes by continental distance. This means that the worldwide division into developed and underdeveloped countries influences the economics of each community. The Communist revolutions that did occur happened in agrarian societies through peasant movements rather than in industrial countries (Wolf 1970).

Dahrendorf (1959) suggests that in more advanced stages of capitalism, ownership becomes a less distinct source of power in favor of those with authority, the managers, because in modern bureaucracies power not only emanates from ownership but also from other kinds of control and decision making. He sees institutionalized authority relations or "imperatively coordinated associations" as the major source of conflict. Dahrendorf defines conflict as "contests, competitions, disputes, and tensions" (p. 135).

Instead of writing about economic organization, Dahrendorf writes of legitimated role relations in imperatively coordinated associations. Within these associations are positions of dominance and subordination called quasi groups. With awareness, quasi groups become conflict groups, which redistribute authority as a result of conflict.

Georg Simmel and Lewis Coser will be mentioned just briefly here as representatives of a branch of conflict theory that tapers off into functionalism. For them, conflict in society serves a positive function in that antagonism and confrontation between two or more groups promotes solidarity and bondedness within each group. Conflict integrates rather than divides. For example, in communities, rival high-school teams promote a togetherness of the community members in the face of other communities' teams. Simmel further connects an increase in conflict with more urbanized conditions (1956). Coser (1956) argues that resolving conflict produces flexibility in systems and a greater capacity for adapting to future imbalances and changes. He defines conflict as "a struggle over values and claims to scarce status, power, and resources in which the aims of the opponents are to neutralize, injure, or eliminate their rivals" (p. 8).

Application to Community

With the exception of Coser, classical conflict theory has been a European product. Its application to U.S. communities has led to the classification of types of community conflict, as well as studies of the elites of communities and of the political economies of cities. The latter two set the background for conflict approaches to community stratification and institutions.

Coleman (1957) synthesizes a number of community conflict studies and generalizes about community controversies. The studies cover such issues as fluoridation of community water (Crain, Katz, and Rosenthal 1969), censuring of school books, desegregation, and religious controversies. These issues contrast with the more recent issues of the 1970s and 1980s, such as nuclear power plants in communities, which have generated strong protest movements and violent confrontation with police and national guards. Coleman theoretically develops the processes and outcomes of community conflict based on different kinds of involvement, different kinds of communities, and how the controversies affect people.

Some crises, such as floods, unite communities, while others divide them. The kinds of controversies that lead to disputes must affect important aspects of community members' lives, must affect different people differently, and must make community residents feel that action can be taken. The main areas of community life involving community conflict are economic, power or authority, values or beliefs, and groups. The three processes — from specific to general, the development of new issues, or from disagreements to personal antagonisms — can lead to unification, division, or defeat. Leaders, preexisting community divisions, and the inter-relationships among community organizations also impact on community conflicts.

Gamson (1966) also studied a number of communities in conflict, especially about fluoridation. He examines the handling of conflict, which can be in a conventional political way or which can go beyond the rules of the game and become bitter. The latter, called rancorous conflict, is found in politically unstable communities where the opponents do not know one another.

Several studies show how elites or small groups of people in communities control the resources and power. One of the earliest is the Lynds' restudy of Middletown. Although their initial work (*Middletown*) was a functionalist approach with detail on the working and integration of the institutions, in the second work, ten years later, *Middletown in Transition* (1937), Robert Lynd discusses the elite control by one family that extracts labor and dominates the community. The X family's power and profits grew with the depression. That one family used greater control of resources to put down strikes and influenced community institutions along chosen lines through its great philanthropy. Lynd linked economics and the concentration of power in the hands of the few.

Floyd Hunter (1953) carried on the elite model of community power in his study of Atlanta, Georgia — "Regional City." He found that just a few people seem to make the decisions in every aspect of community life. The top of the power pyramid consists of business persons. In a restudy of Atlanta (1980), Hunter finds a continuation of the same processes. As will be seen in the stratification section, the radical elite approach has been compared with the more liberal pluralist approach, which has generated some controversy about communities.

Molotch (1976) developed the concept of the "growth machine" to explain how elites promote intensification of land use and growth-inducing resources for their own profits. Lyon et al. (1981) further test the growth-machine model by relating power to policy outputs. When elites attain power, they promote population growth, which yields higher property values and more profits, but does not alleviate unemployment.

Other studies of community elite power in Michigan (Schulze 1958; Clelland and Form 1964) propose a bifurcation of power when managers of absentee-owned or multinational corporations disassociate themselves from community politics.

Vidich and Bensman (1958) offer still another neo-Marxist approach to community, focusing on the false consciousness of community members. They show how in the small town of Springdale, community members, even those in elected positions, have very little control or self-determination in the community because the economic matters that count are decided in urban and national centers beyond the local community. Only one person seems to have any power in Springdale — "Jones" — because of his ownership of a feed mill, which creates obligations from both farmers and village dwellers.

The McCarthy era in the United States during the 1940s and 1950s suppressed conflict theory because of its association with communism, but urban riots, confrontations between policy makers and those opposed to the war in Viet Nam, students' take-over of universities, and other social movements by minorities and women inundated the 1960s with social problems inexplicable by the human-ecology and functional frameworks. Social conditions that did not change with social policies of urban renewal and the War on Poverty mandated conflict explanations and a redistribution of power and resources. Problems of the 1970s and 1980s have included fiscal crises of cities and high unemployment rates, which seem to demand a conflict analysis.

Consequently, more recent studies since 1970 have focused on the political economy of localities and have avoided using the word "community," perhaps because of its connotation of integration and solidarity. The political economy concerns material production and reproduction as these are related to power issues. The most extensive study of the political economy of local areas by Manuel Castells (1977) has recently been translated from French and used for studies of U. S. localities. He suggests that the relation of power to the economy is the central problem of urban space.

Castells sees consumption as the prime focus of urbanism at the stage of advanced capitalism. He criticizes ideological treatments of urbanism that equate problems with urbanization rather than with advanced capitalism, when, in fact, cities have existed throughout history. For example, the rural-urban dichotomy is an ideology, since advanced capitalism experiences no contradiction between rural and urban places; rather a plurality of units reproduce labor power. Even with unequal development of production and means of consumption, urban and nonurban places are intricately bound in the same mode of production and consumption. In advanced capitalism, reproduction of the labor force or collective consumption remains at the local level, while distribution and capital accumulation are a more worldwide system. The forces of production and specifically the spatial organization of the reproduction of the labor force, seen in terms of the dialectic of the class struggle, determine urbanism. Capitalistic urbanization relates to dependence and underdevelopment of Third World communities. Socialist countries such as China and Cuba have prevented much urban population growth.

Katznelson (1975), an American radical political scientist, reaches some of the same conclusions as Castells. As he traces capitalistic transformations of communities, he finds them left with only consumption and reproduction functions. Katznelson advocates the need for analysis "to assess the importance of community as a locus of political struggle and of urban community organization strategies as aspects of a politics of social transformation" (p. 1).

Castells and others have answers for the fiscal crises of U. S. cities. According to Castells, three processes in the history of the United States — metropolitanization, suburbanization, and social-political fragmentation — have contributed to the fiscal, economic, and service crises of cities. Underlying all these is the process of capital accumulation and the specific organization of consumption to reproduce the labor force. Technological invention alone cannot account for the changes, because, for example, the automobile industry deliberately abolished streetcars and cut back other public transportation.

O'Connor (1973), Hill (1978), and Tabb (1978) further analyze fiscal crises in terms of the "increasing socialization of costs and the continued private appropriation of profits" (Hill 1978, p. 217). Social consumption of police, schools, housing, welfare, and the like increasingly become assumed by states, (including local governments) even though those expenditures benefit capitalists. With the removal of capital from older cities, laborers have no work and social costs rise beyond revenue accumulation. The solution of politicians to tax the middle class contributes to the problems and blames the victims for the fiscal crises, rather than the corporations who refuse to pay social costs.

Hill (1974) finds that resources have not been spent where needed. Local areas that lack good wage markets and equitable consumption have the least governmental resources. Fiscal inequality promotes inequality in median family incomes among municipalities in the metropolitan area.

Conflict theory, originally a European product, has only very recently been adopted in the United States (with the exception of the Lynds' 1929 study). First came Coser's (1956) functionalist conflict, and then with the social movements of the 1960s and 1970s Marxist sociology came to the United States. One growing branch of Marxist sociology attempts to analyze the political economy of cities. These historical developments contribute to the elements of the community conflict framework that deal with the divided, contradictory nature of communities (Table 5.1).

METAPHOR

War, games, and economics lend metaphors to conflict theory. Communities seem to be engaged in internal wars and to be the sites of battles and skirmishes. Although, theoretically, more than two sides could be involved, the martial metaphor pictures two groups of soldiers planning strategies and tactics, fighting, and then one violently taking over the other. The sides are not equal, however, because one side has more guns, better bombs — in short, more resources stolen from the other side, which has more people.

The Hobbsean notion of all against all in a battle over scarce resources is somewhat modified by conflict theorists, since one

TABLE 5.1
Conflict Community Dimensions

Dimension	*Description*
Metaphor	War
Methodology	Historical specificity; participant observation; data on income, housing, class composition; reconstruction of inequality, macro conflict
People	
Institutions	Hierarchies dominated by the political economy
Stratification	Class and power
Interaction	Conflict, ideology, alienation
Time	
History	Changes in mode of production; revolutions
Process	Dialectic
Space	
Territory	Scarce resource for profits
Boundaries	Political; point of conflict

group assembles against another group (instead of individuals against one another). Hobbs (1651/1958) says that when two parties want the same thing, "which nevertheless they cannot both enjoy, they become enemies; and in the way to their end, which is principally their own conservation, and sometimes their delectation only, endeavor to destroy or subdue one another" (p. 105).

Community as war relates to Weber's idea of states with monopolies of violence, where states with their armies are seen as battling with other autonomous states. When communities were autonomous states — like ancient Athens and Sparta — they were able to fight against one another, as in the Peloponnesian War. Communities no longer battle one another, but they do have some monopoly over violence in their police forces. In this case the battles are within the community, as when police fight rioters. Analysts dispute whether rioters want to destroy the system, win and take over the police, or simply want more of the resources of the existing system.

While constant violence is seldom a feature of communities, the divisions and preparations for potential battles continue in communities as a cold war or as war games — like chess. The more common community conflict is less violent, as the struggle for power and goods becomes a political game with a highly structured set of rules. For example, Norton Long (1958) depicts community as an ecology of games; "structured group activities that coexist in a particular territorial system can be looked at as games" (p. 252). As with wars, games involve teams, but the emphasis is on the strategies, the calculability of outcomes with winning as a goal. In terms of score keeping and winning, most community games are zero sum. That is, one side either loses everything or gains everything, with nothing in between — such as sharing or compromise.

Conflict theorists themselves do not use the martial metaphor as explicitly as human ecologists and structural functionalists use their biological metaphors. The war image is implicit in conflict theory's borrowing from economics. Communities are like material production and consumption units.

Rather than a single organism or a group of organisms, the community is a resource-managing unit, whose course is not smooth but full of struggles. The starting point is a scarcity of goods, a finite amount of resources, including prestige and status, which in turn leads to an allocation problem of who is to get what. Certain groups attain control over the resources and extract surplus from the rest of the population. Some conflict theorists consider themselves economists in more than a metaphorical sense.

Conflict theory is less metaphoric than other approaches. Literal wars have been fought in cities between police and national guards on the one side and blacks, students, and other protesters on the other. Today armed police with a huge array of artillery and strategies of control accompany any demonstrations or picketing, as force and control perpetuate a disparate order. Elites play serious war games over the lives and welfare of the masses. Marx not only borrows economic terms for sociology; he actually is an economist who insists on including social conditions with economic categories.

METHODOLOGY

The war mataphor and emphasis on economics leads to questions answerable by the methods of conflict theory. First, what are the cleavages and divisions? Communities divide into armies, the players of the game as subgroups rather than individuals, with diverse interests.

Second, what are the battles or issues and what is won? What are the spoils of war? What is the substance of the conflict?

Third, what are the rules of the game and how is it played? What are the tactics and strategies? How does organization take place? How do elites control resources of votes, jobs, media?

The methodology for conflict theory provides ways to study all these. The primary strategy is to focus on the issues and points of conflict and the resulting power structure. A researcher identifies the actors, issues, processes, and consequences, as the structure unfolds. Inequalities produce conflict and a possible redistribution.

The hallmark of conflict analysis is historical specificity and, further, the analysis is dynamic, depicting change. Since change is so important to conflict approaches, placing the conflict in its historic context is of utmost importance. Communities must be examined in relation to the particular nature of the historical period with its unique mode of production and class relations. Consequently, historical economic documents become significant.

Like other approaches to community, the methodology for conflict approaches may involve participant observation. For example, Vidich (1958) spent considerable time living in Springdale and talking to people, but the specific things he observed and the kinds of questions he asked distinguish him from what the Lynds did in Middletown or Warner did in Yankee City. Rather than attempting to be wholistic and amass as many data as possible on the whole community, conflict theorists look for points of conflict; they concentrate on group confrontations and decision-making processes.

Douglas (1976) advocates investigative research, a new type of participant observation that actually pushes contradictions. Participant observation usually involves cooperating with the subjects, but conflicts of interest, suspicion of others, and concealed fronts pervade social life. Consequently, to get beyond the evasions and lies, researchers must be like investigative journalists who read classified documents or like spies who infiltrate the ranks of the enemy. This method is especially necessary in investigating those in positions of power or criminals who have much to hide.

Conflict theorists use a variety of types of data. Many recently published accounts use statistics, census data, and large-scale surveys. For example, Castells (1977) cites population and production statistics. Hill (1974) collected information on fiscal spending by municipalities and median income of residents. Data show unequal distributions.

The analysis presents conflicts, preferably in a way that will lead to change. According to Marx, material production is the starting point of analysis, and economic production generates spatial ordering. Class analysis follows, showing how maximizing profits and exploitative consumption sets up antagonisms. Third, the state, fourth, the international organization of production, and fifth, the world market and crises constitute the order of analysis (1969, p. 48). According to Castells, the product of research links the specifics of the situation studied with the context of historical materialism (1977, p. 3). The conflict analysis results in both abstractions and criticisms; the end product must link theory with practice. Analysis of observations, interviews, and documents collected in Lincoln Park and Zenda will be used to show how the mode of production influences class antagonisms and contradictions within the communities.

PEOPLE

Analysis of the political economy dominates conflict theorists' study of institutions and helps explain the class and power divisions of communities. For them, stratification is the most important aspect of communities. Interaction occurs through conflict or attempts to curb conflict through ideology and false consciousness.

Institutions

Study of the political economy structures conflict theory's analysis of institutions, either as the political economy alone constitutes the urban structure or as the political economy controls other institutions. In a collection of essays on the political economies of cities, Gordon (1971) defines the political economy as the study of "how economic, political, and social institutions determine the allocation of scarce economic resources and goods" (p. xiii). Work practices, together with corporate and governmental policies, add up to produce any given political economy. The political economies of most U. S. communities may be characterized as capitalistic oligarchies. An oligarchy means rule by the few, while capitalism is a system based on profits, private property, and wage labor. For Castells, the economic and political systems, along with ideological systems, are the urban structure. The economic system involves production, consumption, and exchange, while the politico-institution system dominates, regulates, integrates, and represses. Castells equates the political aspect with the institutions of cities, reflected in the power of governmental and juridical organizations. The main function of institutions is to preserve the given state of affairs.

Conflict theory highlights the economies of Lincoln Park and Zenda, with residents dependent on large corporations beyond their control. Zenda differs somewhat in having control of parts of its production, the land and equipment, although these are regularly inspected by health officers from Chicago who can order farmers to have concrete poured on land, buildings removed, and the like. Farmers have no choice in the marketing, pricing, and distribution of their products. In addition, agribusiness is moving in – a German corporation and other companies are buying family farms. Lincoln Park residents have their resources of education and training, but they, too, have little control over how these are used and the price of paying for and selling them. Most of the economic support of Lincoln Park residents comes from outside the immediate area, but pricing, especially on housing, has a tremendous economic impact. Both Lincoln Park and Zenda are subject to the whims of the marketplace for consumption materials and for the price of their labor. Although few Lincoln Park residents are owners of production, many of them do have managerial authority over others.

Community can be seen as a state to the degree that it is a legally formed entity with a monopoly of violence. Zenda village is unincorporated and hence has no monopoly over violence, although the township of Linn does have a three-person police force. Lincoln Park is part of a larger entity, the city of Chicago with its police force and machine politics. People use strategies and tactics within the machine and need to placate and cajole members of the machine to get more consumption services for Lincoln Park. The rules are less routinized, informal, and ad hoc in Zenda, as people organize for specific issues. The township board allocates use of taxes, but for getting resources from nonlocal authorities, the strategy in Zenda is collective behavior and social movements.

Political economies create national and even international institutions, but they do have an impact on local institutions, especially those involving consumption, and within each institution, hierarchies reflect the economic control in the rest of the community. In Middletown the X family's control of the major economic institutions, including factories and retail stores, and their philanthropy lead to control of the politics, churches, schools, banks, and voluntary associations such as the Y.W.C.A. and Y.M.C.A. (Lynd 1937). Similarly, Hunter (1953) demonstrates how the wealth and prestige of a few people in economic and governmental institutions, and to a lesser extent, in religion and educational institutions, determine the policy-making structure of Regional City.

Even though extracommunity institutions serve many political economic functions, the local institutions still must reproduce the workforce in the form of consumption and services that the workplace fails to provide. Consumption is the social appropriation of products, which in turn reproduce the labor force and give what is necessary for it to continue working. Consumption has been organized in commercial institutions, and the state is taking over many consumption products of education, transportation, housing, welfare, and health. Consumption also reproduces the social relations of the means of production, since those exploited for their labor are also the targets of expanded consumption. Workers have their labor extracted, and they also contribute to profits by buying the products. Workers pay double: their labor taken out of their control and then having to use their wages to keep themselves alive. Double profits go to the corporate owners (Castells 1977).

While conflict theorists have critically examined institutions such as schools (for example, Bowles and Gintis 1976) to show how they perpetuate class divisions, or religious institutions to show how they prevent revolutions by being "the opiate of the masses," specific institutions are rarely examined in relation to communities. The example of one institution can illustrate the conflict approach to community. In both Lincoln Park and Zenda the issue of control of local schools has generated conflict and divisions. Contradictions between local control and state control, and class divisions over to whom the schools belong, characterize both communities.

The large percentage of blacks, along with a lack of curriculum geared to the college-bound students of the middle class, has led to exoduses of Lincoln Park residents with school-aged, particularly high-school-aged children. At this stage of the life cycle they either turn to private schools or move to suburbs, where local control of schools can perpetuate class ideology. For example, Fidel (1973) cites 1970 census statistics showing that only a little more than 50 percent of high-school-aged Lincoln Park residents attend public high school, compared with close to 90 percent in northern suburban tracts. The cost of living in Lincoln Park, combined with the cost of private schools, produces a population of only the wealthiest with high-school-aged children.

Waller High School, the only public high school in Lincoln Park, was also at one time the only high school for the slums of the near north side of Chicago. This area south of Lincoln Park comprises some of the poorest neighborhoods of the city, including Cabrini Green housing, the site of so many killings in 1981 that the mayor lived there for a while to demonstrate her concern.

Gradually, as the gentrification process grew, more families with young children wanted to stay and send their children to public schools. These families became active in the LPCA and other social movements in an attempt to wrest the schools both from the school board of Chicago and its exclusive decision making on local schools, and from poor blacks whose criminality and different standards on schooling made the schools unacceptable to upper-middle-class families.

The change in the schools began in one elementary school, with the new white parents becoming active in the PTA and agitating and raising funds to oust the principal and institute new curricula, making the school into a "magnet" school with foreign languages. That is, although it was a public school, students from other parts of the city could apply and be accepted for the foreign language specialization. This approach spread to other elementary schools and then to the high school.

A community organizer in Cabrini Green frightened the whites of Lincoln Park, especially when he attended LPCA meetings and demanded more neighborhood resources for the poor and blacks. The superior class position of Lincoln Park put its residents in control of the bartering system. They offered black housing just north of North Avenue for low- to middle-income persons and promised a good high school for the Cabrini Green area, if the potential agitators from Cabrini Green agreed not to fight the re-districting of the schools, which would exclude Cabrini Green from the Lincoln Park schools and expand the school district farther north to Lake Park.

Drawing plans and making demands on the Chicago School Board led to changes. Around 1979 Waller High School became Lincoln Park High, a college preparatory high school with magnet programs in foreign languages, the arts, science-math, and the International Baccalaureate Program. By 1981 the enrollment had dropped from almost 100 percent black to 59 percent black. Integration and desegregation are the ideological slogans of the school changes.

The situation in Zenda, while more subtle and less dramatic, addresses some of the same issues of who is to control the local schools. People with resources who choose to move out of the city, because of the different quality of the schools and lack of control of schools, may move as far as the lake area near Zenda. The people of Zenda see such people as bringing urban problems to the rural area and they are resistant. The population of ex-urban residents, most of whom continue to work in the city and who reside near the lake, has increased and some of them have run for school boards and tried to have their say in local schools. The people of Zenda want to maintain their own control of schools, so they politic against the new residents and attend school board meetings to monitor and counteract any influence the new residents may have. So far, long-time Zenda residents have maintained control.

What prevents the divisions in the institutions from creating chaos? According to conflict theorists, coercion holds the institutions together and order emerges from struggles rather than from value consensus. Both Weber and Marx examined the interrelation of institutions. For Weber, the rationalism of the capitalist economies integrates military, religious, and political-juridical institutions. Marx saw an irrational, oppressive relation between production and institutions.

Stratification

Every aspect of conflict theory mentioned, every author, the metaphor of war, the questions, and institutions as hierarchies have been about stratification. Stratification is everything to conflict theory and far more important than in any other framework, because conflict theorists see communities as divided and with inequalities among the divisions. Class and power differences are the most prominent divisions, because they are exploitative and change inducing.

Conflict theorists differ on the number and bases of the divisions. Weber analyzes stratification by three distinctions: class, status, and party. Class is economically determined power from market situations, and class interest forms communal action "oriented to the feeling of actors that they belong together" (as opposed to societal action, "rationally motivated adjustment of interests") (Gerth and Mills 1958, p. 183). Status groups, related to honor, esteem, and life-style (the consumption of goods), are typically communities. "Parties have political power through the legal order and seek to influence the existing dominion" (p. 195). Although class, status, and power usually overlap in individuals, sometimes they differ. For example, high-status nobility may be unable to maintain their castles and may lose class level, but not lose as much status level.

Weber defines power as "the chance (of a person or group) to realize their own will even against the resistance of others participating in the action" (Gerth and Mills 1958, p. 180). One type of power is the legitimate power of authority. Three kinds of authority have evolved through history: traditional, charismatic, and rational. In traditional authority, leadership is inherited and in charismatic authority, leadership is based on a strong personality figure. Both of these give way to rational authority, which dominates capitalistic society. In rational authority, leaders are chosen by codified rules.

Later we will discuss divisions in Zenda and Lincoln Park; differences in their authority illustrate some of Weber's terms. Both Linn Township and the city of Chicago have written charters, rules, and methods of procedures that make them rational organizations. Zenda tends to be more traditional and unchanging, with people voting Republican, as their parents did before them. For example, the town chairperson (for over 15 years) occupies a position his father held before him. Leadership in Lincoln Park is more rational, as evidenced by an Independent rather than Democratic city council representative. The people of Lincoln Park deliberately made a calculated choice that went against the tradition of the Democratic machine.

Marx defines classes in terms of the relation to the means of production. He emphasizes the workers and their exploitation by capitalists, the owners of the means of production — two basic classes — although he sometimes discusses the petite bourgeoisie, who own small businesses and may not even employ workers, and the lumpen proletariat, including the reserve army of the unemployed, who go in and out of the labor force and can prevent strikes from having an impact. Applying Marx to local stratification, Castells suggests that urban stratification is based on the distribution of consumption products and on the distribution of housing (1977, p. 171). He defines power always in relation to classes. Drawing from Poulantzas (1968), Castells (1977, p. 243) defines classes as "combinations of the contradictory places defined in the ensemble of the instances of the social structure, power then being the capacity of one class or section of a class to realize its objective interests at the expense of the contradictory classes."

The working class is defined in terms of its social relations (dominated), its labor (surplus extracted), and its products. Workers transform nature by changing raw materials into products. The relation of labor to property is that the capitalist appropriates the workers' products for profits. Production and consumption are joined by exchange and administrative units. Urban politics is the way contradictions are handled, including urban planning and social movements (Castells 1977).

The term "elite" has been used to describe the powerful classes of communities in a Marxist stratification scheme. C. Wright Mills

(1963), a radical American sociologist of the 1940s and 1950s, bases national elites in the United States on the military industrial complex, the interlocking directorates of corporate directors, and their control of military and political leaders. In communities, however, he contends that a single-dimension class structure is inaccurate and advocates a Weberian, multistrand stratification analysis. Mills criticizes the functionalist approach of Warner for not distinguishing different aspects of class. He refers to class as the "sheerly economic" in all its gradations and sources; status is the prestige dimension of ranking, and power is a matter of "who can be expected to obey whom in what situations" (p. 41).

Elitism versus Pluralism

Marx's view of a few people in the upper class who control most of the wealth and power is reflected in the elite view of community structures in which just a few people control the major community resources. The elite view contrasts with the pluralist view, a political science theory that is closer to functionalism. Dahl (1961) and Polsby (1963) have propagated the pluralist view, while Floyd Hunter (1953, 1980) is associated with the community elite theory. Pluralism suggests that communities consist of many groups with specialized interests, who more or less take turns having power as different issues arise. Two contrasting structures arise from the two different viewpoints: a pyramid form from the elite model and an amorphous, changing shape based on factions and coalitions for the pluralists. Hunter defines power in terms of moving people to act (1953, p. 2), while to Dahl, power is the capacity of one actor to do something affecting another actor, which changes the course of events (1961, p. 3). In addition to deriving from two different disciplines, sociology and political science, and sculpting two different shapes of communities, pyramidal and amorphous, the two models of community power also employ different methods.

The elite approach uses the reputational method, whereas pluralists study decision-making issues. The reputational method consists of finding out from newspapers, social registers, and membership lists of civic organizations who are important people, and then, in snowball fashion, asking these important people who else is influential — in Hunter's words, who are the "big" people. From a list of names, Hunter chose judges to narrow the list down to 40 people whom he interviewed. He found that a handful of names were considered important by these 40 people, and he ascertained the relation among them: a homogeneous, coherent group of business persons were at the head of Regional City.

On the other hand, Dahl (1961) examined community issues that arose in decision making, such as redevelopment or education, and found different people involved in each issue. Dahl interviewed 46 people on the issues and found dispersed inequalities and no one group in power. Although a handful of people were involved in a redevelopment project, they were not influenced by economic or other leaders. Not one elite, but several — economic, social, and political — were found in New Haven.

Subsequent debates about the relative advantages and reliability of the methods have been controversial in themselves (Hawley and Wirt 1968). Some maintain that some communities such as younger cities and suburbs are elitist, while others such as big old cities are pluralist (Clark 1968), and others argue that the method used will lead to the corresponding structure (Walton 1966). Conflict theorists suggest that pluralism is an ideology to obscure class relations.

Other variables in community power suggested by Rossi (1960) include the degree of professionalization of public officials, the number of elected officials, the degree of partisanship, and the extent to which parties represent minority interests. Using these variables, he delineates four shapes of power structures in communities: pyramidal, caucus, polylithic, and amorphous. Rossi delineates Regional City as caucus rule, with a larger group involved than in pyramidal rule where virtually one person creates a powerful political machine. New Haven is an example of a polylithic community with a diversity of influential cliques, while the amorphous community has no one pattern. Jackson (1978) looked at other variables of participation by blacks and poor in community action, the form of government, and the frequency of public meetings as factors in political mobilization.

Both Lincoln Park and Zenda have unequal class and power divisions, but Lincoln Park has a greater variety. Many Zenda residents own their own businesses as farmers or merchants and as such, they may employ a few people. Zenda has few divisions internally. In the past when farmers had to employ people, each farm had its own class division of owners and hired hands who usually lived together, the married hired hands in the tenant house, and the unmarried living in the same house as the owner. Machines replaced hired hands who left to work in factories. In owning the means of production, farmers are like the doctors, realtors, lawyers, and merchants of Lincoln Park. The tremendous investment required in equipment and land combined with low profits make the petite bourgeoisie of Zenda less wealthy than the petite bourgeoisie of Lincoln Park. For example the 1970 median income in Linn Township was $8,043, with 58 percent of the population having an annual income under $10,000, compared with only 22 percent of Lincoln Park incomes under $10,000. As another indicator of higher class positions in Lincoln Park, according to the 1970 census, Linn Township had 32 percent white-collar workers and 68 percent blue-collar workers, while Lincoln Park at this same time had 70 percent professionals and 30 percent blue-collar workers.

A recent division in Zenda has been between long-term residents and urbanites who come to live near Zenda. This distinction has blurred, as some farming families have retired to the lake area and urbanites have become active members of local organizations and assets to them.

Lincoln Park has a more diversified economy and more complex relations with politics. People who own controlling interests in corporations, artists, factory workers, and welfare recipients live in Lincoln Park. The most populous class sell their labor to bureaucracies and corporations. Lincoln Park not only has wealthier residents than Zenda but also, at the other end, poorer people, on welfare or dependent on an underground economy of drugs and crime. The poor and rich have clashed in Lincoln Park, as have the radicals and police.

In spite of the superior resources of many Lincoln Park residents, they are sometimes powerless. When the large corporations of the hospitals wanted to expand, Lincoln Park residents were unable to prevent it and lost some of their housing. On the other hand, they have been able to work with the city of Chicago and change city laws regarding zoning and districting.

Lincoln Park also has greater variety of consumption classes than Zenda. Both have renters and owners, but according to the 1970 census, 86 percent of the homes in Linn Township were owner-occupied, compared with 17 percent in Lincoln Park. Now developers in Lincoln Park are making great profits by converting rented dwellings into condominiums. Food and clothing there are higher priced than those in the small towns near Zenda, but most Lincoln Park residents can travel to stores with sales or lower prices if they choose; poorer residents are trapped by the high cost of public transportation.

Elite models can be seen in both Lincoln Park and Zenda, in that a few people consistently hold office and serve on the boards of local institutions, like interlocking directorates, but in both places it seems that community elites exist because of the apathy and lack of interest on the part of most people.

Other Divisions

Discrimination and prejudice further divide communities, within the class divisions, by race, gender, age, and life-style. Markusen (1978) emphasizes that subclasses, divisions in the working class by race, sex, physical separation, and different life-styles, inhibit class togetherness and class action. Issues like gender and race complicate a simple class picture. Both minorities and women face job discrimination and housing discrimination, resulting in differential concentration in communities. Even with increasing resources, minorities are especially segregated in housing patterns. For example, Villemez (1980) finds that blacks with resources (education, occupation, and income) similar to those of whites reside in inferior neighborhoods. Thus the use of neighborhoods as an index of class must take into account the issue of racism. Redlining and discrimination by realtors further perpetuate racism and segregation, according to Pearce's study (1979). Many more minority members and women hold visible political positions in communities — as mayors, judges, and officeholders — as cities become fiscally unmanageable, but most of the community work of women and minorities tends to be behind the scenes, where they are not rewarded either with money or honor (Stoneall 1983b).

Age and gender distinctions seem to be the main divisions in Zenda. Adults are more likely to participate in the protest movements than children or old people. Women do much of the work, write most of the letters, although certain men consistently appear as leaders. Community organizations and activities tend to segregate into women's social groups and men's business groups (fire fighters, town board, and so on), with women providing food and household help and men giving help in the fields during times of crisis.

Lincoln Park is divided not only by many class distinctions but also by racial and ethnic groupings. The improvement in housing discriminates against the poor by forcing them to seek more affordable space elsewhere. The greater heterogeneity in income, occupations, housing values, and race would tend to create less likelihood of class consciousness, although the fact that so many live near one another and work together may facilitate consciousness raising. Other things, such as differences in consumption, life-styles, and stages of the life cycle, may interfere with common class interests.

External Stratification

In addition to divisions within communities, power differences in the larger society affect communities, as Vidich and Bensman (1958) discovered. In one sense, they found just one class in Springdale, which is at the mercy of mass society and decisions and events that occur in the urban and national levels beyond Springdale. In another sense, an elite of five business leaders, or perhaps even just one person, has power in Springdale. In still another way, Vidich and Bensman delineate five classes, based on consumption patterns of savings and investment, that include the old aristocracy, the middle class (mostly composed of rational farmers), the marginal middle class, traditional farmers, and shack people. Newby (1979) notes a further contradiction in rural class relations — keeping taxes down and preventing development of services — which pits laborers against farmers.

Many of the battles Lincoln Park and Zenda have fought have been to preserve their communities in the face of the power of outside economic and governmental forces. These communities are subject to worldwide market conditions, often out of the Chicago financial district, and trade boards that regulate prices for such things as milk and labor as well as consumer goods. People in both places have fought developers trying to bring in additional housing and people. Federal government regulations, spending, and decisions such as where to locate the Air Force Academy, have influenced both, and in addition, Lincoln Park must deal with the power of the political machine of Chicago.

Interaction

Conflict is obviously the major form of interaction, but also important are the interactional modes involving ideology, designed to inhibit conflict and keep lower classes in their place. Without conflict, feelings of alienation pervade, even though they are not always recognizable.

Conflict

Conflict involves a collision and clash of opposition groups with different power and class interests, which, as we shall see in the process section, leads to change. When community groups riot, demonstrate, protest, boycott, petition, and confront other groups, they interact in attempts on the part of the powerless and dispossessed to attain power. In both Zenda and Lincoln Park local groups have confronted outside groups and classes have clashed within the community.

The entire community of Zenda conflicted with the federal government in 1954 when the Air Force threatened to locate in the area. Setting aside 9,000 acres for an academy site would have affected 42 farms and 220 other pieces of property. The newspapers of the time report that 350 people gathered in the Zenda town hall and agreed to picket the site-visitation committee, which they did in addition to writing letters. Later the town chairperson himself went to Washington to protest. The outcome was that the Air Force Academy located in Colorado and the people of Zenda awarded the chairperson a gold watch for his efforts. The Air Force Academy incident set a precedent in that Zenda area residents felt they had control of their community and could prevent any other attempts to take it over.

In a similar series of events in Lincoln Park, the poor, led by a street gang, confronted others to obtain community resources. The Young Lords, a Puerto Rican group, started in 1959 to steal, kill, and sell drugs. Many of its members were jailed, but in 1969 they became politically active with a "help the poor" ideology. The members agitated at DePaul University for a day-care center and asked the Armitage Methodist Church for an office. They took over the church, renovated the basement for a day-care center, and painted murals outside. The police confronted them because of zoning and building-code violations. They next occupied cleared land at Halstead and Armitage and declared it a People's Park.

The Young Lords united with the Poor People's Coalition and a splinter group from the LPCA, the Concerned Citizens Survival

Front, to occupy McCormick Theology Seminary and demonstrate for more equal health care at Grant Hospital. The issues became centered on housing for the poor. The coalition finally persuaded the LPCA to vote for new low-income housing, but the Department of Urban Renewal overturned the decision (Ducey 1977).

Ideology

Ideology — defined as the beliefs or ideas of particular segments of society — prevents conflict and serves the interests of the controlling class. Lower classes tend to believe the ideology of the dominants — that private enterprise, profit-seeking competition is good — and that belief keeps them in line and prevents them from seeing their distinct interests and exploited position. For example, one dominant ideology is that working hard puts a worker ahead, but in a capitalist society only a few get to the top, no matter how hard they work. Advertising is another form of ideology that creates needs in people, who then contribute profits to corporations.

For Castells (1977) ideology is one of the three components of the urban system, the symbolic component, a network of signs. Ideology has obscured the nature of urban problems in modern society by making them seem inevitable, bound up with a concentration of population, and the opposite of rural. Explaining behavior by habitat is also an ideology, since modes of production do not specialize by spatial environment. Seeing capitalistic modes of production as the cause of urban problems breaks through the ideology. Castells defines urban ideology as "that specific ideology that sees the modes and forms of social organization as characteristic of a phase of the evolution of society, closely linked to the technico-natural conditions of human existence, and ultimately to its environment" (p. 73).

Ideologies serve as communication patterns and also legitimation structures. As a mercantile appropriation of signs, ideology is sold and consumed. Consumption patterns reflect class ideologies and stratification. Castells sees "a growing contradiction between the diffusion of the ideology of the urban by the dominant class and the political effects intended as the economic contradictions that it connotes deepen" (1977, p. 464).

Being exploited and not realizing the exploitation because of ideology is a case of false consciousness. Persons with a false consciousness are unaware of objective material conditions and unaware of their class position. Being with others in a similar exploited position and talking about their complaints and dissatisfactions constitute a consciousness-raising or "speaking bitterness" process, which results in a class for itself rather than a class in itself. Once a class is for itself, the people within it are able to unite and change their conditions.

Both Zenda and Lincoln Park share ideological beliefs that hold capitalistic society in place. Other ideologies are unique to the small-business situation of Zenda or the housing situation of Lincoln Park. In both places residents believe that private enterprise and competition is for the best, producing the best products and best working conditions. People just need to work hard enough and they will become rich. Threats to the capitalist system are feared. Ideologies of the benefits of private property ownership dominate both places — ownership of farms and small businesses in Zenda, private ownership of housing, increasing now with condominium ownership, in Lincoln Park. Fear of losing that ownership blinds people to the lack of real control. Sign systems of advertisements, television, and radio, which residents of both communities view, perpetuate ideologies.

In Zenda there is a fear of losing land and control, in local traditional ways, of the interrelated scarce resources of the community. Residents express the importance of continued local control and the moral superiority of the locals. Part of the antagonism toward urbanites in their midst is a fear that they and their corrupt ways may take over. For example, during an election for the town chair in which a new ex-urbanite was challenging the traditional leader, I overheard some women in the store saying that the ex-urbanite was only running so that he could sell his products to the township. "In Chicago, they're used to that sort of thing, but let's stop it here if we can." A similar fear surrounds a German corporation that has bought three or four farms in the Zenda area. The Germans remain in Germany and Americans manage the land, but rumors abound of German take-overs, of building a Volkswagen factory on the land.

Most Lincoln Park residents are newcomers to the area. By their wealth and power to change zoning laws, they have decreased the population of the area and deprived many poorer people of housing and schooling, or pushed them into less desirable public housing. Lincoln Park residents approve many slogans that exonerate them from any wrongdoing. They believe they are improving housing, cleaning up the neighborhood, and preserving its historical significance. They change the schools in the name of desegregation and improvement.

Ideologies of differences among people further prevent class consciousness. Zenda residents fear urbanites and Germans. White Lincoln Park residents stand in opposition to blacks, Mexicans, and Puerto Ricans in their district. Both communities fail to see the shared exploitation by the capitalist economy and the similar interests that they all share.

Alienation

Without consciousness raising, feelings of alienation pervade. Alienation is a negative feeling of separation, estrangement, and "otherness," related to capitalistic production. Under capitalism, workers do not own the materials of production and the product of their labor is taken from them. Workers do not work for the satisfaction of doing a good job, or for the love of their product, but for the money and for what they do outside of work. Separation of worker and product is the first alienation; then competing workers feel separate from one another. The ultimate alienation is self-alienation, a feeling of meaninglessness.

Alienation is less apparent in Zenda or Lincoln Park than elsewhere. In both places most people feel that they have control and live meaningful lives. The poor of Lincoln Park who have no jobs and are losing housing are the most alienated.

TIME

History

Conflict theorists encourage the examination of massive-scale historical processes of change in modes of production, as well as how these revolutions have changed specific communities. The conflict theory of history not only contains stages of periods in the past, but unlike any other framework, also continues into the future.

The major change over time has been in the mode of production, which in turn has modified class relations. Each stage of history produces different class struggles: between slaves and slave owners, feudal lords and serfs, workers and capitalists. Throughout history, one class has exploited another class, though the conditions have varied. Only those classes with a future mode of production have changed history in their favor. The craftspersons and shop owners of medieval times became the capitalists, and the proletariat are destined to become dominant in the future.

A new stage of history arises because of contradictions and antagonisms, but first each stage develops its own mode of production to the fullest. The new stage was originally part of the old stage. The new classes from the emerging mode of production break down the old order. With each new mode of production, a scarcity remains and surplus is preempted by the dominant class. People make history and change themselves and their class relations as they create new ways to dominate nature. Marx envisions a future stability where the mode of production will be based on equality because of the destruction of private property. At this future stage, history will cease to change.

Marx and Weber both extensively analyzed history, but both of them specialized in capitalism, its origin out of the feudal period, its class struggles between proletariat and bourgeoisie, and its future. To Marx's material historicism, Weber adds a mental process or social action of rationalism and relates rationalism not only to the means of production but to a cultural level, including religion. People have become less religious and more rational in the sense that the magical no longer holds mystical appeal for most people. The same force of rational thinking influenced both the development of capitalism and Protestantism. Protestantism values hard work, postponing of pleasure, a frugal life of saving. The savings reinvested in business rather than spent on luxury goods built up capitalistic enterprises. Increasing rationalism has also influenced the type of authority that has come to dominate — rational rather than the traditional or charismatic authority of earlier historical periods. Weber defines rational action as purposeful or goal-oriented. Laws and bureaucracies based on reason and efficiency govern capitalistic Western society.

Prophets were charismatic and took away the traditional authority of priests. Modern society has systematized religion as the Protestant ethic.

U. S. Community History

According to Katznelson (1975), the main thrust of change in communities from feudal to capitalistic was the separation of communal and production relations, the removal of the workplace from the community, which in turn mediates the accumulation process:

> The penetration of cash and market relations into all spheres of life is the major factor that accounts for the shattering of holistic communities and the differentiation of social life into spheres of production (the realm of capital) and market relations (the realm of money). (p. 8)

This separation further obscures class relationships. The community is left as a consumption unit in which the major relationships are money relationships.

Marxist urban analysts have specified histories of cities. According to Castells, capitalism has fragmented cities and caused their disapperance as a relatively autonomous social system, instead of strengthening cities as nonconflict theorists insist. Concentration of capital has led to spatial decentralization.

The history of U. S. cities has some unique elements, including colonization under England and Spain. Many of the earliest cities were chartered from British authority by trading companies and virtually owned and controlled by these separate corporations as mercantile towns. After the American Revolution, the cities became subordinate to the states, but they were still corporate towns with their own elites evolved from company control (taken from Markusen 1978).

Gordon (1978) suggests that the history of U. S. cities has been discontinuous and has changed with varying processes of capitalist accumulation. He delineates three such stages. At first U. S. cities were based on commercial accumulation, since, as with the mercantile towns, many began as places to sell, as trading posts, or as military outposts. Second came the competitive accumulation of industrialism, as factories came to U. S. cities instead of just producing products in England. The third and current stage is monopoly accumulation, whereby corporations dominate cities.

During industrialism, as workers became powerful, the industries moved to the suburbs and scattered the working class. Ashton (1978) relates the development of suburbs to manufacturers escaping from the growing power of political bosses' control of workers. Suburbs, made possible because cities already provide services suburbanites need, could be controlled as separate municipalities. Suburban political independence facilitates domination by a single interest group. Gary, Indiana, a suburb of Chicago, provides the best example, with a working-class population controlled exclusively by the factory owners. Cumbler (1977) studied the change that comes with suburban development in a historical study of two communities in Massachusetts. Strong solidarity was found among the working class when the communities were centralized. When industries fled to the suburbs, the working class lost its cohesiveness. In other suburbs, wealthier people have escaped city problems, leading to an uneven development of the metropolis. Unequal development has led to the abandonment of older cities and suburbs for newer cities in the sunbelt, where expenses are less, labor better controlled, and therefore, there are more profits.

According to Markusen (1978), not only the colonial background of cities but also their expansion of services contributes to the fiscal crises of cities today. Cities ceased to annex new space and instead suburbs incorporated, creating contradictions of political boundaries. This undermines the cities' sources of revenue, especially as the wealthy and the factories themselves move out of cities. This causes a loss of tax base, which is made worse by policy shifts separating local and state taxing. As a result, corporations have power to cause unemployment if not given incentives of less taxes, less regulation enforcement, and lower salaries.

For Castells, the latest stage of capitalism and the spatial organization of cities emphasize consumption. Capitalism needs consumption levels to rise to produce profits. Lower classes, Third World countries, even socialist countries become targets for new markets. Increased collective consumption through the state rather than the market accompanies this rising consumption level. Early in their history, U. S. communities provided roads, sewage systems, education, and police. Gradually they have also added transportation, welfare, housing, and medical subsidies. These services yield too little profit to interest capitalists, yet they are needed for capitalistic interests. Collective consumption builds in a contradiction – supporting the system of capitalism with a system that destroys it. Since the state further serves capitalism through tax breaks, the services deteriorate and fiscal crises set in, interfering with the capitalist system. Conflict theorists predict new social protests for better economic conditions in the 1980s.

Conflict History of Zenda and Lincoln Park

Both Zenda and Lincoln Park began as imperialistic expropriations of land from native Americans, which was used to expand agricultural production. In turn, expansion of agricultural production was possible because of increasing production in the eastern United States, begun as colonies to serve England.

For a short period of time, both areas were subsistence based and somewhat communal, as early pioneers helped one another, though they were dependent on the tools and other materials of production they had brought with them from the East. They were soon receiving new supplies from ships on Lake Michigan and from cross-country wagon trains. After the clearing of land, both places had surpluses of grain and vegetables, which they could sell not only locally but also to the nearby urban areas of Chicago and Milwaukee. As the urban areas grew, particularly Chicago, the agricultural surpluses from both places went to feed the people of Chicago, with the agricultural producers selling directly to individual customers or in open markets in the city.

With the destruction by the Chicago fire, entrepreneurs were able to buy the Lincoln Park farmland and sell it for profit to people needing homes. The land closer to the city center was developed by industry and commercial enterprise and the new residents of Lincoln Park went to work for that industry and commerce. In turn, some people who made money from the postfire boom in Chicago bought land from farmers on Lake Geneva to build summer mansions and a yacht club.

At this time Zenda farmers, as a more profitable venture, began to specialize in milk rather than the whole gamut of agricultural products. Some became entrepreneurs themselves in developing local creameries and soliciting their own customers in the city. This did not last long, as with the advent of the local railroad the larger companies, such as a Borden milk-processing plant in Hebron, could outbuy the farmers and force the local creameries to close. The entrepreneurs who bought from the farmers and sold to the consumers garnered the profits and dictated terms to both producers and consumers. Now the Milk Producers Association buys milk and distributes it to various brand-name companies.

Until almost 1950, the work of Zenda was labor-intensive, with farms run by large families and hired hands and farmers cooperating in harvesting parties. The prosperity of the 1950s, post-World War II, coupled with advertising and the desire for more profits, led farmers to invest their profits in ever bigger and more expensive machinery, which increased their production and eliminated their need for help from other people.

With inflation and increased costs of machinery, fertilizer, and fuel, farmers needed more land in order to make a profit. A few farms have been bought and turned into corporations, including the German corporation. Other farms have consolidated within families; fewer families own and work more of the land. The old farmhouses are rented out to people employed primarily in factories. The remaining smaller farms struggle on, sometimes changing their markets as they switch from dairy farming to grain production.

At the same time that farm production grew, industry began in the village with the boat company and gradually has grown, and some new industry has come. Each of these is owned by one family, some of whom migrated from the Chicago area.

In Lincoln Park ethnic groups brought their own commercial enterprises, hospitals, and churches, although most of the people were employed in factories. A few of the ethnic establishments remained small, but some became big business, enabling the owners to become rich. Others moved on to seek their fortunes outside of Lincoln Park. Wealthier people in Lincoln Park moved closer to the lake or to newer housing in newer neighborhoods, rather than repair an old house when it was not profitable to do so. Instead, it was more profitable to rent dwelling space, dividing it to accommodate more and more people until housing in Lincoln Park became so deteriorated that families no longer rented the single tiny rooms, but only the lumpen proletariat — alcoholics, criminals, prostitutes, and other derelicts — who could get no other housing. The change of production in Chicago from industry to corporations put less skilled workers in Lincoln Park out of work and created needs for more white-collar positions.

Soon suburbs also began to age and attract less desirable populations. The problems in the suburbs, combined with the shortage of gasoline and increasing costs of transportation in the 1970s and 1980s, encouraged those who could afford it to move in order to avoid the loss of property values in the deteriorating suburbs and to gain the potential increase in property in the city because of the location near the lake and near the center of Chicago.

Attracted by the lake location, the potential of the old buildings, and the low price of housing, by the 1950s middle-class people began moving into Lincoln Park. As they became homeowners, they wanted to protect the value of their property, and through the neighborhood associations they began activities that would drive out and eliminate people and establishments — like high rises and chain stores — that would devalue property. As property values were upgraded with the emigration of the poor from Lincoln Park, the attraction of more wealthy people brought small businesses that meet local consumption needs — antiques, fancy restaurants and the like — which also attract customers from other places.

In sum, Zenda and Lincoln Park began not as commercial centers, as in Gordon's theory of U.S. urban areas, but to supply the commercial centers. Then followed quite early in Lincoln Park the stage of industry, which did not come to Zenda until recently. Lincoln Park currently experiences the corporate stage, the source of employment for most residents.

Zenda and Lincoln Park have progressed through changing economic conditions and markets that have reorganized their labor and in Lincoln Park have revolutionized housing interests. Economics in Zenda have changed from individuals selling their own products, to locally owned small businesses selling local products, to bigger and farther away corporations selling Zenda's products. Neither community started in the feudal period, but the history of both places has proceeded from early to late capitalism, Lincoln Park going farther than Zenda. Change in the social organization of labor and consumption is the history from a conflict perspective.

Process

Marx calls the process of conflict and change a dialectic that proceeds by the juxtaposition of opposites or the contradiction of interests: a thesis and its opposite or antithesis. In capitalistic societies, the two sides are the capitalists and the workers. The result of the conflict between the two produces a new situation, a synthesis with new contradictions. In the short term, issues arise, people mobilize, and out of conflict the issue is resolved.

According to Coleman (1957), the dynamics of the conflict are, first, that specific issues change to more general ones and new issues arise. Next, disagreement shifts to antagonism, accompanied by polarization as people take sides. Partisan organizations and leaders emerge who mobilize existing organizations. Sometimes a dominant group co-opts issues to make the opposition seem part of the dominant force, and the resolution of conflict becomes an obscuring of different interests. Coleman defines co-optation as "bringing the opposition inside to voice its criticisms" (1957, p. 17). Co-optation deflates dissatisfaction before the conflict intensifies into violence.

According to Castells, the processes of urban dialectics in the 1970s and 1980s center on issues such as urban services, fiscal crises, and pressure from grass-roots community organizations, which replace the poverty and racial discrimination conflicts of the 1960s and early 1970s. According to him, "the urban process is produced through the interaction between the elements of the urban structure and the variation of urban politics" (1977, p. 379). Often urban crises have been contained by repressive social orders of greater violent strength. Killing and jailing protesters can put an end to protests. Attempts at regulating crises through urban policies generates deeper contradictions; for example, spending on ghetto problems and urban services feed fiscal crises. Financial institutions and capital markets depend on the viability of cities, yet U.S. corporations are unwilling to pay the price necessary to maintain cities other than as armed camps.

Examples regarding land use in both Lincoln Park and Zenda illustrate the juxtaposition of opposing interests. In Zenda in 1975 descendants of a long-time farming family, whose property bordered the lake, threatened to sell it to a development company, which planned to build 500 new houses on the land. This was first made known to the town board, since many kinds of permits were required. Soon the news spread by word of mouth throughout the community. People were angered and started holding meetings at schools and the town hall, which overflowed the meeting places because so many people were against the development and wanted to do something about it. Meanwhile the town board continued to discuss it and hear negative arguments. Protesters placed ads in local papers citing the drain on local sewage facilities, on fire and police protection, and on schools, which could not handle so many people.

The development company then answered with its own ads. Finally the protesters got the town board to put the issue on the ballot, and the development was overwhelmingly defeated. Today the 500 houses have not been built, although the developers are seeking other legal means to go beyond the wishes of the local people, and just a few new houses have been built.

In Lincoln Park the conflict is over a hospital's expansion to take over land that was used for residential housing. The interest of both sides was economic — the hospital wanted to make more profits by being able to accommodate more patients and the residents did not wish to lose land by having property condemned and thus devalue more property as the hospital spread.

Early in the 1950s, with urban renewal, Lincoln Park had fought to prevent institutions from relocating, as a way to preserve community stability, but by the 1970s the upper middle class was entrenched and fighting the expansion of the institutions. In 1972 one of the hospitals wanted to double its area and the LPCA opposed the expansion; they presented demographics and information on needs for hospital beds, which showed that the expansion was not necessary. The hospital threatened to leave Lincoln Park altogether. At one meeting the hospital had all their board members, directors, and doctors, and the LPCA had 3,000 volunteers. A lawyer in the LPCA then found that an environmental impact statement was required, since the Federal Housing Authority was funding the hospital expansion. The FHA representative said that it would not provide an environmental impact statement, so LPCA sued the federal government. The hospital argued that it was not a major federal funding project, and LPCA argued that it was. The court process went on for many months with many continuances, until finally the government conceded and LPCA won.

The hospital, however, then went on to seek new funding. They asked the county to issue bonds and stipulate that the hospital would belong to the county in the year 2007. The next day, the LPCA filed suit against the hospital. The day following the filing, the board director of the hospital contacted the board director of LPCA and threatened to countersue LPCA if it did not negotiate in good faith. Eight representatives from each side met for several days. The hospital said that everything was negotiable except the number of beds; so the hospital agreed to reduce its height by 10 percent and require the approval of the LPCA on the facade and garage; further, the hospital could not expand again without the community's approval. The agreement was drawn up, both sides signed, and the hospital expanded. Both Zenda and Lincoln Park were acting out of economic interests and brought political agencies into the conflict — the courts in Lincoln Park and the ballot in Zenda. As a political unit unto itself, the township of Linn could refer the issue to the ballot, while in Lincoln Park the hospitals already had a stronghold in the community. Both Lincoln Park and Zenda have successfully fought developers. In both places the community interests take the form of social movements with power in numbers attacking economic establishments with power in wealth. In both examples, two sides — the developers/hospital and the community groups — clashed, resulting in some resolution or change.

SPACE

Territory

Instead of space being the independent variable that influences population organization, as for human ecologists, from the conflict view organizations structure space. Productive forces, class struggles, and the layers of social structure (economic, political, and ideological) organize space and influence the location of factories and residences (Castells 1977). The example in the section on process shows how determination of land use derives from class struggles. Every historical period experiences a different organization of space. Space is also one of the spoils of the struggle.

Space as a scarce resource becomes an object of profits and an issue of control. The issue of profits from space becomes: Whose profit and who is going to determine what the profits are? The state often gives to land rights of use value and exchange value. In both Lincoln Park and Zenda the first settlers had to purchase the land from the government. The community garners a kind of profit by taxing space through property or inheritance taxes, yet many corporations avoid these taxes, since communities may offer incentives to corporations to locate in their community to provide employment. Corporations then use space for their own profit. Corporations as well as individuals profit from the sale of land, so that spatial arrangements can reflect income hierarchies. Profit seeking has also affected space through transportation, as General Motor's destruction of the trolley system forced automobile use.

In both Zenda and Lincoln Park the land is used for profits, but in different ways. In Zenda the land becomes profitable by its production capabilities, which require ever better machinery, fertilizers, and so on. In Lincoln Park, and to a lesser extent in Zenda, the land becomes profitable by its market values, which are not static and which can be improved by changes both on the owners' land and on the surrounding land. Space is also at the mercy of market forces that go beyond the control of the local community. Agricultural production organizes Zenda space and upper-middle-class residential use organizes Lincoln Park space.

Since the wealthy and powerful control space, they can use space to control lower classes. For example, corporations have relocated to suburbs, to the south and southwest, and to Third World countries, when labor demands become too much. These spatial moves have divided the labor class. Urban renewal is another example of the determination of space use by the powerful and the removal of the poor, as in Lincoln Park.

Boundaries

The boundaries of capitalism have expanded to create a world-wide system that impacts on local communities. While local boundaries perhaps cannot be seen as economic, conflict theorists pay more attention to the political boundaries of communities than does any other framework. Boundaries may be a source of conflict, sometimes between two communities, sometimes between locals and outsiders. To the extent that communities can expand their boundaries and incorporate new land, they can increase their resources and taxing base. Communities can also set internal boundaries by zoning laws. Most older cities in the United States stopped their expansion with the development of suburbs with their own municipalities.

Neither Zenda nor Lincoln Park is a municipality with legal boundaries. Zenda residents battle to maintain their distinction from urban tourists; their protests have prevented one extension of urbanism into their area. On the other hand, land owned by urbanites near the lake does provide revenue to Linn Township through taxes. Since Lincoln Park's boundaries are based primarily on the community organizations, they could expand for Lincoln Park to include larger units. The community has fought the extension of school boundaries farther south into the area of public housing. Its political units, such as census districts or wards, may also change through political maneuvers. Although Lincoln Park itself does not have legal boundaries, political issues of redistricting corporate values through redlining — that is, realtors determining boundaries — can affect Lincoln Park.

SUMMARY

Marx and Weber, applauding the great transformations of the French and Industrial Revolutions, laid a foundation of conflict theory that has been applied to communities most extensively by Castells. Communities are like the battlefields of wars, whose antagonists must be analyzed and set in historical perspective, influencing conflict theory's more extensive use of documents than in other disciplines. The political economy of capitalism dominates communities and controls local institutions. Conflict theorists emphasize community stratification and inequality above all other community elements. Although interactions occur as conflict, or through ideology which prevents conflict, the concept of alienation suggests that capitalism prevents meaningful relationships from occurring. Historically, the mode of production and therefore the class divisions change. In the process of dialectics, opposing groups conflict and either create or prevent change. Upper classes and political institutions use space to attain profits and control lower classes, just as they use redlining, zoning, and city limits to set boundaries.

Old residents and new residents have divided Lincoln Park and Zenda and in both have battled for land and local control. Both Lincoln Park and Zenda residents are at the mercy of the capitalist political economy for wages and prices of consumer goods, even though some of them are small capitalists. Most people in both places accept the ideology that private ownership and profits are for the best and use their land for profits and increased property values.

Lincoln Park appears to be involved in a later stage of capitalism than does Zenda and to have a more rational authority system.

Measures of class by income and occupation indicate a higher class level for Lincoln Park. Lincoln Park also has a greater variety of class and power divisions and hence more internal battles, whereas Zenda battles more with outsiders.

In response to the emphasis on the large-scale social processes and structures, social psychologists criticize functionalism and conflict theory for failing to account for individuals and their impact on communities. Instead of the structures of communities, such as the political economy, influencing community residents, social psychologists consider how individuals create community structures. The next chapter presents the small research on communities that social psychologists favor.

6

Social Psychological Approaches: Community as Communication

In the preceding three chapters the camera has photographed landscapes and aerial views of community and focused on macroscopic issues of community aggregates, community institutions, and community class and power issues. In this chapter the camera zooms in for some close-ups, some portraits of people interacting in their everyday community lives, and their use of community symbols.

Social psychology focuses on individuals, which the other approaches have not done; the focus on individuals, however, does not neglect society. Social-psychological perspectives examine how society influences individuals and, in turn, how individuals influence society. While interaction between individuals and communities is the key concept, the gamut runs from cognition and the self, to interaction, to the social construction of reality.

Many fields have been called social psychology. This discussion will concentrate on symbolic interaction, because it has been the dominant social psychology of sociology and because it has been used for the study of community. Phenomenology or ethnomethodology and cognitive theory will supplement the social psychology of community. Herbert Blumer (1969) coined the phrase "symbolic interaction," by which he meant "the peculiar and distinctive character of interaction as it takes place between human beings" (pp. 78-79). Reciprocal and symbolic interpretations are the uniquely human characteristics. Symbolic interactionists consider all meaning as socially created and examine how meaning is created and maintained through socialization in interactions. While interaction may be defined as how the actual, imagined, or implied presence of others influences a person's thoughts and actions (Allport 1968), the symbolic title refers to signs that carry meanings (Lindesmith, Strauss, and Denzin 1977, pp. 98-99). A subset of symbolic interaction is the dramaturgical approach, which studies how people present themselves and manipulate to communicate (Goffman 1959).

Phenomenologists and ethnomethodologists study how people categorize and the underlying rules of what is taken for granted. Garfinkel (1967) defines ethnomethodology as the study of how people make sense out of social reality through communication and interaction, and thereby construct reality. Phenomenology and cognitive theory, which considers what people know and how they know it, are both concerned with perception. All of the social-psychological approaches emphasize language.

Social psychology has been applied to community in studies of cognitive mapping, community identities, definitions of community situations, and the social construction of communities through language and symbols. To see how this came about, the development of social psychology will be traced from its beginnings under the influence of classical sociologists to its latest findings. Social psychology also contributes unique metaphors and concepts to the three dimensions of community, as they apply to Zenda and Lincoln Park.

HISTORICAL DEVELOPMENT

Of the classical theorists, Weber and his idea of *verstehen* most influenced symbolic interaction, but the major influences were philosophers, American pragmatists. In a theory of social action, Weber contributes the importance of individuals and subjective meanings in the study of society. He considered individuals to be the basic units of society:

> In this approach, the individual is also the upper limit and sole carrier of meaningful conduct. . . . In general, for sociology, such concepts

as "state," "association," . . . and the like, designate certain categories of human interaction. Hence, it is the task of sociology to reduce these concepts to understandable action, that is, action, without exception, oriented to the actions of participating individual people (quoted in Gerth and Mills 1958, p. 55).

Weber defines social action as behavior to which subjective meaning is attached. When people act, they take account of the behavior of others. According to him,

[social action is] all human behavior when and insofar as the acting individual attaches a subjective meaning to it. Action in this sense may be overt, purely inward, or subjective; it may consist of positive intervention in a situation, or deliberately refraining from such intervention, or passively acquiescing in the situation. Action is social insofar as by virtue of the subjective meaning attached to it by the acting individual, it takes account of the behavior of others and is thereby oriented in its course. (1947, p. 88)

Verstehen, or interpretative sociology, is the method by which social action is known. Weber believes that because its subject matter is humans, social science is not the same as natural science. Unlike natural scientists, social scientists must examine the motives of the subjects and their interpretations. Empathy and reliving the experience facilitate verstehen, but verstehen must lead to a causal explanation. Thus Weber lays a social-psychological foundation of individuals and subjectivity.

Another European, Georg Simmel, also influenced social psychology. Examining forms of social interaction, he showed how numbers made a difference. For example, as dyads differ from triads, so do people behave differently in large groups. Simmel argued that the metropolis affects mental life and produces blasé attitudes, so that people block out the overstimulation of city life and do not seem to care about others. Also, the emphasis on money and problems of dealing with such a vast number of people produces anonymity and a calculating mind (Simmel 1950).

Pragmatism

Symbolic interaction and other social psychologies considered in this chapter are primarily products of the United States, based on the philosophy of pragmatism whose criterion of truth consists of utility and what works. Pragmatists consider what difference it would make if a statement were true, and they look at meaning as a practical consequence. Symbolic interaction concepts such as the self and the influence of other people originated with pragmatism, whose basic tenets overlap with symbolic interaction: people are active and selective of stimuli rather than reactive; meaning resides in behavior directed to objects rather than in the objects themselves; and organisms help shape their environment (Manis and Meltzer 1978). The pragmatists William James and John Dewey directly influenced symbolic interaction.

James downplayed instincts and found that other people help form the self, defined as a human capacity to view oneself as an object. He initiated the idea of multiple selves by delineating four basic selves that everyone has: pure ego, a material self, a spiritual self, and a social self, although individuals have as many social selves as the number of groups to which they belong (1892). While James judged meaning by whether it was good for the individual, Dewey judged it by its benefit to society. He stressed experience and argued that communication and language make society possible (1948).

If Weber, James, and Dewey formed the roots of symbolic interaction, George Herbert Mead can be said to be the trunk of the tree of symbolic interaction. A student of James and a colleague of Dewey at the University of Michigan and the University of Chicago, Mead trained many students in symbolic interaction. *Mind, Self, and Society* (1934), a series of Mead's lectures collected by his students, contains his three major areas of thinking. The mind as a uniquely human phenomenon is able to construct and manipulate symbols; that is, humans give meanings to things, people, and events, which have no inherent meaning. In using the mind, people consider various lines of action, which they covertly rehearse, and then select an overt action. Also, in using the mind, people are communicating with others, taking account of their lines of action, and interpreting the symbols of others emitted through language and gestures. Mead calls this taking the role of the other, which means imaginatively putting one's mind in another person's place.

People can also communicate with themselves, because the self is reflexive and can look back upon itself. Mead analyzed the self into two parts: the "I" and the "me," which interact in a dialectical way. The I is the spontaneous, impulsive, acting part of the self, while the me is the object a person sees during self-reflexion. The me encompasses the Is of the past, which include responses to the attitudes of others. In this way people can symbolically represent themselves as objects.

People are not born with selves; selves develop interactively. Babies use gestures just as animals do, but over time, humans develop significant (self-conscious) gestures, including language. When children play, they are learning roles that they will use in later life. At first they take the role of just one or two others — for example, in playing mother and baby, which helps them to understand and communicate with their own mothers. In later childhood, children are able to play games in which it is necessary to consider several other roles in addition to the player's own, as in Mead's example of baseball. The game stage of development prepares children for the "generalized other" stage of adult life, in which people consider all the other roles in the community in their own actions.

Through taking the role of others, individuals coordinate their activities and perpetuate institutions and society itself. Mead sees society in flux because of the constant impact of minds and selves readjusting meanings; on the other hand, he contends that society exists prior to individuals.

Charles Cooley also learned from Dewey and influenced Mead at the University of Michigan, where he spent his entire life. The two important concepts that Cooley contributes to symbolic interaction are the looking-glass self and the primary group.

The looking-glass self denotes the influence of others in the creation of selves. It is as if other people were mirrors that reflect back the self. First, people imagine their appearance to others; next, they imagine a judgment of the appearance, and from these two, develop a self-feeling. Since each person is a looking glass for another, the image is of two mirrors reflecting back and forth ad infinitum (Cooley 1964).

The primary group consists of others who are most instrumental in forming a person's self, such as the family, play group, and neighborhood. They are the primary in two senses: first, in being the initial, earliest social contact, and second, in being the most important influence in forming the social self. Intimate face-to-face association and cooperation that instill a belongingness or a "we feeling" characterize primary groups cemented by sympathy, the most human emotion (Cooley 1962). Cooley conceives of society as a state of mind arising dialectically through communication. He tends to be more mentalistic and introspective than Mead.

Another early University of Chicago symbolic interactionist, W. I. Thomas, developed the concept of the "definition of the situation," which is crucial in the symbolic interaction approach to society. Thomas's famous dictum states that if people define situations as real, the situations are real in their consequences (Thomas and Thomas 1928, p. 572). People give meaning by acting on their interpretations.

Dramaturgical Symbolic Interaction

Erving Goffman developed a particular kind of symbolic interaction, the dramaturgical approach, from a community study of the Shetland Islands. Using theatrical terminology, Goffman describes how people manipulate self-images to control what others think of them. Use of performances, teams, props, setting, and front and back regions helps to define the situation and heighten communication (Goffman 1959).

Labeling Theory

Labeling theory applies symbolic interaction to the area of deviance (Goffman 1963; Becker 1963), but also has relevance for community. Although all people at times break norms, some people are publicly accused by police, courts, hospitals, and prisons. According to labeling theory this produces a label or stigma that they incorporate into their identities, so they continue breaking norms. Powerful groups' denunciation and punishment of deviants perpetuate deviancy. Labeling theorists engage in micro studies of those outside mainstream society.

Phenomenology and Ethnomethodology

Some see ethnomethodology as a branch of symbolic interaction because both examine the process of giving meaning and taken-for-granted assumptions (Denzin 1969; Meltzer, Petras, and Reynolds 1975). Phenomenology and ethnomethodology, however, have a slightly different philosophical background than symbolic interaction because social phenomenology comes from the philosophical phenomenology of Husserl (1913). He abstractly examined the process of how consciousness creates a sense of an external reality and tried to abstract consciousness from its substance.

Schutz learned from Husserl and made phenomenology into a social theory. To do so, he had to borrow from James and Mead. His central concept of intersubjectivity implies a shared experience, yet because of differing biographies and experiencing from different vantage points, experiences of two people are never the same. By acting as if they understand one another, however, by using reciprocity of perspectives, and by typifying their subjectivity, people are able to create a sense of order and communicate. In addition, people experience multiple realities, including science, everyday life, fantasy, and dreams (1971).

Berger and Luckmann (1968) synthesized even more of phenomenology and symbolic interaction to analyze the social construction of reality. They define reality as "a quality appertaining to phenomena that we recognize as having a being independent of our own volition" (1968, p. 1). In the social construction of reality, subjective reality interacts with objective reality to create new realities. Individuals externalize their subjectivity through talk and habits that become coordinated with the habits of others, institutionalized, legitimated, and reified to the point where people forget they are social creations. In turn, this objective reality is internalized for new members through socialization and the creation of identities and becomes subjective. Objectification, subjectification, internalization, and externalization are continuous processes.

Garfinkel, a student of Schutz and Parsons, created the term ethnomethodology, which he defines as "the investigation of the relational properties of indexical expressions and other practical actions as contingent, ongoing accomplishments of organized artful practices of everyday life" (1967, p. 11). In other words, ethnomethodologists examine the rules by which people see, describe, and explain order to create a sense of reality. We can understand what is taken for granted by making it problematic, as Garfinkel does in his famous breaching activities (those that upset taken-for-granted assumptions by turning them upside down and making them problematic), such as sending his students home to act like guests or sending them to barter with store clerks.

In sum, social psychologists have provided basic tenets to guide studies of communities. Individuals as active meaning givers through their interactions with one another produce selves, identities, and realities. This approach takes account of individuals' feelings and perceptions and their use of symbols and dramatizations to communicate.

Community Studies

Social-psychological applications to community are divided into those that focus on interactions and symbols, especially influenced by University of Chicago sociologists, and those that focus on perceptions, as influenced by cognitive psychology.

Influence of the Chicago School

The combined influences of Park, Mead, and Everett Hughes, who urged students to study their own experiences in the city, produced several generations of community studies. Several early studies were of deviant groups in Chicago — hobos (Anderson 1923), taxi dance halls (Cressey 1932), and delinquents (Shaw 1930) — and influenced more recent urban ethnographies of Italian neighborhoods (Gans 1962; Whyte 1955), black street-corner men (Liebow 1967; Anderson 1978), and suburbs (Gans 1967; Whyte 1956; Seeley, Sims, and Loosley 1956). Starting with Janowitz (1951), community concepts were developed with ethnographies. Janowitz studied local community newspapers in Chicago, which not only symbolize communities but also provide new channels of communication. From his study he developed the concept of the community of limited liability, by which he meant that people are still oriented to local communities, but in varied and partial ways, and they also orient themselves to larger units. For example, many people read both the neighborhood paper and the city newspaper. Greer (1962) followed Janowitz in finding that local groups have viable ways of inclusive belonging.

Gerald Suttles, a student of Janowitz, defines community as an identity that people distinguish from other populations (1972, p. 234). He develops three important concepts — ordered segmentation, cognitive mapping, and the defended neighborhood — which combine symbolic interactionist subjective interpretations by residents with issues of location and space.

In his first book, *The Social Order of the Slum* (1968), Suttles argues that the slum is not a place of chaos and constant violence, but rather that ethnic groups (Italians, blacks, Mexicans, and Puerto Ricans) can share the Addams area of Chicago by finding safety in their own segments — such as age, gender, and ethnic divisions. Ordered segmentation not only keeps order but also provides the mode by which groups unite in conflict. Ordered segmentation is communicated in different ways of talking, walking, staring, and dressing in street life, and in institutional arrangements that provide differential territorial claims.

On the perceptual level, Suttles finds that people map the city, that is, have images for indicating which areas of the city are personally safe to them. Cognitive maps* help people locate themselves in physical space and thereby know who they are and whom they may encounter. He defines them as simplified images of the city, which

> serve us well by reducing the complexity of the urban landscape to a range of discrete and contrastively defined ecological units despite the general continuity, gray areas, and constant changes in any section of the city. . . . A cognitive map of our urban environs is useful for precisely the reason that it simplifies to the point of exaggerating the sharpness of boundaries, population composition, and neighborhood identity. (Suttles 1972, p. 4)

Cognitive mapping is a creative imposition of meaning upon the apparent diversity of the city. It serves to sharpen boundaries and identities of places, to indicate what the city is like and what it ought to be like, and to facilitate decision making in social contacts.

In *The Social Construction of Communities* (1972), Suttles wants to show "how people use territory, residence, distance, and space, and movement to build up collective representations which have communicative value" (p. 7). In the concept of the defended

---

*Suttles's concept of cognitive mapping better fits the cognitive side of social psychology, but since his idea of cognitive mapping is so entwined with his concept of the defended neighborhood, it is discussed here.

neighborhood, he shows how communities acquire an identity and boundaries by their "foreign relations."

> Local communities and neighborhoods, like other groups, acquire a corporate identity because they are held jointly responsible by other communities and external organizations. Thus, I suggest, it is in their "foreign relations" that communities come into existence and have to settle on an identity and set of boundaries, which over-simplify their identity. (Suttles 1972, pp. 12-13)

Defended neighborhoods provide both social differentiation and cohesion.

Albert Hunter, a student of both Suttles and Janowitz, reported a restudy of Burgess's natural areas of Chicago in his *Symbolic Communities* (1974), which combines symbolic interaction with human ecology and organizational approaches. He found that people develop local communities as an orientation to meaningful action. They do this largely through symbols that consist of neighborhood names and boundaries.

> The close associations among the words "common," "communication," and "community" are no accident. The ability to exchange meaning through a shared set of symbols has long been recognized as an integral part of community. (Hunter 1974, p. 67)

Hunter examines the ability of people to name their community, its boundaries, and express attachment to their community as shared collective representations of a definition of reality from which residents act. He correlates these with varying statuses of people and of communities. In his restudy of Rochester, New York, Hunter shows how residents create community through a community organization in spite of a decline in the use of local facilities. He defines sense of community as "cognitive identification of and affective identification with the local community" (1975, p. 539).

Karp, Stone, and Yoels (1977) and Gusfield (1975) are the only community textbook authors to extensively examine social-psychological approaches. Karp, Stone, and Yoels devote an entire urban text to social-psychological issues, discussing images of cities, communal ties, and symbolic communities. According to them, rather than being anonymous and indifferent, people in cities interact and negotiate tolerance of one another. Urbanites seek to minimize involvement and maximize social order (p. 11).

In Gusfield's chapter titled "The Social Construction of Community: Concepts as Existential Types," he suggests that people create communal membership (a particular quality of relationships) through symbolic construction. He defines symbolic construction as "a process of creating and signifying the existence and character of persons and objects by the ways in which human beings conceptualize, talk about, and define them" (Gusfield 1975, p. 24). When people have symbolically constructed community, they share similar consciousnesses and identities that give them claims on other members of the same community as a distinct form of interaction. Thus Gusfield defines community as "part of a system of accounts used by members and observers as a way of explaining or justifying the member's behavior" (p. 33).

Lyn Lofland, Claude Fischer, and Gerson and Gerson also examine community or urban interactions and experiences. Lofland's (1973) study of urban experiences demonstrates that anonymity is not autonomatic, but something people work on by their self-presentation, their use of space and props. Furthermore, people are not entirely strangers, because they do have information about others. Some of the strangeness is eliminated through a perceptual ordering of appearances and spatial locations.

Claude Fischer spans several community paradigms and is best known for his work on networks. His book, *The Urban Experience* (1976), and a recent (1981) article, however, are both social-psychological. In the article he argues that urbanites are more social-psychologically different in their private lives than in their public lives. Publicly, urban dwellers profess a fear and distrust of people different from themselves, but on an interpersonal level, people do not distrust their neighbors and people they know well, even though they are different. In *The Urban Experience*, Fischer compares and contrasts three theories of the social-psychological effects of urban life. The determinist suggests that city life has a negative social-psychological effect; compositionalists argue there are not social-psychological consequences of urbanism; the subcultural position is that concentration of population produces subcultures that influence city life to be different from rural life in both negative and positive ways (1976).

Gerson and Gerson (1976) argue that people order perspectives, which provide guides to action, based on their interactions with others. They explore four place perspectives: temporal (a place's pace and rhythm), monetary, sentimental, and ideological.

Environmental Cognition

Geographers and psychologists have recently combined their knowledge to produce a seemingly new discipline that actually has many affinities with the application of symbolic interaction to community. Indeed, they cite sociologists Fiery and Strauss among the founders of their perspective. Environmental cognition examines the interaction between people and the environment; this interaction occurs primarily in the form of images and perceptions of space that develop through interactions with other people. The environment can refer to a community or to smaller units, such as the layout of a house or paths through a park, or to larger environments. In a statement describing environmental cognition, Moore and Golledge (1976) use many of the same phrases as community sociologists when they say that cognitive processes permit meaning to be given, provide orientation, and suggest action (p. xii). Fiery and Strauss wrote about urban symbols and images, but Kevin Lynch, an urban planner, did the most to inspire this subdiscipline with cognitive mapping as its key concept.

Although Fiery was a human ecologist, he argued (1945) that subjective states were community variables, including sentiments and symbols. He found that in Boston, residents' concern about historical places, such as the Boston Commons or churches, and residents' choices to live in certain neighborhoods determined land use and the layout of the city.

Anselm Strauss (1961), a major proponent of symbolic interaction, discusses popular characterizations of American cities as found in newspapers, history books, and literature. Where ambiguity about cities exists, observers filter the myriad images into manageable units that permit observers to relate to cities. Observers contrast cities and exaggerate certain characteristics. Strauss argues that cities cannot be understood without knowing what the people in the cities think about them.

Lynch (1960) compares the imageability and legibility of cities by asking which cities were easier to view and which facilitated people's pathways. He initiated the method of asking people to draw maps of their environment. In order to compare cities' image-ability — that is, "a high probability for a physical object to evoke a strong image in any given observer" (p. 9) — Lynch analyzes maps drawn by 30 people in Boston, 15 in Jersey City, and 15 in Los Angeles, primarily in terms of five symbolic representations on the maps: paths, edges, districts, nodes, and landmarks. He also considers how these are connected. He concludes that Boston has the best imageability.

Many researchers have followed Lynch in analyses, taken from the concept of cognitive mapping, of maps drawn by residents. For example, Moore and Golledge define cognitive mapping as "the process by which individuals and groups acquire, code, recall, and decode information about the relative locations and attributes of the everyday large-scale spatial environment" (1976, p. xii). Researchers have used Lynch's ideas to see how mapping changes over time (Devlin 1976); to examine mental maps, or preferences as to where people want to live (Gould and White 1974); to analyze the relation of cognitive mapping to spatial behavior and gender differences (Downs and Stea 1973; Stoneall 1981); to demonstrate that not only the environment but also social position affect perception (Orleans 1973).

Proshansky (1978), another founder of environmental cognition, argues that role identities often have spatial and physical elements. He defines place identity as "those dimensions of self that define the individual's personal identity in relation to the physical environment by means of a complex pattern of conscious and unconscious ideas, feelings, values, goals, preferences, skills, and behavioral tendencies relevant to a specific environment" (p. 147). In addition, each person chooses and favors some places over others.

While symbolic interactionists examine how meaning is produced from interaction, environmental cognition emphasizes how selective perception provides order. Combined, these two approaches lay a foundation for analyzing the interpersonal, subjective conscious-ness of communities. Looking at individuals interacting, viewing their surroundings in varied ways, and promoting some of the sur-roundings as symbolic representations of their community lead to a social-psychological approach to community (Table 6.1).

METAPHOR

Unlike the scientific images of previous theories, the humanities influence social-psychological images of people creating communities. Communities are like joint artistic creations, never quite finished, constantly being worked on. The language of construction, drama, and labeling bear out the artistic image.

Berger and Luckmann (1968), Suttles (1972), and others have used the phrase "social construction" to describe the interactive

TABLE 6.1
Social Psychological Community Dimensions

Dimension	Description
Metaphor	Artistic creation
Methodology	Participant observation, life histories, ethnography; data on perceptions, interactions, symbol use; reconstruction of typifications
People	
Institutions	Regularized situations; community symbols; choices of facility use
Stratification	Self-placement
Interactions	Negotiations of definitions of situations
Time	
History	Biography and careers
Process	Cognition, conversation
Space	
Territory	Cognitive mapping; material of community construction
Boundaries	Changing with situations

processes that give people a feeling of reality about a community. Ethnomethodologists indicate that people work to put together meaningful accounts to make sense of their surroundings and other people; they define work as practical procedures by which intelligibility is attained. People accomplish community.

The image is of uniformed workers bustling around with tools to build the reality of community. The main tools of the residents and others are language and definitions. People inherit the tools for construction in an apprenticeship under the previous generation, since people are born into a world where typifications, words, and ideas about communities already exist. The new apprentices learn to perpetuate these, while also modifying them in their own way. Workers are like artists creating a sculpture, a symphony, or a poem, because each community is unique; similarly, each person viewing the art work has a slightly different interpretation and sees a slightly different configuration.

The drama image merely elaborates how people use tools in the social construction of community. The image of costumed people on a stage, using props, settings, and lines, shows how the way people talk, dress, and carry themselves communicates something about themselves, and in an extended way says something about their community and indicates whether they belong with other people or not. In addition to the everyday dramatizing and rituals, traditional collective events may signal both to insiders and outsiders the existence of the community. When asked how they know there is a community, people cite the annual rituals, because they symbolize the community, as signs that the community has meaning for them.

The social construction of community produces interactive and collective rituals that give the community an identity for insiders, a reputation for outsiders, and for both insiders and outsiders, a label. Labeling is another social-psychological metaphor, which implies that a giant rubber stamp has come down on a person or community and branded a word or symbol on the place or person. Sometimes community labeling works like a stigma, in that officials publicize and often chastise communities as a whole for some particular localized attribute, such as the crime rate, or pollution. For example, Krase (1979) argues that being from a slum stigmatizes. Slum residents may be unaware of, accepting of, embracing, or attempting to contradict the stigma image. Thus, community residents attempt to control information about their communities, to hide information that would discredit the community, and heighten and publicize prestige symbols of the community.

METHODOLOGY

Given the metaphor, certain questions must be asked. The emphasis of the metaphors and therefore of the questions is on meaning. Accordingly, the first question is about the establishment of meaning and meaning systems.

What are the interpretative frameworks? What are the meanings of the community and how do people construct and communicate them? What are individuals' definitions of the situation, as conveyed in their actions and talk? Going beyond individuals to the collectivity, what definitions or meanings become ongoing and perceived as more or less fixed culture? In turn, how do people react to these ongoing meanings? Social psychologists focus on the nature of the creative aspect, the process and change.

Another point of focus related to meaning is interaction. How do individuals communicate and exchange meaning? This question forces attention to many channels of community: posture, dress, gestures, space use, language, and paralinguistic styles.

Third is the question of identity and the self. What meanings do individuals give to themselves? How are these meanings related to interaction? Meanings get built up in the individual as personal biographies, although these are constantly being renegotiated. The same is true with the identity of the collectivity − in this case, the community. People redefine and renegotiate its history and meaning. Social psychologists see an interplay between individuals, interactions in situations, and the collectivity. What aspects of the community get incorporated into individuals' identities?

To answer these questions, social psychologists in some way want to know what is going on inside people's heads as well as what goes on between individuals in face-to-face interactions. While some people use pencil-and-paper techniques of questionaires − for example, the Twenty Statements Test* (Kuhn and McPartland 1954),

---

*The Twenty Statements Test (TST), also known as the Who Am I? Test, is based on the assumption of the reflexive self that individuals can look back on

or asking people to draw maps (Lynch 1960) — most social psychologists advocate that meanings of people be understood in their context, which requires participant observation and in-depth interviews. Blumer (1969) stresses sensitizing concepts, which are general ideas about the community to be studied rather than a battery of hypotheses to be tested. The researcher must spend enough time with the subjects to be able to act as a member of that community. The analyst must deal with symbolic representations as a coconstructionist and not as an outside observer imputing meaning. When researchers participate in the same situations as the community members, they are able to take the role of the individuals they are studying and use introspection for further understanding.

Analysis proceeds inductively, as concepts emerge that are directly tied to ordinary people's everyday perspectives. The analysis of qualitative field data consists of an interaction between sociological ideas and everyday life. On the one hand, sociological ideas become grounded in the reality of ordering people's lives (Glaser and Strauss 1967) and on the other hand, new sociological ideas emerge from the data and can be incorporated into the sociological body of knowledge. The end of analysis is the development of second-order constructs, that is, concepts that use the data of first-order constructs or people's knowledge of their everyday lives (Schutz 1971). In other words, a community study using social-psychological frameworks must understand local residents' ideas and perceptions about community and the role community plays in their daily lives.

The author spent a year in Zenda and less in Lincoln Park as a participant observer, and conducted several in-depth interviews on such subjects as life histories, community participation, and definitions. In Zenda 50 people drew maps of what they felt was their community. Friends were also cultivated, who became key informants and regularly expressed their views of what was happening in the Zenda area.

---

themselves in a measurable way. In the TST, subjects are given a paper with 20 numbered blanks. In the span of 12 minutes, subjects are asked to write answers to the question, Who am I? The analysis proceeds in various ways, usually by correlating scores from the test with other characteristics such as group membership.

PEOPLE

Since social psychologists study micro processes, they are less interested in macro structures of institutions and stratification, although through social psychology it is possible to see how institutions and ranking systems are built up and are composed of the interactions of individuals. In turn, social psychologists argue that social structures have no meaning unless they are related to individuals' lives.

Institutions

Berger and Luckmann (1966, p. 64) define institutions as "reciprocal typifications of habitualized actions by types of actors." That is, people develop habits in their ways of doing things that are repeated so often that they become a kind of tradition. People interactively recognize these habits and characterize the habits with specific names of typifications. Social constructionists examine how institutions are created and maintained in daily life. They are basically patterned ways of doing things. Lincoln Park has a greater variety of ways of doing things than Zenda, so we see a greater variety of institutions in Lincoln Park. Institutions are processes of negotiated rules, which change.

Suttles (1968) describes institutional arrangements as a way to perpetuate ethnic boundaries in the Addams area. Ethnic groups can use their own churches, schools, parks, and stores to display their ethnic differences and dramatize their customs, language, food, and costumes. The institutions can also serve as spokespersons or go-betweens for groups.

Taub et al. (1977) found in a southside Chicago neighborhood that rather than residents creating local institutions, outside agencies had to create them to foster communication among neighbors.

> Because there are no obvious points of contact based on informal social networks, external agents seeking to intervene in these neighborhoods must sponsor or even create local voluntary associations as sources of information and legitimation." (p. 425)

From a social-psychological viewpoint, community institutions regularize community situations, use community names and symbols, and indicate a choice pattern of facility use.

Regularization of Community Situations

In Zenda most of the community activity is in informal inter-actions, although residents have formed some institutions. As old-timers talk about creating the organizations, residents visibly form and transform voluntary associations, the major institutions in Zenda, which were started to help one another and to provide sociability. For example, one woman said about the Neighborly Club's beginning: "We were isolated and didn't see each other too much until we started getting together for sewing and making things. Then we just set a regular meeting date each month."

In the 1940s a fire in the village was too big for neighbors to extinguish and fire trucks from other communities could not get there fast enough. Several local men, including the owner of the implement store that had burned, organized a volunteer fire-fighting brigade and persuaded the township board to purchase trucks and other fire-fighting equipment. Similarly, thefts in the area led to citizen demand for police protection, establishing a three-person corps in an office in the town hall.

In 1950 the Zenda Bowling Palace opened and drew most people in the community into bowling leagues, although few had bowled before. In this case a structure developed sociability, in contrast to the other voluntary associations in which sociability became in-stitutionalized in a structure. Many of the original teams still exist, with seeing and playing with friends as important as the sport itself. A 50-year-old farm woman said:

> I'll probably bowl until I'm too ancient to get down there and throw the ball, not because of the bowling so much, but because the social part is so really great. Everybody is so busy and involved in their own little worlds, that you just wouldn't see them. I don't care even whether we win or lose. We sure have a lot of fun.

A 60-year-old farm man also indicated the institutionalization of sociability in bowling:

> I'm on a bowling team. The same five members have bowled together for 26 years. We started when it opened and when it closes, we'll probably quit. Our bowling is really quite a laugh, but we enjoy visiting. They always have to prod us to go up there. "It's your turn now." Then we come back and we talk farming and crops and stuff. We really enjoy it. I'm sure we enjoy the visiting more than the bowling. That's one way of getting together. Otherwise, we don't see each other that much.

The LPCA and the neighborhood associations in Lincoln Park, like the voluntary associations of Zenda, can be viewed as routinized patterns of getting together to oppose outsiders such as developers, to help one another improve the neighborhood, and to socialize with one another. The LPCA has become even more institutionalized than the Linn town government or voluntary associations, hiring a full-time professional staff member and secretary and renting an office, but the founding members still talk about how and why they started LPCA. For example, a retired artist recalls how she and her husband came to Lincoln Park: "We were part of the beginning of LPCA. When we came here in 1948, the area was run down and just beginning to be discovered. We had some friends below Fullerton and they said we should go to some meetings. All the new people went to try to effect some changes."

In Lincoln Park many large institutions, like the hospitals and school systems, seem beyond the interaction of local people. Some residents choose to work with these institutions and make them in some ways their own. One community leader in Lincoln Park worked very hard on schools and practically single-handedly improved their quality. Others choose to work for hospitals by serving on their boards.

Institutions as Community Symbols

Ross (1962) and Hunter (1974) denote community symbols primarily as place names. In Zenda and Lincoln Park, institutions that bear the place names perpetuate the names and communicate them to others. For example, in the rural community, we find the Zenda Garden Club, the Linn Neighborly Club, the Linn Fire Fighters, the Linn Presbyterian Church, and the Linn-Hebron Farmers Club. In the city the Lincoln Park Presbyterian Church, the Lincoln Park Piano Studio, the Lincoln Park Cooperative Nursery, the Lincoln Park Medical Center, and many more names are used in newspapers and make the community known to others. For example, when the Zenda Garden Club won a prize for a bicentennial flower show, it was a source of pride for all in Zenda. Annual festivals especially highlight community formation to participants and others. In Zenda the annual township fair serves this ritualistic purpose, and in Lincoln Park each of the neighborhood associations has an annual event, such as the Old Town Art Fair, the Sheffield Garden Walk, and the Park West Antiques Fair.

Commercial Establishments and Local Facility Use

While other paradigms have documented the loss of local facilities, a social-psychological approach can show how some residents perpetuate their sense of community by patronizing locally owned stores. Suttles (1968) has shown how ethnic differences are maintained by the nature of local stores and how ethnic groups choose to use them. Stone (1954) found that urban shoppers give different meanings to shopping. Two of his types, personalizing and ethical (shoppers choose stores to get personal attention or out of moral obligation to types of stores [anti-big-business]), are ways in which shopping perpetuates a sense of community. These processes also work in Zenda and Lincoln Park.

The Zenda grocery store had been a long-term commercial institution, established within a few years after the founding of the village and owned by only two families. At the time of the study the current owners, who were active church and volunteer association members, had been there over 30 years and lived above the store.

I asked people about their shopping patterns and also learned about the meanings of shopping as a participant observer working in the store. Some Zenda residents chose to do all their shopping at the local store, in part because their parents had done so, but even more to show their patriotism and loyalty to the community and to the owners. Some people go to the store deliberately to be part of the community and all the sentiments its history entails. Most such shoppers have been born in Zenda, and their families have lived there for at least one generation. In trying to preserve the local store, they are also being loyal to small independent business, which is what the farmers and most of the other establishments in the area represent.

The store generates community traditions and rituals. A middle-aged farm woman described the informality of the customer-clerk relationship by saying that if she ran out of bread when the store was closed, she could just telephone the owners. Knowledge of store rituals, such as that customers are supposed to open the freezer for frozen foods, but are not supposed to open the meat case, perpetuate local rules and interactions. With no local newspaper, Zenda residents use the store to post signs or find out news of one another. For example, I observed a man coming to the store to tell the proprietors that his wife had just had a baby, and they, in turn, could inform others. An open cigar box on the counter of the store meant that someone had died and people were being asked to contribute money for the funeral.

In addition to asking people about their shopping patterns, other facility use of the bank and doctor seemed to be related. Just as the Zenda village store was the local facility, the bank in Hebron was also considered local because the officers and workers of the bank were neighbors, and had gone to school with Zenda residents, and because it was easy for Zenda residents to obtain loans from the bank. In 28 families interviewed about facility use, a pattern developed: those who did most of their shopping in Zenda also tended to use the Hebron bank and go to a doctor in Lake Geneva (Table 6.2). Those who shopped outside Zenda showed no pattern in where they banked or received medical treatment.

No one local grocery store symbolized Lincoln Park, although many independent grocers thrive there. As in Zenda, residents can choose to shop outside the community. Some patronize locally owned stores and develop close customer-clerk relations, although, unlike Zenda, in Lincoln Park the customer-clerk relation does not include many associations outside the store. For example, as a 30-year-old professional woman in Lincoln Park said, "We shop at the neighborhood grocery store where everyone knows everyone. I made friends there and we exchange Christmas cookies."

Lincoln Park residents discourage non-locally owned stores in the community; for example, they were successful in preventing the opening of a MacDonald's. While both Lincoln Park and Zenda have lost some local facilities, in both places we find people choosing either to disregard local institutions or to patronize them for their own sense of community.

TABLE 6.2
Location of Shopping, Banking, and Doctor for 28 Zenda Families

| | *Families Shopping in Zenda (9)* | | | *Families Shopping outside Zenda (19)* | |
	Doctor in Lake Geneva	Other Doctor		Doctor in Lake Geneva	Other Doctor
Hebron Bank	7	1	Hebron Bank	5	4
Other Bank	0	1	Other Bank	4	6

Stratification

Social psychologists view stratification, like institutions, on the interactive level rather than as a structure imposed on them, since community stratification is built up from the everyday definitions of residents. People, as part of their self-identity, compare themselves to others and may consider themselves above, below, or equal to others, but this self-placement changes with time and situations. Stratification becomes a matter of defining and interpreting differences among people. Sennett (1970) applauds differences among people because they promote personal growth and individuals find meaning by contrasting themselves with others.

Merton discovered in his community study of Rovere that some residents (locals) turn their attention to the local scene and rate themselves in terms of local people, while others (cosmopolitans) orient to extracommunity people and rank themselves in that milieu. Locals (whom others turn to for decision making) influence by whom they know and cosmopolitans by what they know. Merton defines orientations as patterns of utilizing status rather than the formal contours of status (1949, p. 402).

People's comparisons among themselves are facilitated by how people present themselves. Goffman (1967) discusses how deference and demeanor display power status. Thorne and Henley (1975) document many cases of interactions that perpetuate gender status, such as touching, interrupting, and making eye contact.

Zenda residents know one another well, yet they have developed patterns of behaving differently toward different genders and ages. For example, young people should not initiate conversations with older people, and men "protect" women from doing heavy labor. Lincoln Park residents use many more cues, and most of them are impersonal ways to distinguish themselves from others: clothing, racial types, languages, in addition to gender and age. These make the show of deference more complex, since body language has different meanings for different groups. In Lincoln Park people will respond to a police uniform or a title (like doctor), whereas in Zenda people are responding to a specific younger or older woman or man they have known all their lives.

In addition to interactive cues of status differences, people define certain aspects of communities, and symbols of whole communities become ranked. In Lincoln Park, address, residence, and position connote something about a person's status. Many Lincoln Park residents define having a house near the lake as a prestige symbol, although since most of the housing near the lake is high-rise, others prefer the old Victorian houses as representing the "true" spirit of Lincoln Park. Restoring a house to its original style is a prestige symbol. Elegance of houses or condominiums is an outward display of status in Lincoln Park, whereas Zenda residents pay more attention to how neat and clean yards and houses are. A community feature like a lake, found in both Zenda and Lincoln Park, is defined differently and as a result takes on a different symbolic status aspects for each community. Zenda residents for the most part define their lake as not part of their community.

Interaction

Interaction, as the concept *par excellence* for social psychologists, may be defined as face-to-face reciprocal influence between two or more people (Goffman 1959). Interactions that create selves as well as communities are the focus of most social-psychological approaches and far more important to social psychology than to any other framework.

Definition of the situation and negotiation are the interactional concepts most relevant for the social construction of community. Through interactions, community residents negotiate definitions of the community and then act on those definitions in continued interactions, which further negotiate and modify the definitions. There is a give and take and flexibility about what the community is. Strauss (1978) suggests that in negotiations people bring differences of biography and compromise in order to accomplish something.

Hunter proposes that definitions of situations are necessary for meaningful social action: "for local communities to operate as objects and arenas of meaningful social action, their residents must possess some conceptual image of them" (1974, p. 7). Deseran (1978) has shown how the definition of the situation conceptually clarifies studies of community satisfaction. He also uses the definition of the situation to examine community decision making. "Community can be viewed as an arena in which everyday life events as well as major policy issues become linked to individuals' experiences" (Deseran 1980, p. 25). He examines a rural Louisiana community and the problem of constructing an outdoor movie theater in terms of relevance, factual beliefs, evaluation, and the actions involved. Varying definitions and negotiations are required to build the theater.

In Zenda, community situations were examined by analysis of references to the community in everyday conversations and of responses in interviews to the question: "Do you think there's a community here?" Everyone agreed there was a strong community and gave evidence as to why they thought so. Three types of situations seemed to encompass the references to and evidences of community: opposing, helping, and sociability situations, which can be compared with similar situations in Lincoln Park.

In opposing situations, individuals talk about outsiders and compare themselves with others. Sometimes they actually mobilize social movements against others. The most common causes of opposition are urbanites — tourists — who are now coming to live in the area, referred to as "Lake people" or "city folks." For example, the town chairperson compared the way he ran his office with the expectations of urbanites:

> A great many people, especially what we call the city folks, come out
> here and they wonder why this isn't a full-time job and why I don't have a
> an office and a receptionist and a secretary there to answer the phone.

Other daily conversations depict Lake people as driving too fast and dressing and talking differently.

Lincoln Park residents compare themselves with various neighbors and rely on external cues, because they lack personal knowledge. They notice whether others have the latest designer jeans, heights of heels of shoes, the width of lapels and ties. On the other hand, Zenda residents look less at the outward appearance and are more interested in whether an individual is known personally. In Zenda personal contact is scarce, so people value such contact highly and remember specific incidents. Privacy is scarce in Lincoln Park, so people protect it through public control over personal displays (Lofland 1973). The presentation of self is different in Lincoln Park and Zenda because of these differences in scarcity.

In helping one another, people also create community situations. Various crises mobilize the community, as indicated in these examples from Zenda, which show helping as evidence of community:

I like Zenda. Most people are friendly. If one needs help, anyone would help. When one family lost their boy, everyone helped, even if they didn't know them well. (50-year-old village woman)

There's a sense of community here, especially if someone is sick or hurt or needs help, everybody shows up. When we had our accident, everyone from the village and farm area showed up to help in any way — food, mow the lawn. (30-year-old village woman)

Our neighbor across the road just had a kind of tragedy. His silo burst open. It was a mess. It's really something to see how everyone comes to bat when somebody gets in trouble. (50-year-old farm woman)

In Lincoln Park the helping is more institutionalized in secondary relationships of neighborhood-alert programs to stop theft and other crime. Residents signal to one another through whistles and signs placed in their windows, rather than by personal contact.

When people help, they create a sense of community, but they must negotiate when help is appropriate and when it is to be defined as community. This is illustrated in an example from Zenda. A man well-liked and prominent in the community died. Everyone wanted to help and pay him tribute, but they were prevented from doing so by the widow, who decided the funeral would be private and refused all offers of help. In this case, the definition of community was aborted and changed to a private family affair. Something similar happens in Lincoln Park when the LPCA campaigns to enroll new members in the LPCA or to get neighbors to help in a community campaign such as cleaning alleys. Many residents choose not to belong to LPCA and not to cooperate. They decline to consider themselves part of the Lincoln Park community and may view the attempt to get them to change their alley or backyard as a violation of their privacy.

Community members also negotiate sociability situations, which Simmel defines as a form of social interaction that has no ulterior purpose, which in itself provides satisfaction for the participants (1950) as communal or not. Some sociability is private, with closed parties and closed groups not open to everyone. As has been seen, community sociability often becomes institutionalized in voluntary associations. In the other direction, sometimes the sociability goes beyond the community as, for example, when voluntary associations come under state or national charters. The

Zenda Garden Club at one point had a state affiliation, but when local members were unwilling to follow the state dictates about flower shows and the like, the club members reclaimed it as a purely local organization. They renegotiated the definition of the garden club as part of the community.

Negotiations of definitions of situations show processes of continuous giving of meaning to people, events, and places that create a sense of community. People make choices about their community participation and may define opposing, helping, and sociability situations as their community.

TIME

The social-psychological approach can require the least amount of time of all the community frameworks, since people themselves define what the community is. They could define a fleeting experience as community. On the other hand, since definitions of community that already exist are based on longer-term phenomena, it is more likely that people will view longer-term, repeated events as community, rather than shorter ones. In turn, the continued existence of community traditions and definitions contributes to new members' definitions.

History

Social psychologists focus on short-term interactive processes more than on history. They view history as made up of people's changing patterns of interaction, of smaller units of time inside smaller units, like an onion. Moments lead to daily routines, to weekly and annual patterns, to growth and aging, and to historical periods. Social psychologists examine how people perceive history, especially through the concept of biography, the flow of meaningful life events.

People select historical and current events that are meaningful to their own lives. Only certain aspects of the past stand out. Residents of a community create history by remembering certain events, forgetting others, and constantly reinterpreting the past. Biographies and, therefore, interpretations of past events change through maturation (Gubrium and Buckhold 1977) or through conversions (Berger and Luckmann 1968).

In addition to creating history, people experience their own creation. They are born into an already created world in which they learn the typifications of community. Unless events are given meaning and become part of people's lives, then history and other macro processes do not exist. These events in turn get modified as people interpret and use them.

Zenda residents perceive a longer period of history than do Lincoln Park residents, because their biographies have been bound up in the place over a longer period (as illustrated in the biographical summaries, Appendix B). They see the history of the community as personal and family history. They can recount events from the past that have been told to them in the oral tradition and point to current activities whose origins relate to their own family history — for example, that a great grandmother started 4-H in the community.

Lincoln Park is only the latest of many community locations for its residents, although many know the history of their particular houses. People who arrived in Lincoln Park as long ago as the 1940s are considered unusual, whereas such people would almost be newcomers in Zenda. Many people know about the history of LPCA, which symbolizes for many the origin of the community. The hospitals and other institutions put out brochures on their history and their growth and development are often perceived as long-term processes. In both places individuals must relate the changing organizations or families to their own lives.

Process

Individuals not only perceive history through discrete blocks of activities, but also see everyday life through outstanding events, like time markers that distinguish different parts of the day. People constantly create community through the process of daily rounds and community careers. Goffman suggests that the concept of the daily rounds links individuals to their social situations (1963, p. 91). Everything that happens in a day is not remembered, nor is every event perceived as relevant to the community. In everyday life, individuals not only incorporate events of the past but also project into the future.

The community constantly changes with minute and sometimes traumatic impingements by each community-related interaction that shifts the definition of community. On the other hand, individuals experience a permanence and continuance of the community. According to Weigert, different relationships require different time, although the rules and specific amounts of time are not specified, but negotiated (1981, p. 202). If people spend too much time on communal activities, such as organizations or committees, they may be chided for neglecting their families or work.

The day starts earlier for more Zenda residents than Lincoln Park residents, but their early morning time is usually spent working alone, except on Sunday, whereas Lincoln Park residents go out into the community, riding public transportation, going to work with others. Some of the women's organizations in Zenda meet in the afternoon and people may do other things then, go shopping together, help one another. Lincoln Park's community life lasts longer into the night as people visit night spots and the hospitals continue their work. Most people in Zenda go to bed between 10 and 11. In both communities, what is community time depends on how people define it. Daily rounds have a slightly different rhythm in the two places, with Lincoln Park's lasting into the night, but in both places many community events, meetings, and parties occur in the evening.

Social construction is in some ways more visible in Zenda and Lincoln Park than in other types of communities, because so many residents are actively, self-consciously working to create and maintain a community. Zenda residents work to hold on to their historical community, which is threatened by the loss of local facilities and the influx of outsiders. In Lincoln Park residents work to impose a community where before there had been crime, chaos, and an absence of interest in the community. In their communities, socially constructed through organizing, meeting, talking with one another, residents develop community identities and reputations. For example, the state of Wisconsin labeled Walworth County as affluent because of Lake Geneva and wanted higher state taxes from Walworth. Historical boards gave some of the neighborhoods of Lincoln Park landmark designations. In the Walworth case the people, including some from Zenda, fought in the courts and through writing letters to state legislatures to reject the label, which would have meant higher taxes for them. In the Lincoln Park case several people worked hard by writing letters, documenting the history of buildings, and meeting with influential people to obtain historical designation.

Goffman and others also discuss the idea of careers, the concept that people go through developmental stages of socialization. What careers does a community member have? A child or new resident will be introduced to the customs of the place and to other people. In Zenda this occurs especially through community organizations and through families. For example, many women marry into Zenda, whereas most men are born into it and stay. Husbands' mothers often socialize their new daughters-in-law. When a person knows almost everyone in Zenda, usually through active participation in community organizations, that person is almost a full-fledged member of the community. Coming from a long-term family or marrying into one are also tickets into the community.

Older people in Zenda are phased out of community organizations and become the recipients of their charity, receiving Christmas presents and get-well cards from the organizations. Graduation from high school is when many residents from Zenda leave the area to seek jobs or marriages elsewhere. Few long-term residents leave, but when they do, they are honored with ceremonies and in some ways continue to be part of the community; for example, they may still receive the church bulletin.

In Lincoln Park, new residents are more likely to be introduced to the neighborhood through realtors, and the close proximity to neighbors facilitates meeting people in the area. Many people, however, never know their neighbors and some have no experience of community in Lincoln Park. Those most a part of the community become active in LPCA and its neighborhood components, which begin with property ownership. As with Zenda, active participation in community organizations creates community belongingness.

Community careers end earlier in Lincoln Park than in Zenda. In some ways they are like firecrackers, quick to start, intense and glowing, but soon over. Many residents came as young singles or young marrieds. Until the recent improvement of public schools, those with school-aged children, especially high-school-aged, moved elsewhere to find better schools. Professionals are often transferred to other areas, and even those who remain in the community may have a spectacular but brief career of giving time and energy to the community projects for a while, but then going on to other challenges.

For example, one young man who became very active in the neighborhood and community associations when he bought a house in the area did much for the community. He had been active in Old Town in his early 20s, even though he lived south of that section. He was among the first students at the Old Town Folk School, the Gate of Horn. After he got out of the army, he felt a commitment to Chicago. He lived in an apartment for a few years; then when he decided to buy a house, he chose Lincoln Park because of the big old homes there. In his words,

> Until this point, I never did any community activities or projects. My life had consisted of parties and trips. As a home owner, I was concerned with what was happening. All around my house, buildings were being torn down. I asked neighbors what was going to be built and they told me about the Mid-North Association. I went and joined. I got into it as a matter of self-preservation. I didn't want high rises in my neighborhood. As a property owner, I became conservative. That was the beginning of my intense community activity.

He went from committee member to several officerships in the Mid-North Association and LPCA. He worked hard to prevent high-rises, change the zoning laws to get boarding houses and "unsavory" people out of Lincoln Park, and make the Mid-North area into a landmark district, so that the old, historical buildings could not be torn down. He also improved the financial situation of LPCA and through many hours of planning, going to court, and working on federal and legal requirements, he established a settlement between the community and the local hospitals. After serving the maximum terms in community officerships and receiving awards for his efforts, he saw the need for his skills in health-related organizations that had a broader scope than the community of Lincoln Park. He gave much of himself to the community and then went on to make contributions beyond the community. "The excitement wasn't there because I'm older and the situations aren't crises anymore. I felt the challenges were elsewhere."

Communities change over time as individuals change their definitions of community. Attention to the community comes and goes over a day and over the life cycle. Not all people choose to be involved. The major differences between Zenda and Lincoln Park lie in the perception of pace and length of time. Zenda is perceived to be almost unchanging and lasting a long time because residents remain there for long periods. Lincoln Park is perceived to have a rapid changeover of events and people. Some become very active in community organizations, but then burn out or go on to other, noncommunity activities.

SPACE

Territory

Residents may define community using a minimal amount of space or they may use space as a tool for elaborating their own concepts of community. The world they are born into usually includes some amount of space as the definition of community. Social psychologists examine emotional attachments to land, perceptual organization of territory through cognitive mapping, and the association of space with community symbols.

In Zenda the space is very important because of ownership of the land and sentimental involvement with that land. Residents are familiar with almost all of the community space and have personal attachment to it because of their own and family contributions or because of friends' and neighbors' inputs. The community space in many ways is an extension of themselves.

On the other hand, Lincoln Park residents do not perceive such encompassing space as part of their community. While they are familiar with the maps of the seven neighborhoods, few have traversed that space. Instead, their personal paths often lead them out of the community and into other parts of the city for work, recreation, and friendship. Attachment to space by ownership does modify perceptions, in that property owners wish to maintain high standards for the community to preserve their property's value. Lincoln Park residents also develop pride in their restored houses.

Cognitive Mapping

An analysis of maps drawn by Zenda residents shows that individuals vary in their perception of the space of the community; it expands to the whole world and contracts to just the village. Physical characteristics such as the lake, roads, and political boundaries provide objects for people to use in the construction of community, but people are selective and no one included all the features of the official map. Selection often differed by gender, with men drawing more gridlike maps, while women sometimes made their maps artistic, included schools (no man did), and named specific people's farms (few men did). Women's and men's activities in the community, which are often sex-segregated, help explain the differences. Men more often consult official, gridlike maps as drivers on trips, and women in the voluntary associations often learn arts and crafts and do things for schools (Stoneall 1981).

Since LPCA and the neighborhood associations are not sex-segregated, one may be less likely to find such differences in Lincoln Park. It is probable, however, that different ethnic groups have different perceptions of the community, which would show up on maps. Hall (1966) indicates that different cultures use space differently and have varying definitions of personal space. Poor people, more confined in respect to space in Lincoln Park, may have a different perspective than new people with a cosmopolitan outlook, whose community may not be just Lincoln Park.

Community Symbols

Residents further use space through the names they give it, and as we have seen with institutions, neighborhood and community names are symbols of the community. The social-psychological perspective forces attention to individual differences. In Zenda the contradiction of some people living in Illinois, yet belonging with the Wisconsin village, the fact that many of the rural residents in Wisconsin have an Illinois mailing address, and the differences between the unnamed rural area versus the named village give people a dilemma in saying where they are from (Stoneall 1983a).

Lincoln Park residents also have many possibilities of residential terms to choose from: the neighborhood name, the street address, the community name. They can say they are from the north side of Chicago, from Chicago, or from even larger entities — state or region. It is likely that most people are familiar with Chicago and for people to say that they are from Chicago or its north side would best communicate residential location.

Within communities, spatial areas reflect certain activities. For example, juvenile gangs of various ethnic groups in Lincoln Park make symbolic claims by the graffiti they paint. In Zenda the town hall becomes a symbol of the township and the fair.

Social psychologists also examine community space as a dependent variable. Bennett Berger wanted to test the hypothesis that living in suburbs produces specific life-styles, such as "keeping up with the Joneses." He studied factory workers who had lived in the city and were moved to a suburb because the factory moved, but he found little change in their attitudes about voting, church affiliation, and activity in voluntary associations (1960).

Boundaries

Boundaries, like territory, change with people and situations, expanding and contracting. From the maps drawn by Zenda residents,

FIGURE 6.1
Composite of Boundaries Drawn by Zenda Residents

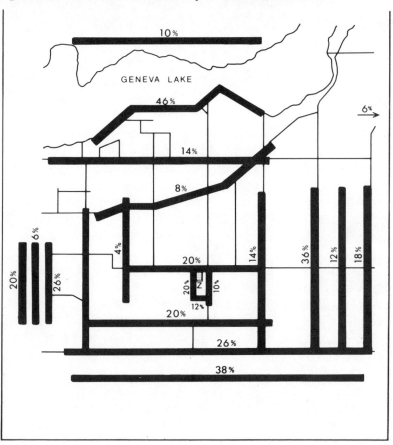

I categorized boundaries in each of the four directions, as indicated in Figure 6.1. The lake to the north was the most agreed-upon boundary, even though the township extends beyond it. Most of the other northern boundaries come closer to the village. For most people, the southern boundary was not the state line, but beyond it. Second was the state line and then closer to the village. Men tended to follow the political township boundaries (at least south of the lake) more than women did; women seemed to have certain people in mind whom they wanted to include in the community and drew their maps according to what roads they lived on. Some women actually named certain family farms as the boundaries; men rarely did this. A core of community in the village stretches out beyond it differently for different people and, in particular, cognitive mapping differs by gender.

Sex-segregated activities also explain gender differences in how women and men draw boundaries. Women's activities consist of meetings and bridge games that are primarily held in people's homes. Their community routes are to neighbors' and friends' houses, so they include these on maps. Men's activities on the township board and as fire fighters direct their attention to the political boundaries, and so these become more noticeable to them (Stoneall 1981).

Lincoln Park residents discount and disassociate themselves from the river to the west and its surrounding factories. Also the housing projects of Cabrini Green just south of Lincoln Park are clearly rejected as not belonging to the community. The lake and park are claimed as part of the community on the eastern boundary. To the north, the boundary is less clear, since it runs into housing and people similar to those of Lincoln Park, with no outstanding distinctive features.

Space and boundaries, then, become part of the community as individuals define them and give meaning to them. Only selective aspects of the physical surroundings are used in the social construction of community.

SUMMARY

Social psychology has forced the consideration of meanings and their communication as the most important part of community. This chapter has included a greater variety of traditions than previous chapters. Backgrounds in pragmatism, phenomenology, and cognitive psychology provide a variety of concepts. Subjective interpretation, primary groups, taking the role of the other, definitions of the situation, symbols, social constructions of reality, and cognitive mapping are all relevant to the study of community. A few sociologists and environmental cognitionists have explicitly examined interaction patterns in communities, community symbols, and how communities are socially constructed.

Communities look like artistic constructions, constantly being worked on, with new artists being trained to continue the process. A stigma or label stamped on the artistic construction adds another image, which gives communities identities and reputations. Through routine habits, individuals create patterns of interactions, some of which they define as the community. Communities are constantly changing in microscopic ways as people modify their perceptions and definitions. Individuals see the community through what is relevant to themselves, their biographies and daily rounds. They also cognitively map their spatial surroundings and use such features as a lake, roads, or people's homes as tools to construct the territory and boundaries of the community.

In both Zenda and Lincoln Park, residents socially construct the community by their definitions and actions in relations with outsiders and insiders. Some evidence stands out in their minds as significant to community, while some does not. Both are continually changing through interactions and their use of names and symbols of their surroundings.

Because of the greater variety of people in Lincoln Park, a broader range of meanings and definitions are given to the community; Zenda is differentiated perceptually by gender and age. The varied backgrounds, which in Zenda have been shared over longer periods of time, produce urban or rural symbols, language, and ceremonies. In Zenda perception is more particularistic. Each person is seen as an individual – except for outsiders, who are stereotyped. Lincoln Park residents cannot know everyone in their community, but they use various signs to tell information about one another.

Lincoln Park acquires a reputation as a fashionable, urban, middle-class residential neighborhood, while Zenda is peaceful and friendly, with a natural beauty. Zenda residents and Lincoln Park residents see negative aspects of one another reflected in their choice of residency. Lincoln Park residents may view Zenda as empty, boring, slow; Zenda residents see Lincoln Park as crowded, fast, unfriendly. In short, people create, define, maintain, and validate the created aspects of community in their interactions of conversing, presenting selves, and symbolizing.

Overemphasis on the subjective side of communities and the difficulty of finding structure or permanency have been the major criticisms of social-psychological approaches. One alternative, network analysis, still takes account of individuals, but uses the structure of their relationships and how connections build larger units, such as communities.

7

Network-Exchange Analysis: Community as Connections

The preceding chapter has focused on the significance of individuals in communities. Emphasizing micro processes, social psychologists view communities as artistic creations. Individuals use their own lives, their interactions with others, and selective perceptions of their spatial surroundings to create community situations.

Network analysis also stresses the importance of the individual, but examines the nature of ties between people rather than what goes on inside their heads. While both consider interactions, network analysts are more interested in their structure than in their content. Network analysis, as the newest approach to community, is rapidly taking the lead. Network analysts consider the flow within structures of connections between persons or between groups or institutions, combined with an exchange framework. Thus, network analysis can be both micro and macro. Exchange theory is added to this discussion, because many network analysts have included it (for example, Kapferer 1969; Emerson 1976; Willer and Anderson 1979). Exchange theory can explain how goods and other items flow through the network connections. In turn, exchange with others requires some connection with others, direct or indirect.

Network analysts use the structure of links among people to explain a particular type of behavior. Mitchell (1969) defines a social network as "a specific set of linkages among a defined set of persons, with the additional property that the characteristics of these linkages as a whole may be used to interpret the social behavior of the persons involved" (p. 2). Boissevain (1974, p. 24) suggests that social networks are "the social relations in which every individual is embedded . . . in an egocentric sense, . . . the chains of persons with whom a given person is in actual contact and their interconnection." Similarly, Whitten and Wolfe (1974, p. 720) give the definition of "a relevant series of linkages existing between individuals . . . a basis for the mobilization of people for specific purposes under specific conditions."

Boissevain suggests that the basic postulate of network analysis is that "people are viewed as interacting with others, some of whom in their turn interact with each other and yet others, and that the whole network of relations so formed is in a state of flux" (1974, p. viii). This leads to communities being defined in terms of linkages. Wellman (1979) calls the network view of community "the liberated community," since local solidarity and territorial relations are not necessary for the definition.

Exchange theory implies a rational giving and receiving of both material and nonmaterial goods and services. According to Blau (1964, p. 6) "exchange is a particular type of association involving actions that are contingent on rewarding reactions from others and that cease when these expected reactions are not forthcoming."

Both network and exchange theory arose as dissatisfactions with structural functionalism. Exchange theory has roots in behavioralism and economics, while network analysis originated in anthropology. The development of network-exchange frameworks will be traced to show that they can apply to community in the model of metaphor, method, and the three dimensions. The linkages and ties, flows of goods and services, and coalitions in Zenda and Lincoln Park become important in this framework.

HISTORICAL DEVELOPMENT

Simmel, American exchange theorists, and British anthropologists have developed and defined concepts leading to network analyses of communities. Simmel inspired modern sociologists to examine the form of social relationships which he calls sociation:

> The study of society may be called "pure sociology" which abstracts the mere elements of sociation. It isolates it from the heterogeneity of its contents and purposes. . . . It thus proceeds like grammar, which isolates the pure forms of language from their contents through which these forms, nevertheless, come to life. In comparable manner, social groups which are the most diverse imaginable in purpose and general significance, may nevertheless show identical forms of behavior toward one another (Simmel 1950, p. 22).

In an essay entitled, "The Web of Group Affiliations" (1956), Simmel suggests that the form or configuration of group affiliation shapes personality.

Exchange Theory

Behavioral psychology and utilitarian economic considerations, according to which individuals act because they get something out of it, influenced both Homans and Blau, the two main proponents of exchange theory. Homans applies behavioralism to the study of society, which he envisions as composed of transacting individuals who build groups. In his first exchange book, using a series of case studies, he introduced four concepts — activities, interactions, sentiments, and norms — that lead to propositions about group events. In one of the studies he analyzes "Hilltown," a community that he defines as a social group, to show how exchange theory can explain social disintegration (the decline of community). In this case, the number and strength of the sentiments that led members of one group to collaborate with others had declined to the point where the community could no longer control members, because they did not punish and reward one another (Homans 1950).

In his second exchange book, Homans (1961) develops six principles of profits and costs, from which can be deduced explanations for particulars. In interactions, all of which are exchanges, individuals calculate profits, costs, and benefits, which, in turn, determine whether exchanges will continue. The first principle states that a person is more likely to engage in action that is rewarded.

Second, if a stimulus has received a reward in the past, then the more similar another stimulus is, the more likely it is that it will be rewarded. Third, the more a person values an action, the more likely it is to be performed. Fourth, the more often a person has received a reward, the less valuable it becomes. Fifth, when people do not receive expected rewards, they become angry and aggressive and value angry and aggressive behavior. When they do receive expected rewards, they value approving behavior. Finally, Homans offers a rationality proposition that when people have choices of action, they will calculate the rewards of each action and the probability of receiving the rewards. People will opt for lower rewards, if they have a greater probability of receiving them. After developing these propositions, Homans then applies them to sets of conditions from simple to complex, from two-person interactions to multiple exchanges. Homans explains institutions and organizations as facilitating predictable and efficient gratification, where reinforcement is generalized into legal and normative orders.

Peter Blau builds on Homans by considering power in exchange. He defines social exchange as voluntary actions of individuals that are motivated by the returns they are expected to bring (1964, p. 91). Although social exchange imitates economic exchange in the principle of maximization of utility, it also differs in that some social rewards, such as positive feelings, cannot be bartered. The two purposes of social exchange are to establish bonds and superordination.

Social exchange consists of trust and unspecified obligations that refer to the return or reciprocation of what has been given. The obligation is unspecified in two senses — first, with the imprecise measurement of equivalency. Givers expect receivers to make returns that equal the giving, but usually these are not exactly the same. For example, if a couple invites another couple for dinner, they expect a return invitation of the same elaborateness, rather than just a snack, but it would be inappropriate to serve exactly the same food. Obligations are also unspecified in the time dimension — they must not be repaid too soon; the return invitation is not for the very next meal. If the time gap is too long, the givers may assume a lack of reciprocity, which could end the association.

Because the obligations are unspecified, givers and receivers rely on trust. Each trusts that the other will reciprocate and, in turn, with reciprocation, the trust strengthens the bonds. Whether or not it is a first occasion, the status of the participants and other aspects of the social context also influence the process of exchange.

Blau does not address all interactions — only those in which rewards are expected and received from designated others. Actors weigh costs of actions, seek profits, and develop reciprocal obligations with norms and sanctions. Social exchanges have the problem of no fixed value or medium of exchange, such as money; instead, people reap gratitude, social approval, esteem, and compliance. Exchange holds people together, but also pulls them apart when the norms of reciprocity and fair exchange are violated. These norms must necessarily be violated at times, since people are involved in so many exchange relations; balance and stabilization in one exchange relation may cause imbalance and strain in other necessary exchange relations.

Blau's major contribution to exchange theory is the addition of power, which he defines as control through negative sanctions (1964, p. 116). With no reciprocity or equality in exchange, the relationship becomes unbalanced, but the imbalance of power balances the exchange. Power is the ability to obtain compliance as the profit of exchange; people become powerful by having more resources. Blau distinguishes power, based on calculated actions, from prestige, which springs from spontaneous evaluations (1964, p. 100).

From social exchange, norms, and stratification, the macro structure develops. As norms and laws of reciprocity develop, leaders become legitimated and do not have to spend so much time negotiating exchanges. Macro structures themselves then engage in exchanges, facilitated by shared values, institutionalization, and more than one level of social organization.

Emerson bridges social-exchange theory and social-network analysis by adding networks to solve some of Homan's and Blau's tautological problems of defining values in terms of actions and vice versa. Emerson omits individuals' values and examines the exchange and the ratio of rewards given as the basic units. He develops a series of theorems, propositions, and corollaries relating exchange to power, the division of labor, stratification, and social circles. It is worthwhile to consider the example of social circles, since it is so central to network analysis.

Emerson borrows the concept of social circle from Simmel and from Kadushin (1966). A social circle involves indirect, somewhat institutionalized exchanges among people with similar interests. Emerson posits that networks become closed with the exchange of the same resources, as opposed to exchange of different resources, which is more open. His theorem states: "The more an exchange approximates an intra-category exchange, the more likely are exchange relations to become closed" (Emerson 1972, p. 75). He conceives of networks as opportunities for exchange.

Network Analysis

British anthropologists Barnes, Bott, and Mitchell pioneered network analysis, which originates in dissatisfaction with structural-functional theory's inability to explain various levels in society. Structural functionalists have also found it difficult to explain the rapid change in what happens when simple societies have contact with more complex ones – for example, when African tribal people migrated to cities (Mitchell 1969).

In studying a Norwegian fishing village, Bremnes, Barnes (1954) introduced the concept of social network, which before had been used only metaphorically. Social-network analysis focuses on interpersonal links rather than groups, thereby avoiding the structural-functionalist limitation of boundary maintenance and equilibrium. In his analysis of Bremnes, he presents the community not as an organism or a solid, uniform block but as several systems overlapping, as in layered transparencies. The third layer of kinship, acquaintanceship, and friendship, which became the foundation for network analysis, was distinguished from the permanent territorial system of administrative units and the industrial system of fishing and farming.

> Each person is, as it were, in touch with a number of other people, some of whom are directly in touch with each other and some of whom are not. . . . I find it convenient to talk of a social field of this kind as a network. The image I have is of a set of points some of which are joined by lines. The points of the image are people, or sometimes groups, and the lines indicate which people interact with each other (Barnes 1954, p. 43).

Persons in any network tend to be social equals and organize activities of mutual help and home entertaining. The networks link Bremnes residents with other parishes. Barnes conceived of network as a multi-dimensional concept and concentrated on the "set," by which he meant a single-person-centered network. "Mesh" refers to the connectedness among the people tied to any one person; small societies are tightly meshed.

While less directly related to community studies, Bott's (1971) family studies make a contribution to network analysis. Like Barnes, she suggests that the scale of the society influences the nature of links and, in turn, the nature of links could explain social action. She found that the structure of ties between wives and husbands — whether the wife's friends are also the husband's friends — relates to the division of labor in the household. In small-scale societies, local groups encapsulate nuclear families, while in urban societies the family is involved in many varied groups. Bott defines networks as a social configuration in which some but not all of the component external units maintain relationships with one another. She sees networks as opened or closed, in that either most people in a community are linked to one another or most people in a network are linked to others outside the network. Friends and the flow of norms are more influential in closed networks.

Mitchell makes the most extensive codification of network analysis by developing and defining many interrelated concepts. Since his conceptualizations are so widely cited, they are summarized and listed here. *Morphology or form* and *interactional criteria* are the two major distinctions of networks. Within morphology, anchorage, density, reachability, and range constitute the subconcepts. Content, directedness, durability, intensity, and frequency characterize the interactional aspects of networks.

> *Anchorage* refers to the starting point of the network. The most common anchorages are ego-centered, beginning with a specific person, but a group can also be the anchor.
>
> *Reachability* is the extent to which people can use their relationships to contact others. How many steps does it take to get from one person to another?
>
> *Density* is the degree to which people connected to ego also know each other.
>
> *Range* means the proportion of ties to ego in comparison with all other ties.
>
> *Content* is the purpose of the linkage, such as friendship or kinship. Content is found by observation of behavior and attribution of meaning by actors. Several contents between two actors is called multiplexity.

Directedness is the degree of reciprocity, whether exchanges flow in one direction or both ways.

Durability refers to how long networks last. Mitchell distinguishes between time length of action or communication sets and endurance of a set of obligations and rights. Durability refers more to the latter. Changes occur as people add to or drop from networks.

Intensity is the degree to which people honor obligations and rights. Strength of the tie is synonymous with the intensity of the tie. Kinship ties and multiplex ties are more intense.

Frequency describes how often and how regular network members have contact.

Mitchell notes that no study uses all of these network concepts. He advocates network analysis because it facilitates understanding behavior in situations, shows the connections within and across institutions, and analyzes "the uniqueness of particular empirical communities" (Mitchell 1969, p. 50).

Mitchell's students undertook a variety of studies using network analysis. These ranged from Boissevain's (1974) study of the entire networks of two men in Malta, one rural and one urban, to Kapferer's (1969) analysis of a dispute in a zinc plant in Zambia. Epstein (1969) analyzes all the people one informant in an African community in Rhodesia encounters in just a few days to show a mix of tribal, kinship, and urban ties (categorical relationships) and sources of prestige. Epstein's distinction between an effective network and an extended network shows that a person can have both loose and tightly knit networks. Boswell (1969) examines how residents of Lusaka, Zambia, mobilize elements of their networks in times of personal crises, using the example of a death. Thus, individual networks vary greatly and are mobilized for a variety of situations.

Other important network studies have been done by Milgram and by Granovetter. Through a field experiment of asking people to deliver a letter indirectly to an unknown person through direct, known contacts, Milgram (1967) discovered the "small world phenomenon," that people need go through an average of only five other people to be connected with anyone. Granovetter (1973) examines how people use ties to obtain jobs. His notion of the "strength of weak ties" suggests that having several weak ties is more conducive to job attainment than having strong ties with a few people.

American Community Studies

Network analysis has also been applied to American communities. Wellman, Fischer, and Macionis continue the viable study of communities by minimizing the strict requirement on space and local solidarity. Webber (1963) has suggested that there can be "community without propinquity"; that is, people can be tied to one another in a community way without living in the same place.

The application of network analysis to community includes examination of a sample of residents' ties (Macionis 1978; Wellman 1979; Fischer 1982) or certain kinds of community ties, usually of community leaders (Laumann and Pappi 1976; Laumann, Marsden, and Galaskiewicz 1977; Galaskiewicz and Marsden 1978; Galaskiewicz 1979).

Wellman and his associates at the University of Toronto have advanced community studies by network analysis. Craven and Wellman define community as "those bounded sets of links and nodes, all of whose members are connected either directly or via indirect paths or short length" (1974, p. 74). Using network analysis, Wellman (1979) addresses what he calls the "community question": How do large-scale divisions of labor in society affect primary ties? The community question concerns whether communities can still exist in the light of major changes in society brought about by industrialization, urbanization, bureaucratization, and the like. The community has been termed lost or saved by various authors; Wellman proposes the liberated community, freed from solidarity and territorial connections, but still having important primary ties. In his study of an East York community in Toronto, Wellman finds the community saved through the importance of kin and help from neighbors, and he finds the community liberated through differentiated networks. Wellman's latest approach is to detail the networks of a small sample (33 people) from his East York study. He reports for the first time negative aspects of networks and a series of dyads rather than extended connections. "People may not like their ties and community may not be nice" (Wellman 1981).

Also to dispute the decline of community, Fischer and his associates analyze the 1965-66 Detroit Area Study and a 1967 national survey conducted by the National Opinion Research Center. Instead of dismissing territory as a network tie, they present space as one of many constraints on networks with their key concept of choice-constraint. They examine the proposition that "limitation on the number of potential social relations available to individuals leads to more communal social relations. Communal refers to relations of intimacy and moral commitment, the sort of relations sociologists generally assume to be important for psychological well-being" (Fischer et al. 1977, p. 7). In addition to territory, the life cycle, class, ethnicity, and age constrain networks. The findings of Fischer's research do not support their proposition, but they do not find a decline of community. According to them, "the disintegration of the monolithic community has perhaps led to the proliferation of many personal communities, each more compatible and more supportive to the individual than ascribed social groups" (1977, p. 202). The change is that people now have more choice in their ties, but boundaries still exist.

Fischer's latest research (1982) surveyed networks in different types of communities in northern California. He uses the analysis of this survey to ask theoretical questions about the decline of community and the existence of subcultures in urban areas. He considers many characteristics of respondents — especially their location in the central city, metropolitan area, town, or semirural area, as well as class, occupation, life-style, marital status, age, and gender — and many kinds of ties, including kinship, friendship, work, ethnic, religious, and voluntary associations. Fischer also examines the connection of the ties to psychological well-being and attitudes to communities. People in nonurban areas are closer to kin, and people in urban areas are closer to nonkin through self-selection. Fischer argues that population concentration accounts for the community differences in networks.

Macionis (1978) also considers communities in relation to friendship patterns, which are more elusive than other community ties of neighbors and kin and go beyond locality. He finds friendship more voluntary, active, autonomous, and dyadic than community relations. In friendship, modernites find community in the form of networks rather than local groupings.

Community organizations with their interconnections may be the anchorage of network analysis. Galaskiewicz and Marsden (1978) examine resource transactions among community organizations and find asymmetric transactions in money, information, and moral support. Galaskiewicz (1979) further relates community organizations' centrality in exchange networks to their influence in community affairs.

Network analysts also study community elites and their ties to one another. Burt (1977) examines role sets and resources of elites with stratification. Communication among elites influences outcomes of community issues, according to Laumann and Pappi (1973) and Laumann, Marsden, and Galaskiewicz (1977).

Network-exchange analyses are new approaches, although they have been influenced by Simmel. British anthropologists, exchange theorists, and American community studies use network analysis in reaction to structural functionalism to show that complicated connections among people minimize any possible loss of community. Their development of concepts and their empirical studies make unique contributions to this book's theoretical model of people, space, and time (Table 7.1).

METAPHOR

Network analysis and exchange involve sets of connections that form varied images, including the network, sociogram, and market exchange. Network analysis itself was originally a metaphor rather than an analytic tool, in which threads or wires, drawn as lines, connect people or organizations, drawn as dots, to one another.

Networks relate to an electronic image — the connections are wires conducting messages and other exchange contents. The people at nodes, which are knots or points of connection, are like light bulbs that turn on for specific occasions. For example, with a death in the family, certain of a person's connections will show up; if that person needs to borrow money, a different configuration of people will be involved. Similarly, in radio and television, companies control chains of transmitting stations — networks.

Each community and each person forms a different configuration of links. The nodes and wires consequently create a variety of shapes — a net, a web, a star, a wheel, or chains. Some people are indirectly linked to a series of others in a chain that may be like a fence, sturdy and lasting, or more ephemeral and as easily broken as a paper chain. Others are directly related to several others, each of whom may have few other connections. The person at the center seems to form a star or wheel with all the connections. Some of the wires will be more concentrated than others, forming clusters, or many stars may group together in bunches. Some nodes are interconnected by several wires, signifying a variety of role relationships. A community looks like dots connected by lines, which form varied patterns within and beyond the community territory.

Sociometry furnishes a similar image to network analysis, as a tool of psychology to assess friendship, leadership patterns, clique formation, and task performance in small groups — usually in a classroom setting — by asking people whom they like best or whom they consider to be the leader. Sociometrists administer questionnaires

TABLE 7.1
Network-Exchange Community Dimensions

Dimension	Description
Metaphor	Dots and lines; electronic
Methodology	Surveys, interviews, observations; data on numbers and shape of connections; take a point and trace through links to test hypotheses about communities
People	
Institutions	Specialized networks; links within and between
Stratification	Unequal exchange; coalitions, distributive justice
Interaction	Form and content
Time	
History	Integration and disintegration of links and patterns of exchange; processes affecting nature of ties
Process	Activation of network; exchange; cost; frequency and duration
Space	
Territory	Liberated from
Boundaries	Set by analysis; otherwise, boundless

that ask respondents with which person present they would like to do some particular task. From the questionnaire sociometrists form a sociogram, which uses a geometric figure to represent each person and that person's choice of others. A statistical analysis, often using matrices, is used to correlate connections with task completion or efficiency. Network analysis applies the principles of sociometry to larger groups such as communities and sees them as also forming friendship connections or being directed toward a leader.

The metaphor from exchange theory is that of the marketplace. People in their communal lives are like shoppers trying to get the best buys and maximizing their transactions of buying and selling goods, services, and sentiments. People attract and repel one another according to rewards, investments, profits, punishments, or costs incurred. Using rational decision making, they form contracts with one another, implying an impersonal relationship based on strict legal rules and regulations.

As the contracts are traced, the image of exchange networks becomes apparent. Communities emerge from the exchanges among people. From Homans, the tracing of the contracts leads to groups, and then a larger society with a codification of norms. This build-up of groups and communities can also revert back to separate groups and individuals, as in his study of Hilltown (1961). According to Blau (1964), competition in the marketplace will lead to specialization. From Blau's image, we can see exchange networks coming together to form coalitions and extract compliance from others less powerful.

METHODOLOGY

From the metaphor, the combined network and market image, questions must be asked about the structure and processes of exchange networks. First, what are the variations in the forms and structures of networks? Are they closed or open? What are the density, extensiveness, frequency, duration, flow, and direction of the networks?

Second, what is being exchanged? What are the contents of the networks? These can range from material benefits and goods to sentiments and exchanges of affect. Are there different networks for different exchanges?

The third area concerns distributive justice. How do people place value on goods, services, and affect? How is agreement attained on the value of exchange? Answers to these questions often come down to the notion of common culture; people are acculturated to evaluate things similarly.

People will measure cost by foregone alternatives. People will ask what they are giving up, what they could do instead? How it should sell on the market is a way to judge. This is in contrast to the Marxist labor theory of values, in which the value of a commodity is the labor put into it, the value added. Distributive justice implies that in order for exchanges to continue, the ratio of costs to benefits is equivalent and that exchange relationships are based on equality. As Blau (1971) has discussed, exchange relations may in fact continue on an unequal basis. Where equality does not hold, one of the parties is likely to feel frustrated and taken advantage of. Such persons will be less willing to engage in exchanges and will become aggressive and look for alternatives. Blau points out that power produces feelings of frustration. The distributive justice question, then, is how equality or the appearance of equality is derived and maintained.

A final question concerns the methods and starting point of the analysis. Is the starting point with a larger unit, such as a community in which the ties within and beyond it are then traced? Or does the network analyst start with individuals and try to trace community links among them?

Methods of studying exchange networks range from qualitative, anthropological techniques to highly technical mathematical models. Anthropologists, who developed the key concepts of network analysis, rely on observations and informants. They may analyze specific situations, as Kapferer did in seeing how network ties influenced taking sides in an argument. His analysis was based on his observations. Boissevain and Epstein used only one or two persons and examined their networks.

Wellman and Fischer used questionnaires. Wellman and others asked people to name three to six best friends or people close to them outside of the household, and state the characteristics of these friends and friendships. Fischer asks more about tasks — for example, who would watch your house while you are out of town, or with whom do you share interests?

The analyses that use technical graph theory are less applicable to community than statistical analyses that describe and correlate density and other aspects of network structures with community activities, such as helping or loaning. The analysis is used to describe the networks of a person or several persons in one place and correlate them with community activities.

PEOPLE

While the starting point of network analysis may be dyads and individuals' links, it rarely remains at this level, but goes on to reveal the emergence of larger social groupings and their linkages. In general, network-exchange analysis includes both macro and micro levels of the community. Institutions and stratification emerge out of links because of the need to standardize and regularize.

Institutions

Network-exchange theorists examine the emergence of institutions from networks and exchanges. Specializations in networks and exchanges lead to institutional differentiation and provide a contrast between Lincoln Park and Zenda. Links within institutions and between institutions further distinguish the exchange-network approaches to community.

Development of Institutions

Exchange theorists analyze the rise and fall of institutions, beginning with individual exchanges and ending when rewards are absent in such exchanges. Homans defines institutions as patterned interactions; Blau defines them as formalized, indirect exchanges. Both agree that institutionalization helps to implement goals and to provide norms that regulate and thereby facilitate exchanges.

In Homans's view, a small group needs capital in the form of organizational innovations or surpluses of resources for institutional elaboration. The capital generates more complex and indirect inter-meshings of behavior. Development of rules forms the second major step in the development of institutions; larger sizes of groups lead to more formal rules. Blau adds that in addition to formal rules values are transmitted in socialization and the dominant group is interested in the survival of the patterns with institutionalization (1964, p. 76).

The next major step in the development of institutions is their differentiation, which comes about because of different goals and different kinds of exchanges. Homans contends that institution-alization allows more complex transactions, which specialize in specific kinds of exchanges, but that institutionalization simplifies links. Homans further argues that new institutions may arise out of subinstitutional conflicts within institutions. That is, institutions that are not patterned may not fit with the old institutions, but survive in newer ones, as was the case with labor unions.

Blau proposes four kinds of institutions based on different values: integrative with particularistic values, distributive with universalistic values, organizational with legitimating values, and finally, counter-institutional, like Homans's subinstitutional inter-actions, which have unrealized values.

Both Blau and Homans see changes and cessations of institutions. No longer providing rewards to their participants, the counter-institutions and their rigidity contain the seeds of destruction of institutions. According to Blau, the norms then regulate and restrict people's exchanges with a rigidity that can lead to elimination or change in institutions.

Examination of exchange networks in Zenda and Lincoln Park can help in understanding how institutionalization has occurred in both in similar ways. The Neighborly Club in Zenda and the Old Town Association, two organizational institutions in Blau's sense, serve as examples.

Before the Neighborly Club, one of the oldest voluntary associa-tions in Zenda, women visited one another and exchanged news about their families and neighbors, information about household tasks, and discussed their shared activities of churchgoing and shop-ping. By then, the houses were built, the land cleared, and people were beyond the subsistence level. They had a surplus of time and a goal of sociability. These visiting ties soon regularized into monthly meetings, as women took turns being hostesses, and soon regular speakers, refreshments, and business meetings were scheduled. Committees and rules that constrained members were developed.

Another Zenda organization, the Thimble Club, began with women meeting to sew and later changed to playing games of bunco and 500. By 1975 there were no longer enough members who received rewards from playing bunco with one another, and the organization disbanded.

The Old Town Association started with ties among neighbors who talked about ways of improving the neighborhoods. Then they negotiated with the city government: if residents renovated Old Town homes, city officials would change zoning laws. With differentiation, they soon also institutionalized the art fair in an exchange with the public for funds to keep their organization going. The institutionalization of the organization made it possible to impose on the whole neighborhood regulations about garbage, parked cars, and the like. Many people who found no rewards in neighborhood improvement stayed out of the organization, and some even left the neighborhood.

On the other hand, the greater specialization of institutions in Lincoln Park, because of differences in exchanges, provided a contrast to Zenda. The population size of Lincoln Park and its location in an even larger city population gives a greater variety of people and possible exchanges. An example that shows the difference between Lincoln Park and Zenda in institutional exchange is the diversity of skills. In Zenda, people possess a wide variety of work skills and less specialization; for example, one man does construction work, excavating, gardening, and snow plowing. On the other hand, in Lincoln Park, people choose to live in apartments or condominiums to avoid having to participate in a variety of tasks such as shoveling the walk, mowing the lawn, gardening, painting, repairing. They do not want such skills and are willing to pay on the market to have someone else – the janitor, gardener, repair person – do these jobs for them. More people and more specializations are needed to promote such a life-style.

Links within and between Institutions

Network-exchange analysts also consider the links within and among institutions. Once institutions have emerged, it is possible to study the links within any one institution. Network analysts have studied political institutions (discussed in the next section on stratification) more than any other. Bott (1971) points out that with network analysis it is no longer necessary to consider balance or integration in institutions; rather, one can see them as a convergence of links.

The norms within institutions are specialized, so some network analysts criticize a structural-functional institutional approach, since the network approach reveals more levels of relationships and several normative frameworks. Mitchell claims that analysis of institutions is an abstract representation of its component systems of relations and an abstraction of contents from the multiplex relations (1969, p. 45). Boissevain sees institutions as networks of choice-making individuals competing for resources (1974). According to Fischer et al., having networks in local institutions, especially voluntarily, contributes to a feeling of belonging (1977). No community institutions are totally self-sufficient, since by definition they are designed for specialized needs. Hence, the networks of people within any institution connect to other institutions. On another level, institutions themselves can be viewed as exchanging entities with their own networks. Blau argues that for such macro exchanges, shared values — instead of interpersonal attraction — become more important and the exchanges are more institutionalized than spontaneous. Since macro exchanges are based on micro exchanges, analysis of macro exchange must be multilevel. Macro exchanges can also create imbalances, which are potential sources of conflict.

Examination of ties within institutions in Zenda and Lincoln Park also reveals distinctions in the two communities. The smaller size of the institutions in Zenda, as well as the multiplexity of links, make it possible for everyone within an institution to know everyone else and therefore to be linked as friends or acquaintances as well as institutional members. The ties of people within the church, for example, overlap with ties in voluntary associations, in schools, in commercial relations, while in Lincoln Park, the institutions are so highly specialized that the ties within them are unique for the one institution only and consist of people whose residence is often outside Lincoln Park. Links within the medical institutions and institutions of higher education are examples. A small proportion of the people within any institution are linked to one another and ties are more tenuous.

Ties among people and macro exchanges among institutions link community institutions with one another. One Lincoln Park resident told how his network ties and additions in them led to his participation in a series of organizations. When he bought a house in Old Town, he started talking to neighbors about neighborhood improvement, and they influenced him to join the LPCA. His involvement there led him to negotiate with hospitals and meet hospital personnel. Because of these ties he was invited to become a board member of one of the Lincoln Park hospitals and there joined a health-planning organization and developed a program of medical care for the elderly.

Most institutions in Lincoln Park develop a specialist in relating to other institutions. The hospitals have public relations staffs and even the LPCA hires an administrator, one of whose tasks is to provide information about LPCA and negotiate among Lincoln Park organizations as well as with city officials.

In Zenda, people themselves are the links among organizations. Most people belong to several community organizations. The links are more informal than in Lincoln Park. When I worked at the store, I observed women who had just served a dinner for a funeral provide details of the funeral to the store proprietor, who was a member of the same church. She in turn could describe the funeral to others who entered the store. The tie between the church and store was quite visible through specific persons.

Institutions themselves can exchange. For example, at a Linn town board meeting, a representative from the Boy Scouts announced a pancake supper. In another instance, the town board allocated funds to the fire fighters for a new truck. This control of resources allows the town board to give to other groups and thereby retain its power.

LPCA has exchanges with schools, churches, and other community organizations, some of which are themselves members of LPCA. LPCA has helped the schools get more funds and students of higher academic standing in exchange for a change of policy in the schools.

Thus, in both Lincoln Park and Zenda the exchanges and ties among people help form organizations. More institutions and a greater specialization of institutions are found in Lincoln Park because of the greater variety of exchanges. Sometimes very specialized positions are created that link institutions to one another. The institutions themselves exchange and have their own networks.

Stratification

The concepts of power, authority, coalitions, status, and distributive justice distinguish network-exchange approaches to community stratification. They base ranking in society on differences in power, which come about through an imbalance in exchanges or a one-way flow through networks and become institutionalized in authority. Coalitions, which structurally appear as links among different kinds of people, facilitate getting rewards in exchanges. A network structure in the shape of a star or wheel also provides potential power. The status from continuous power has implications for interactions, with the fairness of unequal interactions considered through the concept of distributive justice.

Power and Authority

Power, like all aspects of stratification, arises out of the nature of exchanges. Some people accrue more valued resources than others, or some people's behavior changes more than that of others, creating an imbalance. Those without rewards have nothing to exchange but respect and compliance with those with the resources, creating a dependence on one another, but for different resources. Homans argues that the upper ranks give scarce resources and lower ranks give plentiful resources. This exchange somewhat balances exchanges, but never enough to create equality. According to Blau, giving advice creates obligations, while giving orders uses up obligations through compliance; higher rank itself is a reward. A collective recognition of deprivation can lead to opposition and change.

Blau defines power as an imposition of will through the use of rewards or negative sanctions (1964, p. 117), while Homans argues that both actors must be considered in the definition. Homans defines power as a change in the reward exchange such that B is rewarded less than A, and B changes behavior in a way favorable to A (1961, p. 83). Homans also discounts the intentionality of power; that is, people do not choose to become powerful.

Blau lists four conditions that affect the exchange of benefits and services. First, A and B may exchange benefits and services; second, B may obtain services elsewhere; third, B may take services from A by force; and fourth, B may do without services. The four issues create dependence or power and also have implications for the social structure (1964, p. 124).

A network representation of power portrays it as a unidirectional arrow. The tip of the arrow points to a person receiving only and not giving. The one-way flow puts that person in an overpowered relationship with the other.

Authority is a more stable, pervasive view of power. According to Homans, authority is the extension of power through indirect exchanges. A issues a command, but B insists that C comply, as illustrated by a ruler who delegates authority to his guards. According to Blau, authority comes with the establishment of norms, which benefit those who have established power by eliminating the competition and fostering integration. Those with power initiate the establishment of formalized rules. Opposition and conflict may come with authority, because some people do not receive the rewards they expect.

Power and authority are illustrated in Zenda by the town chairperson whose interest in the political position led him to accrue more information and use this imbalance to perpetuate his power position. In Lincoln Park the differentiation of resources distinguishes its relation to the political machine of the city of Chicago.

Zenda has a minimal range of power differences compared to Lincoln Park, since resources are more equal. Some in Zenda, however, have access to external resources. The town chairperson of Zenda is also on the county board and as such receives information pertinent to the community. Because the Zenda town chairperson has held the position so long, as his father did before him, experience and skills in running the township have accrued to him, which can be monopolized and used as a source of power. He also has access to other external sources such as information on revenue sharing about which he and the town board can make decisions for the community. In some ways the capacity to control resources that lie without the community may be the best source of power.

In Lincoln Park the political machine is an exchange system for the city of Chicago, controlling resources and services in support of the party. Thus, fixing potholes, providing more police surveillance, and the like are distributed unevenly in the city. If people have independent wealth and the ability to pay for these services without depending on the city machine, then they are less likely to support the machine politics. This is true for Lincoln Park residents who have elected an Independent alderman and do not need the Democratic machine. Further power differences are based on the ability of some to engage in more advantageous exchanges than others. Lincoln Park residents pay others to administer and wield power.

Authority exists in both Zenda and Lincoln Park because of the formalization of norms through laws and through indirect exchanges. For example, in Zenda the township has liquor licenses to distribute, but police enforce the licensing. Lincoln Park has formalized power positions both with ward representation and a representative of the Democratic machine, who relate to people in giving favors more indirectly through ward workers and the LPCA.

Coalitions

Coalitions are temporary alliances among factions or groups with varying interests to obtain power and exchange rewards (Blok 1973; Boissevain 1973). Formation of coalitions relates to network ties. When leaders of interest groups have direct ties with one another, coalitions more readily form. Further, the alignments people enter into in such situations as disputes relate to past links and to anticipated rewards in future exchanges (Kapferer 1969, p. 209).

In both Zenda and Lincoln Park different factions at times unite; people who belong to different churches or different political parties may come together on issues that threaten the community. For example, several factions of the Zenda community fought the coming of the Air Force Academy. Similarly, different neighborhoods and political party members unite in Lincoln Park to regulate developers and try to prevent high-rises and chain stores. The structure of the neighborhood association leaders also serving on the LPCA board facilitates the coalition of neighborhoods.

Status

Power develops out of exchange interactions and, in turn, affects the content of continuing interactions within a status and between statuses. Drawing on psychological principles of attraction of similarity, Homans argues for status congruence; that is, people of the same status will interact together more and more interaction will produce greater similarity among them. From Fischer et al.'s (1977) network viewpoint, classes appear as a greater density of ties among some people and a separation of ties from other clusters. Further, he suggests that class position limits and shapes opportunities for the selection and maintenance of ties.

The higher-status groups conform more to norms, according to Homans. Fischer adds that the resources of upper classes help them reap rewards from one another and exclude others. In his Northern California study, he found that more education contributed to the formation of larger networks. Further, a power elite can be measured by the relative closeness of the powerful to one another, in contrast to their separate ties to constituents.

The small size of Zenda, which facilitates dense networks and interconnection, also contributes to their being of the same status, whereas with Lincoln Park too big for everyone to interact, more heterogeneity in status prevails. Status congruence is found within organizations in Lincoln Park.

Distributive Justice

People may perceive that the allocation of services and rewards through society is unfair. They arrive at their decision of unfairness by comparing themselves with others on costs, rewards, and investments. Homans equates distributive injustice with relative deprivation; it is a problem for the weak and can lead to hostility.

Distributive justice concerns allocation of rewards by socially defined characteristics. Homans defines it as expectations that rewards are proportional to investments. Norms of fairness develop that are applicable to more than one dyad and thereby civilize the market of exchange as people learn to expect equivalent returns. Without similar rewards, norm violations and imbalances with tensions are created. Social-exchange theorists use the example of income comparison among workers.

Berger et al. (1972) add a structural status dimension to distributive justice: people of similar rank expect similar rewards. They define the structural aspect of distributive justice as the process by which, independently of the comparisons of one individual with another, meaning is given to rewards and expectations are formed about their allocation. Distributive justice also applies to status values, which are evaluations of worth or honor.

Urbanites are moving into the Zenda area. Some of them work to get on school boards, the township government, or other boards, which locals perceive as unjust. In comparing previous board members with the new arrivals, they see the former as long-term community members, often farmers who had been active in community affairs for several years. Their positions on boards serve as rewards for their long service to the community. When new people, whose interest in the community has not become apparent, are elected to boards, residents perceive injustice, which adds to the hostility toward new residents. Poor tenants who are forced to live outside of Lincoln Park, with the change to condominiums or improvements of buildings, form a potential source of distributive injustice because of the unfair allocation of housing, which forces them to lose their homes.

Interaction

As with social psychologists, to network-exchange analysts interaction is the most important part of the community paradigm, but they emphasize different aspects of interaction, especially their form and indirect nature. Exchange-network analysts vary in the extent to which they consider all interactions. Homans theorizes about interactions inclusively, but others specialize in exchange interactions or transactions. For example, Blau restricts his notion of social exchange to interactions oriented to ends, but omits interactions dominated by irrationality or unconscious motives (1964, p. 5).

With the most extensive discussion of interaction, Homans uses behavioral-psychology principles of punishments and rewards to define interaction as one person's activity stimulating or "setting off" another person's activity (1950, p. 101). While communication is synonymous with interaction, no words need be spoken. Defining frequency of interaction as "when action is social, that is, when the action of Person is rewarded by the action of Other, we speak of frequency of interaction" (1961, p. 176), Homans contends that frequency of interaction is distributed unevenly in a group. Frequency of interaction, or the number of interactions per day or year, produces differences among people, according to a series of propositions developed by Homans.

First, frequency relates to sentiments that refer to internal states manifested as observable units of behavior. With increased frequency of interaction, sentiments become stronger; liking for each other, especially, will increase. Liking a person in one group will "spill over" into liking that person in another group. Equals have a higher frequency of interaction. Further, group members like each other more and have a higher frequency of interactions when they decrease interactions with other groups and develop negative sentiments to outsiders.

Origination of interaction also has implications for relationships. Homans defines origination of interaction as action that initiates a series of exchanges between two persons after a period in which no interactions existed (1961, p. 199). The person who originates an interaction usually values the interaction more, but if that person is always the initiator, the two persons will no longer be equals, for the originator will experience a decrease in status and will feel respect or hostility for the other. If two people originate interaction for another person, the two will tend to have less interaction with one another. With a decrease in specialization of activities, the field in which to originate interactions becomes limited.

Homans also delineates shapes and flows of activities and sentiments that can be passed along among a group of people, much like passing a squeeze through a circle of people holding hands. Interactions within organizations or communities form a pyramid, with those of higher ranks interacting with more people. An increase in the size of a group leads to a greater number of chains between the leader and others. This greater range lowers the amount of interaction those at the lowest ranks have with leaders.

Other exchange and network analysts are more limited in their discussion of interactions. For example, Boissevain specializes in transaction as a type of interaction. He defines transaction as "interaction between two persons governed by the principle that the interaction must be equal or greater than the cost (value lost)" (1974, p. 25). His idea of transaction is that it can be unilateral, while Emerson (1972) views transactions as more reciprocal, suggesting that interactions are mutually reinforcing or rewarding instances of exchange. In Boissevain's view, people are manipulating interaction, playing "a strategic game with each party trying to gain value or at least break even" (1974, p. 158). Transaction implies exchanging to win something.

Network analysts consider both the content and structure of interaction, although often they equate exchange content with interaction. Indirect exchanges of obtaining help or political obligations can occur through a series of links. Characteristics and definitions of contents and structure of networks from Mitchell were presented earlier in this chapter. Kapferer suggests three aspects of interaction — the exchange content, multiplexity (the number of contents), and the direction of flow (which was discussed under stratification). For example, in his study of a workroom, he found five exchange contents: conversation, joking, job assistance, personal services, and cash assistance. Wellman (1979) looks at helping exchanges — daily assistance and in emergencies. Other contents of intimate ties are sociability, obligation, and propinquity.

Other network analysts equate content of networks with role relations such as mother-daughter, teacher-student, friend. This concept of role differs from the structural-functional definition in that for most network exchange theorists, roles are in flux and vary according to situations, although Blau mentions that expectations come to be associated with certain roles.

Rather than trying to illustrate each aspect of interaction separately, it may be useful to analyze the networks of two individuals, one from Zenda and one from Lincoln Park, to illuminate the interactions in the context of the major interactions of a single person and further substantiate the continued claim that Zenda has greater overlap in networks and more multiplexity.

The examples are both women in their 30s, both married. The Zenda woman has two school-aged children. She came with her family to a Zenda farm as a young child and has lived in the village since her marriage. Most of her network ties are people whom she knows from living in the community. The ones she spends the most time with are her family and her immediate neighbors. Her brother, his wife and sons, and her parents still live on the family farm and she sees them or talks to them daily. Her sister, husband, and children live about 40 miles away, and she does not see them as much, but talks to them almost weekly. The family members meet for dinner at one another's houses on holidays, including birthdays, they baby-sit for one another, and her son helps on the farm. She and her mother go to garage sales and sometimes give each other things they pick up at the sales.

Three immediate neighbors, one on each side and one across the road, are her good friends, with whom she does many things, such as going shopping and out to lunch. She baby-sits for the friend who teaches piano, and both she and her daughter have taken piano lessons from the friend. They pay each other money for these services. Next door is a young couple and they visit back and forth, borrow tools and household goods, and share advice.

A few times they have held joint garage sales, and sometimes both families go out for pizza.

Her other neighbor is a 90-year-old woman whom she helps a great deal. She is paid to keep up her lawn and take care of her finances, but she also visits regularly, almost daily, and often brings supper to the older woman, who sometimes gives her dishes and has promised to will her piano to her.

Three of her friends live on farms. She participates with them in activities at the children's school, goes shopping with them, and attended exercise classes with two of them. One of these friends bought the village grocery store in 1979 and hired her to work there part-time until the store closed. Another friend is someone she worked with in a factory in another town, when she got out of high school. They talk to one another or visit almost monthly. She and her husband about twice a year visit a couple they have known since high school, who live in a nearby town.

Other people in the village are relatives of the friends or acquaintances seen at the post office, store, or school. Over half of her network resides in the Zenda area and most of the ties involve multiplex exchanges of many things. Most of her network know one another; many of them belong to the Zenda church and participate in other community events with one another.

The Lincoln Park woman came there as a young adult from a southern state, where her parents and sisters live, and she rarely sees them. She works as a health-care professional in a Lincoln Park hospital and puts in long hours because of her prominent position at the hospital, where she knows many people and considers them her friends. She does not see them outside of the hospital, with the exception of one couple and the doctor she mainly works for, with whom she travels to other hospitals throughout the city. She is also working on a master's degree at a school in another part of the city and considers many of the students there also her friends. She is active in many professional organizations that take her traveling throughout the city and elsewhere, which is typical of many Lincoln Park residents whose professionalism dominates their networks. She knows many health professionals in a variety of different contexts, none of them communal. Exchanges of advice and information constitute the network flow. She also is friendly with independent grocers where she shops and with whom she exchanges Christmas cookies. One couple from work and one couple from her husband's work are their best friends, but they do not have time to see them much outside of work, not even once a month.

The Lincoln Park woman knows a great many more people than the Zenda woman and most of them do not live in the same community. The interactions tend to center on health professionals and have little relation to the physical setting of Lincoln Park, other than the hospitals. The rural network is smaller, limited more to local ties, with multiplex exchanges and close ties within the network, a denser mesh. This comparison also illustrates Fischer's findings (1982) that in small places people interact more with kin.

In addition to the differences in sources and multiplexity of ties, Zenda and Lincoln Park also differ in the degree of formality and the extent to which they are purely market ties. The example of the local store shows the lack of formality in giving credit. In Zenda charge accounts are opened and closed at request with no forms to fill out, no credit checks, no identification cards needed, and people pay when they can. In Lincoln Park, while a few of the locally owned stores may have such a relationship with customers they know well, the impersonality of the marketplace is more likely. Rarely is charging allowed and if it is, it may be based on a national system of credit cards. Check cashing in the city, if allowed at all, requires several identification cards with a picture.

More informality exists in nonmoney exchanges in Zenda. For example, some people with surplus produce such as strawberries, raspberries, and apples may bring them to the store to be sold, but they take groceries, rather than money, in payment. In Lincoln Park there are chains of exchanges, so that people are not linked directly, but through money which passes through many hands. Zenda exchange is more direct and less mediated by money, as people exchange work, borrow items, or do services for one another. Whereas the market prices (based on national and international processes) reign in Lincoln Park, more bartering occurs in Zenda, where a bushel of beans may be exchanged for a haircut, or one farmer will help another bale hay with reciprocal repayment.

TIME

While network-exchange theorists visualize long-term, historical processes, these are ultimately related to individuals' exchanges.

Over time, individuals build up network ties and patterns of exchange that become normative and institutionalized. Nevertheless, the continued flux of the micro interactions create conflict and change in the macro processes. Macro historical changes also influence the nature of ties.

History

While it appears that Homans has a cyclical view of history, since he discusses the rise of Hilltown with increased prosperity and increased population, and then its disintegration through lack of interaction among people, he actually agrees with Blau that history is dialectical. The exchange dialectics of history do not completely coincide with conflict theory dialectics, which view contradictions of class relations. Instead, both Blau and Homans see conflict, opposition, and disintegration as intrinsically connected with integration, institutionalization, and organization, all necessary parts of social change.

Homans views history as always related to individuals' rewards and punishments. Over time, the rewards and punishments stabilize into norms that regularize exchanges and institutions, which by definition imply patterns of exchanges that last through time. The section on institutions pointed out that Homans believes that surpluses began the civilizing process of institution building, which facilitates more complex interactions and differentiation of institutions.

Although communities seem to equilibrate after these initial developments, disintegration and conflict are always possibilities. Homans relates the downfall of the community of Hilltown to a decrease in interaction among the residents. He describes equilibrium and statics as special cases of change. The two main types of change he delineates are social disintegration and social conflict. Disintegration produces anomie and disorganization, while social conflict produces alternative groups, as when criminals oppose standardized norms by reversing the norms in their own communities. Homans also sees that sometimes it is possible for a leader to direct the long-term change of a group.

Blau defines dialectics as alternating patterns of intermittent social reorganization. Integration leads to status patterns of inequality. Because of the complexity and interdependence of the social structure, incompatability of parts changes back and forth with pressures to change. Blau suggests that institutions reflect history in daily life, since they are part of the past that has lasted. Even so, they can be changed. In addition to the built-in nature of complex social structures, power imbalances also create pressures to change, so that those who lack power can escape their hardship.

On the other hand, once institutions are created, they resist change and so do some groups of people, especially those who benefit from having power and vested interest. This resistance to change is a rigidity that promotes conflict. To change social institutions requires "strenuous and prolonged struggles by opposition movements" (Blau 1964, p. 388). Opposition catalyzes social change, although some change — such as technological development — does not depend on opposition.

Another part of the dialectics of history is the interaction between history and everyday, short time. Historical changes, such as industrialization and modernization, make little sense to most network-exchange analyses, unless the macro changes are manifested in individual behavior. For example, Mitchell (1969) refers to analyses of urbanization in Africa by the shifting of network centers from hometown to urban ties.

Fischer et al. (1977) document three historical changes that impinge on networks. First, rather than an increase in geographical mobility, they find a change in who moves; in the past the poor moved, but now the middle class and upper classes are more mobile. Second, technological changes of improved transportation and communication have facilitated constructing and maintaining ties outside the local community. Third, the influence of neighbors has declined.

We can see instances of the simultaneous disintegration and integration in Zenda and Lincoln Park. Many community arenas that were exchange centers for Zenda have disappeared, while others have been added. After 1976 the Zenda Fair was no longer an annual event, but became sporadic, put on some years and not others, depending on the willingness of people to organize it. After 1981 there was no longer a grocery store, some voluntary associations disbanded, and in 1982 the bowling alley closed. Similarly, in Lincoln Park some community events have decreased; church attendance has fallen. At the same time, new forms of integration and institutionalization occur in the form of classes in the Zenda area, for example, "stretch and sew" and exercise classes offered at the town hall. The factories in Zenda have grown and now employ a larger number of people and more local people. More recreation organizations are entering Lincoln Park.

An example from Zenda illustrates change in ties with the movement from one community to another, not so much with urbanization, but as part of the settlement of the West. Letters from a young couple who moved to the Zenda area in the mid-1800s, written by the wife to her parents back on a farm in New York, is revealing. For the first few years, the people referred to in the letters were friends and relatives back in New York, but the pioneer woman's increasing mention of local people and events indicates her gradual integration with others as other pioneers came and the community of Zenda was formed. In the last letters, references are entirely to local people (Cornue Letters 1848-1858).

Process

The short term consists of activation of networks and exchange flows. Day-to-day social exchanges must actually last longer than a day, in the sense of being repeated, to form social rather than economic ties. Homans uses time to distinguish social exchange from barter, which consists of a one-time exchange. As such, it is only economic rather than social, for social exchange requires repetition to evolve into a social relation. Also, actors are not interchangeable in social exchange as in economic exchange.

The distinction between barter and social exchange can be illustrated by sale activities. Some people in both Zenda and Lincoln Park like to go to garage sales, which are sometimes purely economic transactions of bartering for a bargain. As people begin to know the others at the sales, going becomes more a social event, with exchanges not just of used goods and money, but also of visiting and exchanging information on giving sales and getting the most out of them.

Once the social exchanges have begun, they may be modified, with new behavior added and old patterns eliminated or changed. Rewards and punishments, as well as changes in the environment and changes in perspectives, influence a change over time of interactive behavior.

Social relations can be temporary, such as coalitions where people come together for a single controversy only. That particular configuration of people may never be together again, yet for a short period they are united in exchanges. Their coming together is related to previous connections among at least some of them.

Time becomes an investment, a cost, or an opportunity in a social relation. Blau characterizes time as the most generalized cost. It is an opportunity cost because of alternatives foregone, in which time could be spent in a different way. Time is a scarce resource because its amounts are limited, but its use value can change, depending on availability. Blau uses the example of workers asking experts for advice. Experts invest time in this because it gives them admiration and prestige, but there are trade-offs in what other time demands the expert has on the job, the number of workers asking for advice, and the number of experts. With an increase in the number of experts, the advice of any one is reduced in value, decreasing the value of the experts' time so that experts will have to spend more time giving advice to get the same amount of prestige as before. This promotes competition among experts.

Some people have more time than others to spend on the community, such as nonworking women with grown children and retired people. This may make them experts on the community, but since they have a surplus of time, others who have less time may be more valued when they are able to give their attention to community matters.

Blau sees an unequal distribution of time in a group, which is allocated "among members in accordance with their estimated ability to make contributions to its welfare based on initial impressions" (1964, p. 125). Reciprocity in one interaction leads to an imbalance in another part of the social structure. A community consists of constantly shifting patterns of reciprocity and imbalance. Boissevain adds that those who have more time to manage social relations are more likely to have multiplex relations (1974, p. 157).

Blau also applies issues of time to power and leadership. Power is expended in use, but it can be held over a period of time by not forcing obligations and thereby maintaining others in debt. In an informal group with no defined goal it is difficult for a leader to obtain power, because there is not enough time to help and obligate each member separately.

Frequency and duration are important time dimensions of networks, with frequency indicating repetition within a specific time frame and duration indicating lasting through time. Boissevain suggests that duration is more important. The people seen everyday for a short term may not be willing to give as much help as a family member or long-term friend who may be seen only yearly. According to Wellman, frequency of contact with intimates produces a greater likelihood of assistance (1979, p. 122). In Zenda duration and frequency are probably stronger than in Lincoln Park, because of lack of mobility and greater probability of seeing the same people daily. Work contacts in Lincoln Park are frequent.

The short term is an exchange of immediate gratification for one party, with a postponement of gratification for the other party. People will give to help another with the thought that they may be helped in the future — a sort of insurance. For example, in Zenda, when one farmer's father was in the hospital and dying during the plowing season, several other farmers got together and did his plowing, even though they all needed time for their own. The farmer could not pay them back, nor did they expect it, but they have some assurance that the same would be done for them in a similar situation.

Sometimes the help returned is indirect and may not even be returned to the person who gave it. Postponements in Zenda can sometimes last several generations. One community member will help another because of something their grandparents shared. In Lincoln Park, because of greater mobility, exchange may be out of a more general civility that is not as personal and specific as in Zenda. Instead, people have a mutual sense of what good people do as a characteristic of the system and not of specific families or people.

SPACE

Territory

Of all the paradigms, network-exchange approaches require the least amount of space and indeed can conceive of communities (in the sense of interpersonal ties) of people who share no space. Many exchange theorists make no mention of space or environment, and some network analysts only argue against the necessity of space. Barnes (1954) delineates the territorial system of Bremnes as the domestic, agricultural, and administrative part, which he distinguishes from the network system of informal ties.

Homans notes three aspects of the environment: physical, technical, and social (1961, p. 88). Such things as the shape of a room and geographical position influence the formation of cliques. Changes in the environment such as economic fluctuations or migration rates may change interaction patterns within a community.

Blau relates space to preventing collective experiences of power imbalances by separating people. With less spatial division, people will collectively experience the power of superordinates, and this may lead to an opposition movement and an impetus for change.

Wellman, Fischer, and Boissevain view space as an influence on the structure of networks. According to Wellman, it is still possible to find many ties within the confines of a community. He maintains that assistance from those spatially residing near a person in East York has not declined, but that the spatial range has increased to the whole metropolitan area. Boissevain analyzes place of residence and the climate as distinct aspects of the physical environment that impinge on networks. By residence, he means rural or urban and he hypothesizes that rural networks are denser and more multiplex. The hotter climates facilitate more activities in public and more casual contact, while networks will tend to be small in colder places.

Mobility also influences networks in that when people move, they extend their networks and can know people in more than one place. It also takes more energy to create new ties and maintain old ones in a new place. Fischer et al. suggest that changes in technology — such as automobiles, airplanes, telephones — have made it easier to maintain ties over distance. In fact, long-distance ties must be valued more, since they cost more to maintain. People have more choices about their localities now than they have had in the past (1977).

Fischer et al. do not believe that spatial restrictions promote community relations: "Dense networks were not particularly likely to come of ascribed social contexts Toennies emphasized — kinship and locality — any more than out of more freely chosen ones — work and voluntary associations" (1977, p. 202). Dense networks come as people select rewarding social relations out of the context in which they live. Fischer finds a historical change of more and more frequent long-distance ties because of changes in technology.

Today the middle and upper classes are more mobile geographically and able to afford the technology to keep in touch over long distances.

Telephone, radio, and television make Zenda and Lincoln Park more alike in their ability to instantly talk to others almost anywhere. To get tangible items and face-to-face interaction with long-distance links may be easier for Lincoln Park than for Zenda, because Lincoln Park has access to better mass transportation. Its residents can reach longer distances more easily because of their proximity to bus and train stations and international airports. Because travel is easier, they are able to have more diverse and long-distance links.

I know of no one in Zenda or Lincoln Park who has ties only within the community; everyone also has ties beyond the space of the community. The difference in Lincoln Park and Zenda is in the proportion of network ties that are local. The concentration of kinship ties, relation to neighbors and others in the community because of living there a long time, and connections at school, church, and other institutions, all promote internal ties in Zenda, while the greater mobility, both in terms of residency in and out of the community and of daily commuting outside the community, lessens local ties in Lincoln Park.

Land and location can be seen as contents of exchange, a type of community for which contracts are made. Both Zenda and Lincoln Park have market values, but they are different. Property values and the cost of living are higher in Lincoln Park. In Zenda, the prices attached to homesteads reflect family tradition and sentiments, rather than market values.

Boundaries

Network-exchange ties are literally unbounded, since they may be traced from one person to the rest of the world and back again. They are not bounded by space, patterns of subsistence, shared values, or perception. Theoretically, the whole world, as in Milgram's small world (1967), can be a community, a global village (McLuhan 1964).

For purposes of analysis, researchers themselves limit networks to closed or partial networks or to activity fields, such as Kapferer's consideration of a workroom or exchange analysis of dyads. Mitchell (1969, p. 40) explains how analysis binds networks:

> This difficulty [unboundedness] is resolved by fixing the "boundary"
> of the network in relation to the social situation being analyzed;
> the analyst traces links from ego to the constituents themselves in
> as much as the links are necessary and sufficient to throw light on
> the problem studied.

Network analysts consider lack of boundaries a benefit of their
perspective. Types and contents of exchanges may also be a limiting
factor to networks, since where norms of exchange cease to operate,
a different culture exists as a kind of boundary.

Boissevain delineates several boundaries or zones within each
personal network, based on degrees of intimacy. They rely primarily
on subjective criteria, and range from intimate to effective (pragmatic considerations) to nominal (acquaintances) to external (1973,
p. 47). Boissevain also proposes that the environment can limit
networks — that small-scale, isolated communities will be more
"bounded," which means that most people's ties will be in the
community and few will extend beyond it.

Ties in both the communities studied here extend over long
distances without any boundaries. For example, two families in
Zenda have relatives in Ireland, and one of the families even went
on trips there to visit. Some Zenda retired couples and widows
migrate to Arizona each winter and others from Zenda often visit
them, thus creating an extension of the Zenda community that
leaps over a great amount of space. Lincoln Park ties extend even
farther, even as far as Japan, and many people have ties in Mexico.
Even those not from another country usually have siblings, if not
parents or children, in other states. If actual lines of ties could be
drawn, the average length of lines in Lincoln Park would be found
to be considerably greater than for those in Zenda, making Lincoln
Park residents' ties less bounded by the immediate location.

SUMMARY

Network-exchange analysis is a very recent phenomenon and
does not have a long history other than its inspiration by Simmel
and the 1950s exchange theories of Homans and Blau. British anthropologists defined terms and carried out original research, while
Fischer and Wellman are currently making the most extensive applications to American communities.

For network-exchange analysts, communities look like dots and lines of people connected in various ways, with exchange flowing through the lines. Institutions and stratification patterns form from these connections of interaction and from norms of fairness. Historically, network exchanges institutionalize but also may end when they are no longer rewarding. Changes in technology and other historical processes change the nature of links. People daily activate their networks as needs arise, with others investing time in exchange for prestige. Long-lasting ties lead to more help than frequent ties. Networks can be liberated from ties to land, although people continue to form some ties locally, whether the kinship ties of rural areas or the chosen ties of urban areas.

Lincoln Park and Zenda differ in the nature of their ties, with more multiplexity and local density in Zenda and greater numbers and extent of ties in Lincoln Park. Zenda exchanges are personal, often nonmonetary, and money flows back and forth between individuals, in contrast to the more rational, entirely monetary exchanges in Lincoln Park. Ties and exchanges in the latter more easily relate to new people outside the community, whereas tracing links in Zenda usually leads back to the local group.

Network-exchange approaches conclude this study of community paradigms. Each has given a different picture of Lincoln Park and Zenda and, as such, are selective and partial. Critics often accuse individual theorists of omissions as well as denigrate their logic and political implications. The final chapter will examine criticisms and practical applications of the theories.

8

Conclusion: Criticisms, Synthesis, and Applications

This study concludes with three final considerations related to the community frameworks: critical evaluations of the perspectives; questions of whether they may be synthesized; and, last, a brief discussion of the impact of these frameworks on the practical community arenas of community planning, development, and organization. First, the major criticisms of each school of thought will be briefly examined.

CRITICISMS

Each framework has been presented both as applicable to communities and as standing alone, each acceptable in its own right, but we cannot leave these frameworks critically unexamined. We must make judgments about their adequacy, especially in comparison with the other frameworks.

Human Ecology

Critics question the logical connections in human ecological thought. They further criticize the causal variables, such as subsocial

251

forces and the zone theory. Alihan has written a whole book on the subject (1938) and many others have published articles. Wilhelm (1964) attacks human ecologists for tautological reasoning and mixed-order data. Tautological reasoning consists of explaining a phenomenon with variables or proofs that are part of the given phenomenon. Such proofs are true by definition, and therefore go in circles without getting anywhere. For example, Duncan's population-organization-environment-technology combination defines the ecological complex, then measures one or more of the four to explain the others (Duncan 1964). Human ecologists show an interrelationship among these four and then explain the connection by the same complex of variables. Wilhelm also suggests that human ecologists mix inappropriate units of analysis: material phenomena (technology, geography, and population) with non-material phenomena (such as organization). He maintains that human ecologists need a common basis of interaction between physical and social data. Human-ecology variables are also faulted; indeed, Alihan criticizes all human-ecology variables for being unclear and inconsistently used (1938).

Critics accuse human ecologists of ecological, geographical, biological, or environmental determinism, all negative labels. Hollingshead (1947), among others, claims that all these "natural" forces are tempered by sociocultural phenomena and that human beings may not be equivalent to plants and animals. Alihan further questions the distinction between the biotic and the social, between the community and society. Human ecologists define community as the animallike, spontaneous activities of humans that have connection to territory and distinguish community from society. They assume that rational acts are less territorial, but in their studies the distinctions between community and society, between rational and spontaneous acts become blurred.

One specific kind of ecological determinism is that location in a specific zone of a city – specifically, distance from the center of a city – will determine land use, ways of life, class, or various rates. Davie (1937) did not find this relationship in New Haven. Fava (1968) further argues that each zone has become so permeated and heterogeneous, with industrial parks, apartment buildings, and shopping centers found in all zones, that the zones no longer have meaning. Alihan suggests that according to human-ecological reasoning, the most stable and most highly valued land ought to be closest to the center of the city and the least stable the furthest from the center, whereas in fact, human ecologists find the reverse. Nor are natural areas indigenous to all cities, as Hatt (1946) found in a study of Seattle. Human ecologists of the Chicago School are chided for believing that Chicago can be the model of other cities.

Competition is the main dynamic assumed by human ecologists, and Alihan questions competition as a primary determinant. She especially criticizes human ecologists' emphasis on competiton as unplanned and unconscious by citing instances in which they equivocate over whether whether competition is planned or conscious. Bernard (1973) further points out that competition has not worked for blacks who have not been succeeded by new groups and become part of more prestigious housing areas, largely because racism supersedes any ecological process. Hawley (1950) criticizes the concept of competition, which is generally inferred on a post hoc basis, for not being empirically observable.

In addition to faulty causal reasoning, human ecologists commit sins of omission. Their very macro, subsocial approach omits individuals, while at the macro level they have disregarded conflict and political forces. Data cannot reveal details about any one individual in the aggregate, since to do so would commit the "ecological fallacy." Individuals' choices and uses of symbols are lacking in most human-ecology studies, with the exception of Fiery, whose work was less emulated and less incorporated into mainstream human ecology.

Logan and Sterns (1981) and Shlay and Rossi (1981) suggest adding collective action, zoning ordinances, and other political ideas to human ecology. Politics and power seem neglected, even though some authors have attempted to add political dimensions. Other omissions are class and class conflicts. According to Bernard (1973), external social, economic, and intellectual conditions have changed so radically as to be impossible to incorporate into human ecology. Further, many of the processes delineated by human ecology are now controlled and regulated by policy.

Structural Functionalism

Structural functionalism has been the target of more criticisms than any other paradigm; indeed, network analysts and others interpret their development as reactions to the inadequacies of functionalism. Predominant among problems with functionalism are faulty logic and omissions.

Critics fault functionalists for being teleological and tautological in their causal explanations. Teleologic means end-directed reasoning based on a goal, with the end assumed to have caused the processes and structures leading up to it. Functionalists argue that systems exist to attain certain goals. For example, they claim that a community system is working toward integration or that a community's need for social control causes it to have political institutions. Without documenting the causal chain from one point to another, the reasoning does not hold.

A related problem exists: that of taking the organismic metaphor too seriously, with no clear criteria for the assessment of life, death, or diseases of social orders. For example, Sorokin (1928, p. 208) long ago suggested:

> If we take off these analogies and the identification of society with an organism from these theories, there remains very little in them. Their originality and specific nature disappear; and through that, disappears the school itself.

Tautology is a kind of circular causal reasoning in which a statement is true by definition and therefore cannot be explained. Tautologies are vacuous explanations that do not reveal anything new, but repeat what the item is in different words. Saying that parts of the community are necessary for its existence and proving it by the fact that the community is still existing is circular. A community's survival is equated with equilibrium, but the equilibrium is proved by survival. Functionalists blur the distinction between cause and function. The theory contains implicit assumptions of what is needed for survival without being definitive. A functionalist would have to list all the substitution possibilities and conditions that could fulfill any particular function. It is also difficult to list all the values of a society, which are rarely entirely agreed upon. Criteria for the fulfillment or nonfulfillment of requisites could counteract the tautology (Turner 1978).

Functionalists' emphasis on order, on stability, and on every structure having a purpose leads them to use language that omits or faults activities that do not support the existing structure. Other than evolutionary changes of gradual adaptation, change is seen as something wrong with the system or as deviance that must be corrected for the system's survival. In their emphasis on consensus, functionalists leave out revolutionary change and ignore contradictions and conflicts. These lacks and emphases make them seem conservative and proponents of the status quo. Merton answers these criticisms by arguing that functionalists can analyze dysfunctions, disequilibria, dynamics, and history as well as Marx (Merton 1949, pp. 39-40).

Social psychologists criticize the functionalist portrayal of individuals as internalizing agreed-upon norms and values through socialization. Assumed roles mechanistically seem to determine how each person acts in an oversocialized (Wrong 1961), robot way. Functionalists leave little leeway for individualism, choice, or negotiation of norms and values, and they never reveal the origins of consensus. Stokes and Hewitt (1976) suggest that while internalization occurs, most of everyday life is not governed by internalized norms. In considering macro-level integration, the functionalist approach is holistic and abstract and often lacks grounding in concrete situations. It does not say much about ordinary people in everyday life, where few interactions are based on internalized norms.

Finally, the wholism of functionalism leads its proponents to assume that communities are lacking if they do not have a complete set of institutions. Such communities must be dying. Since most smaller communities in the contemporary United States — such as Zenda, or parts of cities like Lincoln Park — are functionally incomplete, their significance may be downplayed by functionalists.

Conflict Theory

Conflict theory has long been distrusted and criticized, and recent criticisms have been leveled against Castells's urban Marxist approach. Conflict theory's omissions and methods of argument are equally condemned.

Some people criticize and fear Marxist theory in the light of current Communist states whose totalitarianism and lack of freedom seem undesirable. The idealism and practicality of equalitarianism is further questioned by those who doubt the feasibility of equality. Where are the revolutions and the conflict for workers' interests?

Most revolutions of the twentieth century have been peasant-based. U.S. workers in mid-century are generally complacent and well paid.

Conflict theorists tend to emphasize economic and class explanations above all others. In so doing, they tend to minimize explanations that others consider to be crucial to understanding communities. The omissions include order and stability, individuals' subjective meanings, and even the local place.

Functionalists believe that conflict and change are not as common or significant as conflict theorists argue. For human ecologists, competition rather than the more extreme conflict seems a better community variable. Both functionalists and human ecologists view conflict as rare, with order and integration more common in communities, which change with gradual adaptations. Others accuse conflict theorists of being biased, therefore not scientific and not sociological. Social scientists should not criticize society, but should study it, present it as it is.

Conflict theorists often downplay the perceptions and feelings of individuals, claiming that these lack objectivity. Most people in their everyday lives do not realize their true class position and the economic conditions of exploitation, because the capitalist system contrives to separate workers and obfuscate their position through ideology.

The economic determinism and historical determinism of conflict theory omit other causal possibilities. Blumer (1969) makes this criticism in noting that the assumption is often made that people are a product of the forces of society, rather than people with selves who selectively give meanings through their interactions. Manning concurs with Blumer in criticizing a conflict approach. In trying to simplify "the complexities of social meanings, it tends to see politics as a reflection of interests and not the converse" (Manning 1973, p. 2). The conflict approach fails to take into account the two-way nature of economic structures and individuals' perceptions of them. This points to a disagreement at the individual level, so that the impact and nature of the economic structure and of conflict itself are filled with ambiguities, disagreements, and negotiated meanings. This criticism of a conflict approach is that it does not give enough recognition to the individual and interactions. Saunders (1981) argues that Castells is especially guilty of neglecting subjective meanings, and this makes his theory inadequate.

Conflict explanations based on the political economy often extend to a wholistic world view. For example, closing factories in one community connects with exploiting labor in the Third World, or transportation costs related to Arab oil countries. Conflict explanations constantly move beyond the local place, so that it becomes almost insignificant, one of Vidich and Bensman's points in *Small Town in Mass Society* (1958). Saunders (1981) suggests that conflict analyses lead to worldwide considerations, leaving in question whether there are distinctly community or urban phenomena.

Conflict theorists who do argue for urban distinctions base them on unique urban classes, such as Rex and Moore's housing classes (1967). Housing classes are criticized for being indistinguishable from other classes, and therefore exhibiting no distinct phenomena — merely reflecting the classicism and racism of the greater society. Castells (1977) argues that urbanism is an ideology and that urban and rural areas do not differ.

Fischer (1978) argues against Castells's contention, citing rural-urban differences in attitudes, beliefs, and networks that go beyond class distinctions. Fischer also contends that while economic variables may explain a great deal, it is still important to study ecological variables. Human ecology should not be entirely dismissed.

In addition to the lack of clarity on the concept of class, other conflict concepts including outcomes of conflict, collective consumption, space, and political economy are deemed unclear. How class is to be defined, how many classes there are, and even further divisions within classes have generated controversy and lack of agreement. It is not certain how classes are to be identified, and people equivocate over the number of classes. Turner (1978) contends that the units of analysis are not clear for conflict analysis. For example, the conflicting parties range from individuals to nations, which vary in the nature of conflict. Further, Turner notes the confusion over whether conflict theorists are examining the causes of conflict or the outcomes of conflict.

Saunders (1981) criticizes Castells, who, it will be recalled, distinguishes urban structures by a particular organization of space that involves collective consumption. Saunders suggests that the concept of collective consumption is unclear and needs specification. He further questions whether space is necessary for all forms of collective consumption and gives the examples of social security payments, family allowances, and pension schemes, which lack spatial referents. Castells ignores the specific setting and the structure of space.

Saunders also censures political-economy approaches to urban problems. These approaches elide capital accumulation with consumption and do not make firm distinctions that would uncover varieties of class struggles. While Castells tends to omit production, political economists tend to omit consumption. Both must be seen, but they must also be considered separately.

According to Saunders, Castells and other conflict theorists at times become tautological and teleological. They become tautological in trying to explain everything because then they have nothing with which to explain. Conflict theorists need counterfacts, ideas that are outside the original concept. "As long as the theory purports to explain everything, it explains nothing" (Saunders 1981, p. 208). More specific examples of tautologies include the ex post facto arguments about the continuation of monopoly capitalism. The state must be acting on behalf of dominant capitalists' interests or capitalism would not continue. It is also tautological to say that every gain of the working class helps the interests of capital. These tautologies lead to a lack of criteria for empirical adequacy.

According to Saunders, the state both responds to working-class interests and simultaneously safeguards elite interests. Pluralism and elitism separately are inadequate, since a dualism prevails. Castells and others fail to explain how the state responds to the contradiction of interests of workers and elite. They become teleological when they define urban systems as heading toward some goal (such as a socialist state) without including any purposive agency.

In sum, critics have accused conflict theory of being idealistic and unscientific. Conflict theorists further focus too much on classes and the political economy, to the detriment of the importance of order, individuals' meanings, and local communities. The concepts of class, space, collective consumption, and the political economy are imprecise and unclear. Finally, some arguments become tautological and teleological when conflict theorists try to explain everything and when they explain the continuation of capitalism by its continued existence.

Social-Psychology Approaches

Critics denounce social-psychology approaches for their theory base, methodology of participant observation, for leaving out macro-level phenomena, and for some distorted views of individuals.

Huber (1973) critiques symbolic interaction as not having a theoretical base in the sense of testable hypotheses. She suggests that because symbolic interactionists approach phenomena without a clearly formulated theory and expect the theory to emerge from the data, they induce a bias from themselves and from their informants. Researchers have no criteria for judging either which informants have the correct answers or the observer's own selection of observations. Many factors can sway the findings. She further asserts that the emergent bias supports the status quo: "When truth is expected to emerge from interaction, then what is taken to be true tends to reflect the distribution of power among the participants" (Huber 1973, p. 875). Such studies are impossible to replicate, nor can the assumptions be tested.

Turner (1978) further argues that social-psychology approaches are descriptive rather than causal explanations. Many of the concepts such as self, expectations, and symbols are almost impossible to measure. The attempts at measuring — verbal accounts of concepts — may not accurately reflect either behavior or attitudes, since they do not distinguish the concept from the actor. Intuitive accounts are too individualistic and, therefore, not accurate or adequate.

In agreement with Turner, Bell and Newby (1974) claim that community studies are no better than novels because they are subjective, noncumulative, and innumerative. To Effrat (1974), the qualitative methods of most community studies are impressionistic, difficult to quantify, and idiosyncratic. The sex, age, class, and ethnicity of researchers provides differential access to people of communities.

The problems of theory are part of the problems with methodology. Much of social psychology, particularly studies based on participant observation, are considered descriptive, impressionistic, and retrospective, lacking explanations, theory, and scientific bases. These same criticisms are leveled when structural functionalists or conflict theorists also use participant observation. Many sociologists distrust the method of participant observation because procedures are not specified and scientific techniques of random sampling and statistical tests are not conducted.

Social psychology is by definition micro-based, so social psychologists are faulted for leaving out macro-level phenomena or not clearly indicating the relation between micro and macro phenomena. Classes, institutions, and history are not clearly seen from this viewpoint. Focusing on micro levels makes it difficult to understand how powerful organizations develop and impose definitions and ideologies on others with less power. The political economy perpetuates inequality beyond the efforts and effects of single interacting individuals. Some social psychologists remain so close to their observations that they seem incapable of generalizations. Much of social psychology lacks permanent dimensions, making it impossible to consider a lasting social order or history. If everything is in flux, nothing permanent can remain.

Finally, some critics like Gouldner (1970) fault Goffman's and Garfinkel's images of human beings. Goffman (1959) brings us the conning impression manager who constantly manipulates — the bureaucrat. He reveals nothing on how people change the structures within which they manipulate. On the other hand, Garfinkel's (1967) characters are whimsical dupes who trust in a nonexistent reality. Meltzer, Petras, and Reynolds (1975) sum criticisms of Blumer and Chicago School symbolic interactionists as an unattained ideal of understanding human behavior.

Network-Exchange Analysis

The recency of network-exchange applications to community has precluded extensive criticisms of a framework that has not yet solidified. In-house fighting has led to criticisms within the framework. The hodgepodge of terms, the mathematical emphasis on morphology, the prominence of rationality, problems with social support, the absence of a time dimension, and even lack of a theory have plagued this framework.

Mitchell (1969) sought to codify definitions and terms in order to develop theory, but subsequent uses of network analysis have not been consistent in their use of terms, resulting in what Barnes (1972) terms "a terminological jungle." Centrality, reachability, power, and prestige in relation to networks have all been defined and measured in different ways (Burt 1980).

Network analysts emphasize the form and numbers of connections in networks, in the name of greater precision, but the mathematical nature of network analysis has led to problems. According to Killworth and Russell (1976), no one can remember all one's ties with other people. This leads to problems with sampling from total networks and with measuring what is sampled. Network analysts debate the merits of asking respondents to name all their friends (for example, Wellman 1979) versus asking them about specific content areas such as to whom they go for advice (for example, Fischer et al. 1977) Both of these techniques involve interviews and/or questionnaire whose accuracy is questioned. Further, with more people in the network and more aspects of the network examined, the combinations become unwieldy, forcing network analysts to specialize and, therefore, leave out some aspects of the network. For example, interconnectedness or mesh becomes extremely complicated with more people involved.

Some network analysts get so involved with the measurement that they lose track of the actual persons involved and end up saying very little about them. The structure of ties is usually emphasized to the exclusion of content, thereby leaving out the meaning to those involved. The emphasis on form rather than content omits individual's interpretations.

Those who do include content, such as exchange theorists, overemphasize rational calculations. It is difficult to see how interactions are based on rational calculations of rewards, and it is questionable whether all interactions have such a basis. Blau explicitly limits his discussion to interactions that do involve rational calculations, but then, it seems, he has omitted the majority of interactions.

Another content area of network analysis has been social support, which also has the problem of inconsistent definitions, measurements, and the question of how many exchanges are based purely on positive giving. Network analysts omit negative aspects of relationships.

The complexity of network analysis has forced researchers to concentrate on networks at one particular time. As such, they are purely static approaches that miss changes over time.

All these problems centralize in one major difficulty: Burt (1980) cites lack of theory as the greatest impediment to the development of network analysis. "In the absence of theory . . . arbitrary decisions regarding system boundaries and measures of relational form/content are difficult to assess" (Burt 1980, p. 133). Much of network analysis is descriptive, applied ad hoc, and does not generate hypotheses or permit causal arguments to develop. Because of the varieties of network analysis, a single corpus of knowledge has not developed.

While exchange has a more centralized theory, it can be tautological. Exchange theorists explain in tautologies when they define value, rewards, and actions in terms of one another. Homans (1961) claims that these become separate on an empirical level, whereas according to Blau (1964), values and actions are part of one another on an empirical level.

Overview of Criticisms

Faulty arguments, imprecise concepts, and difficulties in measurement plague all the frameworks, particularly as they apply to the study of communities. General criticisms range from community theories not being scientific to being out-of-date paradigms. Bell and Newby (1974) denigrate community studies for being more like prescriptions for the good life rather than generating hypotheses and measurable outcomes. Bernard (1973) claims that new scientific revolutions are needed in order to understand the complexity of today's communities.

Problems in logic and sins of omission summarize the criticisms leveled against the five schools of thought in this book. Theorists have been careless in defining their terms and have reasoned in circular, dead-end fashions. Most community frameworks have failed to be scientific theories in the sense of having a body of propositions from which to draw hypotheses. Prior hypotheses are rarely tested in community studies, further hindering a development of scientific theory.

One possible exception to the lack of theory is the broad question of whether communities still exist. This question has been answered indirectly by most community studies and directly by some hypothesis testing. The five frameworks answer this theoretical question in different ways. Human ecologists continue to find communities by the concentration of aggregates, which shift to different positions. Functionalists are having a more difficult time finding the integrated local institutions and look more to the past to find true communities. Conflict theorists find that communities function to replenish the labor force, but fiscal crises, exoduses of employment sources, and other problems have hindered them from doing so. Social psychologists discover community when residents are able to give meaning to their surroundings. And network analysts test the community question through the nature of ties among people.

In addition to theory, omissions have been cited as problems with each of the community frameworks. Community analysts have viewed communities on either the macro or micro level. Each framework has emphasized some aspect of community to the neglect of other aspects. Can we put these together and emphasize all parts without omitting any?

Given the criticisms of the five orientations, we ask two additional questions. First, are the theories synthesizable in a way that overcomes the criticisms of omissions? Second, given that the frameworks do not make good science, are they useful in other directions? Even if they do not advance science, can they be applied to practical policy areas of community?

ISSUES OF SYNTHESIS

All of the frameworks, distinguished by slightly different historical backgrounds, are useful for studying and understanding communities, but each also has limitations — emphasizing certain aspects of a place and omitting others. Can we put these varied perspectives together to give a complete, whole vision of the community? Are the perspectives like the blind men examining the elephant, each feeling a different part and generalizing to the whole? Since each framework emphasizes a different part of the model (like the parts of the elephant), let us compare the parts across the elements and then, finally, the whole, to see whether any synthesizing is possible.

Metaphors

Several of the frameworks model themselves after scientific disciplines. Human ecology and functionalism use biological metaphors, from groupings of organisms to one organism. Conflict and network-exchange metaphors are chosen from applied disciplines of economics and electronics, with a marketplace image appropriate to both of them. Social psychologists alone are indebted to artistic images with their emphasis on symbols. It would be difficult and would take many leaps of imagination to combine the metaphors into one, although human-ecology and structural-functionalist images are very close, and human ecology, conflict, and network-exchange approaches are directly tied to economics.

Methods

The metaphor leads to formulation of questions, which are answered by a variety of techniques and analysis. All the frameworks tend to be eclectic in their techniques and use a variety of strategies. All but human ecologists have used participant observation, and all have interviewed to gather data. While historical data are essential to conflict theory, they are downplayed by some. Human ecologists use census data extensively. Conflict theorists, functionalists, and network-exchange analysts also utilize survey data and other statistics, such as rates of production. Experiments have no role in community studies. The eclectics make the data-gathering techniques of the frameworks nearly synthesizable, except that they are being used to answer different questions and therefore the analyses diverge.

The analyses and questions reflect the particular emphases of each orientation, which focus on certain aspects of community while other aspects remain in a dim background. Human ecology focuses on aggregates in competition and symbiosis; functionalism on local institutions integrated by shared norms and values; conflict theorists on divisions; social psychologists on interacting, meaning-giving individuals; and network-exchange analysts on the nature of ties among people and exchanges within them. Trying to answer all these questions simultaneously in one study seems an impossible goal.

People

For all the frameworks, people are central to communities, but what aspect of people is most important differs greatly. Human ecologists, functionalists, and conflict theorists prefer large aggregates of people, while social psychologists focus in depth on fewer people. Network-exchange theorists seem capable of dealing with small and large numbers of people.

Institutions

People organize some institutions in almost all communities — to work, consume, worship, learn, govern, and so on — but this structure of activities is far more important to functionalists than it is to others. Conflict theorists focus on the political economy, but to them it is a worldwide system rather than differentiated organizations. Human ecologists, social psychologists, and network analysts all minimize the importance of local institutions.

Stratification

Communities range from a minimum of hierarchies to widely ranging pyramids to turn taking by interest groups. All the frameworks, with the exception of some social psychologists, include community stratification, but they differ on their interpretation of it. Stratification holds the most significance for conflict theorists, as class struggles are the major dynamics of communities. Human ecologists see stratification as a primordial, subsocial force of dominance by some populations or locations. Functionalists interpret stratification as a necessary, integrative mechanism of allocating rewards. In contrast, conflict theorists criticize the exploitive nature of stratification and seek to change stratification toward greater equality. Network-exchange theorists find stratification neither beneficial nor detrimental, but seek to understand how it works through coalition building.

Interactions

Interactions primarily have a micro-level, face-to-face connotation and, as such, they are most important to social psychologists and to network exchange. Human ecologists consider a subsocial, indirect mutual influence and for functionalists the norms of roles govern interaction. For conflict theorists, micro interactions are less important because they tend to be blurred by ideology. Network analysts examine the form of interactions and specific exchange contents.

Time

All communities change, but which part and how much of the change is noticed varies. For some, a long-term change may be more important than a short-term change.

History

The role of history varies from a long, gradual process defined by functionalists, to more abrupt or cyclic changes from conflict theorists and human ecologists, to very little consideration of history by some social psychologists and network analysts. Functionalists and human ecologists are reconciled when they both consider evolution and adaptation, but these natural processes would be very difficult to combine with the class struggles of conflict change.

Process

Conflict theorists' ideas that communities are constantly in conflict is the opposite of functionalists' view that communities are integrated by consensus. The competition of human ecology comes somewhat between those two. For social psychologists and network analysts, processual change is more a micro process of giving meaning and activating networks.

Space

Territory

Space includes physical surroundings and boundaries. Space and the environment constitute a major community component for human ecologists. Social psychologists examine how residents use their surroundings to socially construct images and symbols of community. For functionalists, the surroundings are just a backdrop and for conflict theorists, they are scarce resources to be fought for. Network analysts argue that space is not necessary for communities, since people can be tied to one another across long distances.

Boundaries

Space is bounded by several limits, depending on the orientation: values for functionalists, economics in conflict theory, physical boundaries and a kind of economic interdependence for human ecologists, and the attention of individual residents for social psychologists. Networks are unbounded and have to be closed by the researchers' aims, a particular number of people, or a particular content area.

Overview of Synthesis

Each framework focuses on a different aspect of each dimension, emphasizing some things and leaving out others. While in some cases syntheses are possible, in other cases the ideas so oppose one another that there seems no way to unite them. We can consider how each framework may fare with the other frameworks.

Human ecology is sometimes thought to be a component of functionalism; their metaphors, use of evolution and adaptation, make them compatible (see Saunders 1981). To the extent, however, that functionalists examine communities in a static way and human ecologists dismiss values and norms, they do not belong together.

Human ecologists and conflict theorists share economic interests, but the analysis and political-economy interests of conflict theory contrast sharply with human ecologists' (like Hawley's) doubt of the existence of stratification in American communities. The idea of the Chicago School has often linked human ecology with symbolic interaction, but the Chicago School seems to dichotomize into studies of either the group dynamics or the aggregate statistics. Suttles (1968) attempts to combine both in his study of the Addams area of Chicago, yet he is best at delineating micro interactions and differences in body language and clearly falls into the social-psychological side. Fischer (1977; 1982) attempts to combine human ecology and network analysis by examining networks in different places and different kinds of communities. The combination makes a contribution to network theory, but focuses less on human ecology issues.

Merton (1949) argues that conflict and functionalism are two sides of the same coin, although it is difficult to see how all parts of a society simultaneously contribute to conflict and change and to order and stability (Dahrendorf 1973). Symbolic interaction and functionalism are sometimes considered part of the same orientation. They both make extensive use of the concept of role, and both seem to agree that consensus holds society together, but interpretations of roles range from mechanical control of the person to something to be manipulated. Social psychologists examine how consensus comes about and the ephemeral nature of it, both of which functionalists omit. Conflict theory, social-psychological approaches, and network-exchange analysis all criticize functionalism and claim to be alternatives to it.

Although some conflict theorists claim to bridge macro and micro considerations with their examination of alienation, for example, their approach contrasts with considering interactions, negotiations, and meanings to actors. The difficulty conflict theorists have in analyzing individuals also hinders joining with the power-status interests of network-exchange analysis.

A few studies, such as Bott's (1971) and Kapferer's (1969), have simultaneously analyzed the numbers of people known and their connection with how individuals define situations. More often, network analysts delineate statistics on the form of relationships and leave the content to symbolic interactionists.

In sum, the frameworks as a whole do not seem synthesizable with one another, except in some areas. Communities, then, must be examined with particular questions in mind. Practical application of community frameworks are also forced to focus on specific interpretations of community.

IMPLICATIONS FOR PRACTICAL POLICIES

This section considers applied fields that utilize community frameworks. A background in community theories is essential for professionals in these fields to understand communities and particularly to define community problems. The frameworks vary not only on what are community problems but also on what causes them, and this has implications for whether insiders or outsiders, professionals or lay persons must be instigators of change. Applications take the theories one more step in their attempts to create change.

Leaving out more specialized areas, the focus is on community planning and community organizing as they have been practiced in the United States; issues of development or underdevelopment, as they apply to Third World countries, are omitted from the discussion. This brief presentation forces a more general approach, which glosses over many of the nuances in community applications. With these qualifications, the argument is that urban planning has been based on a human-ecology foundation and community action on a structural-functional base. Conflict theorists criticize urban planning and community action programs and suggest social movements to shake the foundations of systems that go beyond local units. As of now, social psychologists and network-exchange analysts have had little to say about community policies.

Urban Planning and Human Ecology

Urban planning corresponds to human ecologists' interest in space and resources. Further, the history of urban planning closely follows that of human ecology.

Theoretically, the classical human-ecology approach implies that urban processes are natural, subsocial, and need no intervention. On the other hand, the human-ecology connotation that space influences behavior intimates that changing space can change behavior. This has been the basic assumption of urban planning.

Although some kind of planning has been seen in every city throughout history, urban planning as a discipline and as a profession associated with local governments did not begin until the twentieth century. Before that, a laissez-faire attitude prevailed to let cities grow and develop naturally. The impetus for urban planning came from military strategies (Madge 1968), while Gans argues that the deterioration through aging of cities stimulated reforms (1968). These reforms led to architects' City Beautiful Movement in the 1890s, which brought parks and other amenities to cities. In 1909 the first National Planning Conference was held, followed by the American City Planning Institute in 1917 and specialized training at Harvard (Reps 1965).

According to Gans (1968), the first planners were architects and engineers. While early planners were concerned with streets and patterns of open space, the institutionalization of planning accompanied more interest in housing and vertical space (Reps 1965). Early engineers helped lay out towns for the benefit of land speculators and contractors (Gans 1968).

The assumption of planners has been that changing space can solve problems. For example, Rodwin (1960) defines the city planner as the diagnostician and advisor on the physical environment of the city. The problems have been defined especially in terms of slums and poor housing. To get rid of slums, urban planners tore them down for urban renewal. Inner-city neighborhoods were replaced with high-rises, often for wealthy residents or new commercial or industrial areas. The federal government aided local planners from 1949 through the 1980s by the Housing Act, Urban Renewal, and the Model Cities programs. Sometimes entire new communities were planned, such as Greenbelt, Maryland, or Forest Park, Ohio (cf. Miller 1981 for a detailed study of the planning of one community).

After developing a master plan — often a five-year plan, based on population projections — the urban planner uses the major tactics of zoning and eminent domain, both of which occur through political processes; the dominant species influences weaker groups. Zoning regulates land use and requirements in housing, while the power of eminent domain can condemn land to be converted for use as policy makers see fit.

Just as later human ecologists gave more importance to resources than to space use, so urban planners have evolved beyond a physical determinist view to see that the problems of slums are broader than housing. This kind of urban planning adopts a systems approach and overlaps with community action. Gans's (1968) definition of planning, based on assessing and coordinating means and ends, reflects a functionalist approach.

Social Action and Functionalism

The community as a system that can act and that consists of subsystems — mainly institutions — describes urban-planning and social work approaches to community, based on a functionalist foundation. In this perspective, communities change to greater horizontal integration (Roland Warren 1978) and to reforming the flows through the system. Various system goals have specific intervention tactics.

I take the concept of community action primarily from Roland Warren's (1978) discussion, although the phrase has been used in other ways. Community-action theory (for example, Sutton and Kolaja 1960) consists of attempts to distinguish community phenomena from noncommunity phenomena. Sutton and Kolaja find three distinguishing features of community action: it involves problems related to the locality where people live; community actions have an impact on most of the people who live there; most people of the locality participate in some action. Poplin (1979, p. 256) defines community action as "voluntary efforts of local citizens to achieve a goal" and includes Alinsky (1969) as an example. It will be argued here that Alinsky belongs with conflict approaches.

Warren's idea of community action is sometimes called community organizing, which Ross (1967) defines as adjusting welfare resources and needs. According to Warren, historically communities have changed toward stronger vertical ties and weaker horizontal ties. Change agents need to coordinate task performance of units that have their separate goals. Warren conceives of the action system as an additional system that arises ad hoc for meeting particular needs.

Braeger and Sprecht (1973) use community organizing as a broad term to encompass means of dealing with organizations, while social action is a more specialized term for a way for groups to change power distribution. They describe three historical periods of social-welfare policies. The whole process of developing specific helping institutions began with philanthropy on the part of both wealthy individuals and charitable organizations, particularly churches. From 1900 to 1930, community welfare councils and agencies developed that were based on private philanthropy. Beginning in the 1930s, with federal policies to help during the national depression, welfare agencies became part of the public domain and developed bureaucratic and technical approaches to solving community problems. After 1950, a participatory approach of getting the needy to do things for themselves was advocated.

Roland Warren (1978) develops a number of strategies and tactics for bringing about change. He first analyzes the general process of change a system experiences, starting with a given environment that has dysfunctions but also has patterns that can be used for action. Second, the action itself is initiated through a definition of goals. Third, the action expands by flowing through the system until, fourth, the action system is completely in operation. Finally, the system is transformed and the action system no longer needed.

The specific tactics for change depend on the goals. Regardless of goals, Braeger and Sprecht suggest that change agents must first develop constituencies through socialization, building primary groups and organizations. They also discuss problems in dealing with sponsors and issues of control of resources. Actual tactics are taken from Warren (1965) who lists four goals, four responses, and four modes of intervention. The last two goals, responses, and interventions overlap with a conflict approach.

The first goal, adjusting and rearranging resources, has the response of consensus and a collaborative mode of intervention. For example, funding from one source is transferred to another source through mutual agreement. Second, a goal of redistribution of resources meets with responses of difference in campaign tactics, such as political maneuvering, bargaining, and negotiation. Third, contest or disruption is used for the goal of changing status relations and this response is dissensus. Finally, a reconstruction of the whole system includes the intervention of violence and a response of insurrection. Warren notes problems with change in that institutions created for change may develop their own separate goals. This goal displacement is overcome by focusing on the horizontal integration.

Many people have criticized urban renewal and community action projects both from nonconflict and from conflict viewpoints. For example, conservatives believe that these projects have been a waste of taxpayers' money, and liberals, like Jane Jacobs (1961), believe they destroy the diversity in cities. The radical view is that these projects have been merely reforms, which have not gone far enough in changing the system and have not altered class positions. Castells cites the damage done in destroying housing for the poor without adequately replacing it (1977).

Community Social Movements and Conflict Theory

Urban racial riots of the 1960s and earlier were unexpected and inexplicable by functionalism. Conflict theory came in vogue because it could explain the violent social change, which began with the movement for black power and spread to other powerless groups. Conflict theory also explains why policies developed to cope with these movements have not alleviated the problems that contributed to the violent outbreaks.

According to Castells (1977), social movements form a dialectic with public policies such as urban renewal. Ideally, social movements influence the social structure to change the mode of production and property arrangements as well as power relations. Social movements form organizations that crystallize social practices. The organization engages in intervention (political, economic, and ideological) and confrontation, with a host of tactics including petitions, demonstrations, and marches. Castells cites examples of social movements in response to urban renewal and housing problems where residents refuse to move. The problem with many urban social movements is that they become too specialized, rather than forming a broader base to radically change the entire system.

Alinsky (1969) demonstrates the need for residents themselves to become aware of their own problems and engage in action that gives power to the people. He views democracy as confrontation and says that any organization must be a people's organization based on conflict. As with Castells, for Alinsky the conclusion is in the streets.

Social-Psychology and Network Approaches

Social-psychology and network-exchange approaches to community are both in their infancy and as yet have no extensive schemes for community change.

Many aspects of social psychology feed into larger schemes. For example, Braeger and Sprecht (1973) mention promoting primary groups in initiating community action, and Warren cites the importance of symbols. Kevin Lynch (1960) studied the "image-ability" of cities, to be able to plan for cities better. Some people have attempted to change residents' attitudes — for example, Cummings and Cummings's project to change attitudes toward mental illness (1957).

Fischer (1982) in his recent book on networks discusses the policy implications of helping people decide where to move and helping them establish new networks. Social-work courses and policies are beginning to devise strategies for people to develop support networks (see Collins and Pancoast 1976; Gottlieb 1981).

Rural-Urban Comparisons

Urban renewal had an impact on cities' housing problems, even though, according to Castells (1977), in the United States 64 percent of deteriorated housing is outside the metropolitan area and 60 percent of deteriorated housing is in rural areas. Rural planners may face demographic situations and attempts to control populations, improve jobs, and protect the environment. Sometimes rural areas cope with economic retrenchment through tourism.

Others, like Zenda, dislike the tourism around their locality (Carlson, Lassey, and Lassey 1981). Lincoln Park has been much involved with urban renewal and through zoning changes has created an almost complete change in housing and the kinds of people who live there. Specialized professionals who work for the city and the community, as well as lay task forces seeking historical preservation, safety, and community improvement, characterize the Lincoln Park planning situation. In Zenda plans have been part of the township government, such as obtaining revenue sharing and controlling the pollution of the lake, but these have been minimal and have not affected much of the community.

In Lincoln Park community action is more visible. Specialized professionals from the city welfare agency, with an office on Lincoln Avenue, form a subsystem of the city. Although county agents work near Zenda, no one in Zenda has been in need of agency welfare. In poorer rural areas, such as Appalachia, community action would have a stronger need. Zenda residents, as in many rural areas, share a philosophy of taking care of themselves without the need of professionals or outsiders.

In both the rural and urban locality, community movements have been strong. Zenda has attempted to prevent change in the form of development or nonagricultural enterprises. Lincoln Park has encouraged social movements for change toward middle- and upper-class housing in spite of other social movements in the 1960s to do more for the poor. Both communities engage in confrontation, although in general their tactics have been attempts to negotiate with authorities rather than violence or threats. Both communities also fight developers to keep the community as they want it. Social movements in both Lincoln Park and Zenda have tended to be preservative rather than change-producing.

To conclude, while the five approaches may not be scientific theories, they nevertheless have proved useful for understanding various concepts about communities, for understanding the varied facets of the particular communities of Zenda and Lincoln Park, and for applied fields.

Appendixes

APPENDIX A
1970 Census Data on Linn Township and Lincoln Park*

TABLE A.1
Age Distributions
(percent)

Age	Lincoln Park	Linn Township
−5	5.9	7.8
5-9	5.4	8.4
10-14	5.1	11.0
15-19	4.8	9.7
20-24	12.8	5.1
25-34	21.9	11.0
35-44	11.4	12.0
45-54	9.9	12.5
55-59	4.9	4.5
60+	17.9	18.0

TABLE A.2
Year Moved to Area
(percent)

Year	Linn Township	Lincoln Park
1968-70	42.0	50.9
1965-67	15.0	18.7
1960-64	17.0	12.3
1950-59	11.0	9.1
1949 or earlier	15.0	9.2

*1980 Census data was not available.

275

TABLE A.3
Occupations

| Occupation | Linn Township | | | | | | Lincoln Park |
| | Males | | Females | | Total | | Males |
	Number	Percent	Number	Percent	Number	Percent	Percent
Professional, technical	44	8.7	23	10.5	67	9.25	31.1
Managers, administrators, except farm	75	14.9	23	10.5	98	13.50	8.7
Sales workers	12	2.4	6	2.7	18	2.49	6.9
Clerical	19	3.8	35	16	54	7.50	23.6
Craftsmen, foremen	68	13.5	0	0	68	9.40	7.1
Operatives	30	6	32	14.6	62	8.60	9.8

Transport equipment operatives	5	0.9	7	3.2	12	1.66	2.4
Labor	59	11.7	0	0	59	8.20	
Farmers and farm managers	41	8.1	0	0	41	5.70	
Farm laborers and foremen	61	12.0	13	6	74	10.20	
Service workers	33	6.5	42	19.2	75	10.40	10.4
Private household workers	6	1.2	28	12.8	34	4.70	0.6
Occupation not reported	52	10.3	10	4.6	62	8.60	
Total	505	100.0	219	100.0	724	100.0	

TABLE A.4
Nonwhite Populations in Lincoln Park

Year	Black		Other	
	Number	*Percent*	*Number*	*Percent*
1930	143	0.1		
1940	132	0.1	130	0.1
1950	205	0.2	1,648	1.6
1960	1,358	1.5	2,874	3.2
1970	4,904	7.2[a]	3,141	4.6[b]

[a]Linn Township: 0.1 percent
[b]Linn Township: 0.41 percent

APPENDIX B

Selected Autobiographies

These four autobiographies, of a woman and man from each community, are not randomly chosen; active community participants were selected, who could reveal the most about Zenda and Lincoln Park. The two from Lincoln Park are the oldest and longest-term residents interviewed. The Zenda woman is somewhat atypical in that she and her family took over the family farm, but she has a long family history in Zenda, as does the Zenda man, one of the most respected persons in the area. I have edited the biographies and removed names from them.

Zenda Woman

My grandfather came here from Cleveland, Ohio. His father was from England and his mother from France. He lived to be almost 95, and he was sharp even though he just had a third-grade education. He read a lot. He came here by train with my grandmother who was also from Ohio, dealt in cattle a number of years, and then eased out as he set up his three sons in farming. They had five children around the turn of the century, and my grandmother died when the children were very young. Grandfather bought this farm for my dad. My mother has lived here since she was seven years old and now she's 75. My aunt lives down the road and I have several cousins in Hebron and this area. I have two sisters, one in another state, and one with a prominent position in a nearby town.

I was born in 1928 in the house across the road from the grammar school that I attended for eight years. It was small; only three of

279

us graduated from eighth grade together. I was never real active in 4-H or any activities. Mother didn't drive and Daddy was always working. Our childhood seemed so vividly uncomplicated. We didn't do a whole lot outside of the things we did together as a family.

I went to Lake Geneva for high school. When I was of high-school age, the districts in the area weren't divided like they are now. We could go where we wanted to go. We all went to Lake Geneva, and my cousins down the road went to Hebron. I got a ride to school with one of the neighbor boys, and then as we got more involved in extracurricular things at high school, it got to be a real hassle to participate, so I lived in town with a minister and his wife for my senior year, a beautiful Scottish family that spoke with a brogue, and they were so dear. Their daughter and I were the best of friends.

When I graduated from high school, I worked in Hebron and then got married. I met my husband through a friend I worked with, and we corresponded while he was in the service. We lived in another town for about a year and a half, but he had always wanted to farm, so when I was expecting, my dad, who of course didn't have any sons, was just thrilled when his son-in-law wanted to farm, so they asked us to come here and farm, and at that particular time, Daddy was set up very beautifully. He had a hired man in this house where we're living now, and we lived with my folks for a year, because my husband never really farmed on his own, and he was learning how. The first of March, we moved over to a farm on the state line, and then just a few months after we had moved, and everything was going well, my dad got caught in the hay bailer, and he had his arm crushed, and it was real bad. Of course, all the work from the farms, then, with Daddy being in the hospital, fell on the back of the hired man. He kind of put the pressure on Dad for more wages than he could afford to pay, so Dad had a sale and sold all his cattle here with the exception of the young stock. Then we moved here and took over the farms. Daddy struggled for a couple more years in and out of the hospital, then he developed intestinal problems, and passed away. He was only 51 when he died, and of course, was most happy that we were here to take over the farms that he so dearly loved.

We have two daughters and a son (born around the 1950s). They all live in Wisconsin. Our son is studying agriculture and he sounds more like he's going to come home and continue on.

We were real active in the church for all the years we raised our family. Then I was also involved with the Garden Club for about eight years, including being an officer, but I had to quit because I was really too involved with schools and church. We've both been enthusiastic bowlers. My husband is a fireman, and we've served on the school board. I've been driving the school bus; this is my ninth year.

On the farm, I've never helped out as far as milking is concerned. Even though I've been born and raised on a farm, I'm not all that keen on the animals, but I help out in the fields in the spring. In fact, I helped put in all our crops this year. I drove one of the big tractors through the planting and haying season. When the children were younger, we always had a single man that lived with us. Then when we've been alone, I've always helped out with milkhouse chores.

We feel the church is very important and also the family, and we have a nice, close friendship with four of us couples that do many things together. We've vacationed together, and over the years we've shared good times and bad times. I guess that's what makes friends close. I certainly don't mean that they're our only friends, but we're all in the same church groups.

Lincoln Park Woman

I first lived on the near north side when I came from Indiana to Chicago to go to art school. I came to Lincoln Park in 1948. Before that, my husband and I had lived closer to the Loop, but the building was going to be torn down.

When I knew the building was going to be torn down, I said, "there's an area [Lincoln Park] I'd like to explore. I like the restaurants there and the iron railings, and the foreign look on houses. Let's go look there." We found three buildings joined, and we were going to do them over until we faced the facts of life. We couldn't get a bank loan because west of Lincoln Avenue was run down, and the banks refused to fund us. We showed them the hospitals and the need for housing, but we couldn't move a mortgage. We found out the price to rehabilitate a small backyard and decided it was a lost cause. Some friends wanted to buy with us. Three couples were going to buy a place because in those days, if you rented out, you didn't get much. This area was respectable, but dowdy, and lots of people found houses had lots to offer. Then we heard about this place and got it just in time. Our friends helped us get settled, and they bought a double house on Fullerton.

After art school, I worked free-lance, had a studio in the Loop, did a lot of work for Marshall Fields, drawing fashions for newspapers. That was in the mid 1930s and the depression was still hanging around. My husband (now dead) was connected with the direct-mail business and wrote promotional things.

This house was once a servants' quarters for some people on Fullerton. One woman lived here in the 1880s and had a house of ill repute on Dearborn.

When we got here, LPCA was just starting. We got a memo about it and felt we should go. My husband was secretary of LPCA for a while. When we first moved here, we didn't know people in the neighborhood until we went to LPCA meetings. There were only about 10 of us at first. A lot of people resented us and said we were trying to get rid of them; it became true because taxes and property values went up.

We're having our 19th annual antique fair. Before that, we had get-togethers. We called it a Petunia Day and had a street fair. My husband said he liked antiques, and ever since it has been an antiques fair.

I helped get petitions to have a branch library built here. Now I help tutor English as a second language for some people (Spanish-speaking) who live west of Lincoln Avenue. They couldn't afford to live on this side of Lincoln because the rents are too high. I have lots of friends in the neighborhood and around the corner. The man across the street is in the Chicago Symphony. I used to belong to the Home Fashion Group when I had my studio downtown. I belong to a church group, although I don't go to church. I'm in the exercising and literature groups.

The city pays attention to us because we're a strong community. The police are very helpful, and when we had rats, the alderman came. We have good garbage collection. The only trouble with the area is these hospitals want all the space they can get.

Lincoln Park Man

My family history goes back to Saxonia and Bohemia. My parents became Swiss, and I had six uncles in the hotel business all over Europe. I was born in Zurich, Switzerland, in 1901. I graduated from a famous school of arts and crafts in Switzerland and had four years of practical training at the art institute there, the oldest printing firm that dates back to the fifteenth century. After that, I had some practical experiences in various Swiss towns. In 1922, I wanted to perfect my English for working purposes in publishing; so I came to Indiana where my brother had migrated. Then I came to Chicago to study with a printing school and took the four-year course in two years. I worked in different plants and also taught printing.

Part of the reason why I became interested in the preservation of buildings and neighborhoods was because after the end of World War I, there was a trend in Europe to tear down old cities, not only in Switzerland, and people organized against the bulldozer and by popular movement, they stopped it and retained the old cities. They said, "Why would Americans want to come to Europe and use the hotels if there are no old buildings?"

I helped with the Chicago Fair of 1933, the Century of Progress. I was with a printing firm almost 20 years before starting my own organization in graphics design which keeps me very busy, and I travel around the world giving workshops and lectures.

When I first came to Chicago, I lived with some people on the north side until I married and lived in Evanston. My first wife died young and my second wife was involved in theater. We got into preservation because she was always interested in a house in Lincoln Park, a three-story house built just after the Chicago fire by a physician from Germany who wanted to be a brewer and came here where there were several breweries. The area at that time was called Cabbage Gardens. The owner raised several thousand dollars to contribute to Chicago planning. My wife had lived in the coach house there. As a wedding gift, we decided to buy the estate.

At about the same time that we bought the house, the Old Town Triangle Association was formed by a group of neighbors, not just to preserve the declining, near-slum neighborhood but also to begin rehabilitation of old buildings. Our motive in buying our house was to preserve it, and we still spend huge amounts to preserve it. The association put in two or three years of concentrated revitalization and improvement of homes, streets, planting trees. We fought the bulldozers. The foundation of Old Town goes back to the beginning of the National Trust for Historic Preservation. One of the by-products of the Old Town Triangle Association was the beginning of the art fair, primarily to raise funds for improvement of the community, not only physical, but we also support Menominee Club which takes care of youngsters from broken homes or whose parents work, and we put a lot of money into local schools to build a library or study center. My third wife got very interested in the landmark movement and got together with neighbors to get land-mark designation for Old Town.

Meanwhile, we wanted to form an organization that would include more than one neighborhood, because we were so small that we couldn't stop the decline of surrounding neighborhoods, so about 20 of us in 1954 formed the Lincoln Park Conservation Association. By that time, we had gotten enough results with the improvement of one or two neighborhoods so that we formed LPCA with the first president, the son of the city architect. We had several influential cornerstones of the Chicago Historical Society, McCormick Seminary, DePaul, and several historical churches which were well-established institutions and at that time, strong supports of the concept of neighborhood preservation.

We're the only old-timers left because so many young people from affluent suburbs began to move into the city and take over the conservation idea. I'm not really close to any people outside of my family (one son) because my work keeps me so busy. We have a summer home in Wisconsin.

Zenda Man

My grandfather brought the whole family from Germany when my dad was 14 years old. He first came to Hebron where he worked for a farmer. Sons had to go into the army in Germany, and that's why they left. Grandfather died shortly after they arrived here, and the three boys had to take care of grandmother and them-selves. Each bought a farm, and all of them farmed around here. Dad bought this farm from someone else. My mother's family moved here from Chicago to farm when she was about 20, and she married my father shortly after. I have two brothers and two sisters; all of them live in towns near here.

I was born in this house in 1903. The neighbor and I were born the same day within half an hour apart and had the same doctor.

They said the doctor was running back and forth. They used to thresh with steam threshers, and they were threshing across the street at that time. Just as soon as they knew that either one of us babies were born, they started blowing that old steam whistle.

For school, I went two years down the road here. It was a one-room school with double seats. Two people sat together in the same seat. It had a woodshed out back where they kept the wood to build a fire with. There used to be a house across the street. That's where we went to get our drinking water. Always two kids went to get the water, and if they wanted to take a long time, they went to the furthest house. Then third grade, that school closed, and I started at the Zenda School. I went through the ninth grade in Zenda, and that's as far as I ever got. My dad was sick and we rented out the farm and moved to the village for two years when I was ten years old.

We belonged to the first 4-H, or it was the Boys' and Girls' Club, they called it. It turned out to be the first 4-H in the state. At that time, the state would send out a little bag of corn, probably enough to plant half an acre, or something like that. We all learned about corn and planting.

I used to take the horse and wagon and take the milk to the village when I went to school mornings. I'd put the horse in the barn that we rented just this way from the church. Everyone of the houses had barns at that time. That way I could haul the milk to the factory and haul the kids to school at the same time.

I had to milk cows ever since I was 12 years old. I had to help with the milking and help with the chores nights and mornings. Summertimes when school was out, we had to be out with the rest of them. As soon as you were big enough, why you got out and worked. There was no law that you couldn't work until you were 16 at that time.

I worked for my dad until I got married in 1923. My wife and I have known each other all our lives because our parents both went to the church. First we rented a farm and then another until we bought this farm from my dad, and he moved to the village. We have five children born around the 1930s, and they all live around here. My daughter lives next door. She has seven kids and most of them live nearby. My son farms down the road, and he has several children now starting to take over farming.

After the milk factory in Zenda closed, around 1930, we hauled milk to Hebron, but then we switched over and went to Lake Geneva.

They had a higher grade of milk so that they paid a special premium for it. If you kept the bacteria down and cooled it to a certain temperature, you could get up to 40¢ more a 100 pounds. That made quite a difference in those times. We hauled milk there until the plant closed, and then we went to Woodstock. Then somewhere in the 1950s we put in the bulk tank, and the truck picks it up.

We used to get together with the neighbors to do threshing, silo filling, shredding; all of that was done with a bunch of neighbors getting together. Since the combines came, around the 1940s, our threshing ring broke up.

Now this is how I spend my days. I get up at 3:30 in the morning, have a glass of milk and a couple of cookies and go out and start the morning chores, get ready to milk, feed the cows, get the milking stuff ready. I try to be in the barn by 4 usually and try to start milking by 5, get the cows fed and everything. It takes us an hour and a half to milk. Right now we're milking 40 cows. When we get up to 48, which is as much room as we've got, it probably takes an hour and three quarters, or two hours. I have a high-school girl who helps with the milking. She comes at 5. She washes up the pails, milkhouse stuff and cleans up all that, feeds the calves, and then she goes home and goes to school. I clean the barn, haul out the manure and then I come down and have breakfast, probably about 8:30. Around 9 o'clock, I go out and do the rest of the chores, turn the cows out, feed them, bed them, get them back in and scrape up the floors and everything. That takes me 3 to 4 hours. Then by that time, I have lunch. Then whatever. If I have extra work to do or if I have to go for repairs, or sometimes just lay around until 3:30 and start chores again. We try to be through — we feed and milk and wash up again — by 6:30. In summertime, the schedule is pretty much the same, only we've got to crowd in some fieldwork in between. There's a man who works in the shop in town and in summers, he'll work on weekends and evenings sometimes.

Evenings, I may have church meetings. Sunday morning at church we see a few people, but we don't see people like we used to. Outside of church, there's the fair once a year maybe and the church auction. I don't belong to any other organizations.

Bibliography

Abu-Lughod, Janet. 1969. "Testing the Theory of Social Area Analysis: The Ecology of Cairo, Egypt." *American Sociological Review* 26: 393-98.
——— . 1971. *Cairo: 1001 Years of the City Victorious.* Princeton, N. J.: Princeton University Press.
Aldrich, Howard. 1975. "Ecological Succession in Racially Changing Neighborhoods: A Review of the Literature." *Urban Affairs Quarterly* 10: 327-48.
Alihan, Milla. 1938. *Social Ecology: A Critical Analysis.* New York: Columbia University Press.
Alinsky, Saul. 1969. *Reveille for Radicals.* New York: Vintage.
Allport, Gordon. 1968. "The Historical Background of Modern Social Psychology." In *The Handbook of Social Psychology, Volume 1*, edited by Gardner Lindzey and Elliot Aronson, pp. 3-56. Reading, Mass.: Addison-Wesley.
Anderson, David. 1971. "Cemeteries." *Chicago Sun Times*, February 4, p. 62.
Anderson, Elijah. 1978. *A Place on the Corner: Identity and Rank Among Black Street Corner Men.* Chicago: University of Chicago Press.
Anderson, Nels. 1923. *The Hobo.* Chicago: University of Chicago Press.
Arensberg, Conrad. 1955. "American Communities." *American Anthropologist* 57: 1143-62.
Ashton, Patrick. 1978. "The Political Economy of Suburban Development." In *Marxism and the Metropolis*, edited by William Tabb and Larry Sawers, pp. 64-89. New York: Oxford University Press.
Barnes, John. 1954. "Class and Committees in a Norwegian Island Parish." *Human Relations* 7: 39-58.
——— . 1972. "Social Networks." Addison-Wesley Modular Publication 26: 1-29.
Barry, David, and Plant, Thomas. 1978. "Retaining Agricultural Activities under Urban Pressures: A Review of Land Use Conflicts and Policies." *Policy Sciences* 9: 153-78.
Bates, Frederick, and Bacon, Lloyd. 1972. "The Community as a Social System." *Social Forces* 50: 371-79.
Becker, Howard. 1963. *Outsiders.* New York: Free Press.
Bell, Colin, and Newby, Howard. 1974. *Community Studies: An Introduction to the Sociology of the Local Community.* New York: Praeger.
Bell, Wendell. 1953. "The Social Areas of the San Francisco Bay Region." *American Sociological Review 18: 39-57.*
Berger, Bennett. 1960. *Working Class Suburb.* Berkeley: University of California Press.
Berger, Joseph; Zelditch, Morris; Anderson, Bo; and Cohen, Bernard. 1972. "Structural Aspects of Distributive Justice: A Status-Value Formulation."

In *Sociological Theories in Progress*, vol. 2, edited by Joseph Berger, Morris Zelditch, and Bo Anderson, pp. 119-46. Boston: Houghton-Mifflin.

Berger, Peter, and Luckmann, Thomas. 1966. *The Social Construction of Reality*. Garden City, N. Y.: Anchor Books.

Bernard, Jessie. 1973. *The Sociology of Community*. Glenview, Ill.: Scott, Foresman.

Berry, Brian, and Kasarda, John. 1977. *Contemporary Ecology*. New York: Macmillan.

Blalock, Hubert. 1972. *Social Statistics*. New York: McGraw-Hill.

Blau, Peter. 1964. *Exchange and Power in Social Life*. New York: Wiley.

———. 1971. "Justice in Social Exchange." In *Institutions and Social Exchange*, edited by Herman Turk and Richard Simpson, pp. 56-68. Indianapolis: Bobbs-Merrill.

Blok, Anton. 1973. "Coalitions in Sicilian Peasant Society." In *Network Analysis*, edited by Jeremy Boissevain and J. Clyde Mitchell, pp. 151-66. The Hague: Mouton.

Blumer, Herbert. 1969. *Symbolic Interactionism*. Englewood Cliffs, N. J.: Prentice-Hall.

Bogue, Donald. 1949. *The Structure of the Metropolitan Community*. Ann Arbor: University of Michigan Press.

Boissevain, Jeremy. 1973. "An Exploration of Two First-Order Zones." In *Network Analysis*, edited by Jeremy Boissevain and J. Clyde Mitchell, pp. 125-49. The Hague: Mouton.

———. 1974. *Friends of Friends*. The Hague: Mouton.

Boswell, David. 1969. "Personal Crises and the Mobilization of the Social Network." In *Social Networks in Urban Situations*, edited by J. Clyde Mitchell, pp. 245-96. Manchester: University of Manchester Press.

Bott, Elizabeth. 1971. *Families and Social Networks*. 2d ed. New York: Free Press.

Bowles, Samuel, and Gintis, Herbert. 1976. *Schooling in Capitalist America*. New York: Basic Books.

Braeger, George, and Sprecht, Harry. 1973. *Community Organizing*. New York: Columbia University Press.

Brown, Richard H. 1977. *A Poetic For Sociology: Toward a Logic of Discovery for the Human Sciences*. Cambridge: Cambridge University Press.

Burgess, Ernest. 1925. "The Growth of the City." In *The City*, edited by Robert Park, Ernest Burgess, and Roderick McKenzie, pp. 47-62. Chicago: University of Chicago Press.

———. 1926. *The Urban Community*. Chicago: University of Chicago Press.

———. 1927. "The Determination of Gradients in the Growth of the City." *Publications of the American Sociological Society* 20: 178-84.

———. 1928. "Residential Segregation in American Cities." *Annals of the American Academy of Political and Social Sciences*, vol. 140: pp. 105-15.

Burt, Ronald. 1977. "Positions in Multiple Networks." *Social Forces* 56: 551-75.

———. 1980. "Models of Network Structure." *Annual Review of Sociology* 6: 79-141.

Carlson, John; Lassey, Marie; and Lassey, William. 1981. *Rural Society and Environment in America*. New York: McGraw-Hill.

Castells, Manuel. 1977. *The Urban Question: A Marxist Approach*, translated by Alan Sheridan. Cambridge, Mass.: M.I.T. Press.

Caulfield, Mina Davis. 1969. "Culture and Imperialism: Proposing a New Dialectic." In *Reinventing Anthropology*, edited by Del Hymes, pp. 182-212. New York: Random House.

Cavan, Ruth. 1928. *Suicide*. Chicago: University of Chicago Press.

Chicago Historical Company. 1882. *History of Walworth County, Wisconsin*. Chicago: Chicago Western Historical Company.

Clark, Terry. 1968. *Community Structure and Decision-Making: Comparative Analyses*. San Francisco: Chandler.

Clay, Phillip. 1979. "The Process of Black Suburbanization." *Urban Affairs Quarterly* 14: 405-24.

Clelland, Donald, and Form, William. 1964. "Economic Dominants and Community Power: A Comparative Analysis." *American Journal of Sociology* 69: 511-21.

Coleman, James. 1957. *Community Conflict*. Glencoe, Ill.: Free Press.

Collins, Michael, and Pancoast, Diane. 1976. *Natural Helping Networks: A Strategy for Prevention*. Washington, D.C.: National Association for Social Work.

Collins, Randall. 1975. *Conflict Sociology*. New York: Academic Press.

Commission on Chicago Historical and Architectural Landmarks. 1981. *Landmark Neighborhoods in Chicago*. Chicago: Commission on Chicago Historical and Architectural Landmarks.

Comte, Auguste. 1896. *The Positive Philosophy of Auguste Comte*, edited and translated by Harriet Martineau. London: Bell.

Cooley, Charles Horton. 1962. *Social Organization*. New York: Schoken.

———. 1964. *Human Nature and the Social Order*. New York: Schoken.

Cornue, Sarah, and Cornue, Daniel. 1848-58. Unpublished letters, furnished by Cornue family.

Coser, Lewis. 1956. *The Functions of Social Conflict*. Glencoe: Free Press.

Cottrell, Fred. 1951. "Death by Dieselization: A Case Study in the Reaction to Technological Change." *American Sociological Review* 16: 358-65.

Crain, Robert; Katz, Elihu; and Rosenthal, Donald. 1969. *The Politics of Community Conflict*. Indianapolis: Bobbs-Merrill.

Craven, Paul, and Wellman, Barry. 1974. "The Network City." In *The Community: Approaches and Applications*, edited by Marcia Pelly Effrat, pp. 57-88. New York: Free Press.

Cressey, Donald. 1932. *The Taxi Dance Hall*. Chicago: University of Chicago Press.

Cumbler, John. 1977. "The City and the Community: The Impact of Urban Forces on Working Class Behavior." *Journal of Urban History* 3: 427-42.

Cummings, Elaine, and Cummings, John. 1957. *Closed Ranks: An Experiment in Mental Health Education*. Cambridge, Mass.: Harvard University Press.

Dahl, Robert. 1961. *Who Governs?* New Haven, Conn.: Yale University Press.

Dahrendorf, Ralf. 1959. *Class and Class Conflict in Industrial Society*. Palo Alto, Cal.: Stanford University Press.

———. 1973. "Toward a Theory of Social Conflict." In *Social Change*, edited by E. Etzioni-Halevy and A. A. Etzioni, pp. 100-13. New York: Basic Books.

Darwin, Charles. 1859/1968. *The Origin of Species*. Baltimore, Md.: Penguin.

Davie, Maurice. 1937. "The Pattern of Urban Growth." In *Studies in the Science of Society*, edited by George Murdock. New Haven, Conn.: Yale University Press.

Davis, Allison; Gardner, B. B.; and Gardner, M. R. 1944. *Deep South*. Chicago: University of Chicago Press.

Davis, Kingsley. 1949. *Human Society*. New York: Macmillan.

Davis, Kingsley, and Moore, Wilbert. 1945. "Some Principles of Stratification." *American Sociological Review* 10: 242-49.

Dean, Lois. 1967. *Five Towns: A Comparative Community Study*. New York: Random House.

Denzin, Norman. 1969. "Symbolic Interaction and Ethnomethodology: A Proposed Synthesis." *American Journal of Sociology* 34: 922-34.

———. 1970. *The Research Act*. Chicago: Aldine.

Deseran, Forest. 1978. "Community Satisfaction as Definition of the Situation." *Rural Sociology* 43: 235-49.

———. 1980. "Community Development and Images of Influence Structures." *Journal of the Community Development Society* 11: 23-34.

Devlin, Ann. 1976. "The 'Small Town' Cognitive Map: Adjusting to a New Environment." In *Environmental Knowing*, edited by Gary Moore and Reginald Golledge, pp. 58-66. Stroudsburg, Pa.: Dowden, Hutchinson, and Ross.

Dewey, John. 1948. *Reconstruction in Philosophy*. Boston: Beacon Press.

Douglas, Jack. 1976. *Investigative Research*. Beverly Hills, Ca.: Sage.

Downs, R. M., and Stea, D., eds. 1973. *Image and Environment; Cognitive Mapping and Spatial Behavior*. Chicago: Aldine.

Ducey, Michael. 1977. *Sunday Morning: Aspects of Urban Ritual*. New York: Free Press.

Duncan, Otis Dudley. 1961. "From Social System to Ecosystem." *Sociological Inquiry* 31: 140-49.

———. 1964. "Social Organization and the EcoSystem." In *Handbook of Modern Sociology*, edited by Robert Faris, pp. 36-82. Chicago: Rand-McNally.

Duncan, Otis Dudley, and Duncan, Beverly. 1955. "Residential Distribution and Occupational Stratification." *American Journal of Sociology* 60: 493-503.

Duncan, Otis Dudley, et al. 1960. *Metropolis and Region*. Baltimore, Md.: Johns Hopkins University Press.

Durkheim, Emile. 1895/1950. *The Rules of Sociological Method*. New York: Free Press.

———. 1893/1964. *The Division of Labor in Society*. New York: Free Press.

———. 1912/1965. *The Elementary Forms of Religious Life*. New York: Free Press.

Dye, Thomas, and Garcia, John. 1978. "Structure, Function, and Policy in American Cities," *Urban Affairs Quarterly* 14: 103-22.

Effrat, Andrew. 1973. "Power to the Paradigms." *Sociological Inquiry* 33:3.

Effrat, Marcia Pelly. 1974. "Approaches to Community: Conflicts and Complementarities." In *The Community: Approaches and Applications*, edited by Marcia Pelly Effrat, pp. 1-32. New York: Free Press.

Emerson, Richard. 1972. "Exchange Theory, Part II: Exchange Relations and Network Structures." In *Sociological Theories in Progress*, vol. 2, edited by Joseph Berger, Morris Zelditch, and Bo Anderson, pp. 38-87. Boston: Houghton-Mifflin.

————. 1976. "Social Exchange Theory." *Annual Review of Sociology* 2: 335-62.

Engels, Friedrich. 1844/1958. *The Condition of the Working Class in England*, translated by W. O. Henderson and W. H. Chaloner. Palo Alto, Cal.: Stanford University Press.

Epstein, A. L. 1969. "Gossip, Norms, and Social Network." In *Social Networks in Urban Situations*, edited by J. Clyde Mitchell, pp. 117-28. Manchester: University of Manchester Press.

Ericksen, Eugene. 1979. "Work and Residence in Industrial Philadelphia." *Journal of Urban History* 5: 147-82.

Erikson, Kai. 1966. *The Wayward Puritans*. New York: Wiley.

————. 1976. *Everything in Its Path: Destruction of Community in the Buffalo Creek Flood*. New York: Simon and Schuster.

Everts, Baskin, and Stewart. 1873. *Combination Atlas Map, Walworth County, Wisconsin*. Chicago: Everts, Baskin, and Stewart.

Faris, Robert, and Dunham, H. Warren. 1939. *Mental Disorders in Urban Areas: An Ecological Study of Schizophrenia and Other Psychoses*. Chicago: University of Chicago Press.

Fava, Sylvia. 1968. "Ecological Patterns Reviewed." In *Urbanism in World Perspective*, edited by Sylvia Fava, pp. 145-53. New York: Crowell.

Fidel, Kenneth. 1973. "An Ecological Comparison of Lincoln Park and Selected North Suburban Areas." Paper presented at the Annual Meeting of the Illinois Sociological Association, Macomb, Illinois, November 1973.

Fiery, Walter. 1945. "Sentiment and Symbolism as Ecological Variables." *American Sociological Review* 10: 140-48.

Fischer, Claude. 1976. *The Urban Experience*. New York: Harcourt Brace.

————. 1978. "On the Marxist Challenge to Urban Sociology." *Comparative Urban Research* 6: 10-19.

————. 1981. "The Public and Private Worlds of City Life." *American Sociological Review* 46: 306-16.

————. 1982. *To Dwell Among Friends*. Chicago: University of Chicago Press.

Fischer, Claude, et al. 1977. *Networks and Places*. New York: Free Press.

Fly, Jerry, and Reinhart, George. 1980. "Racial Separation During the 1970s: The Case of Birmingham." *Social Forces* 58: 1255-62.

Foley, Donald. 1952. *Neighbors or Urbanites*. Rochester, N. Y.: University of Rochester Press.

————. 1954. "Urban Daytime Population: A Field for Demographic-Ecological Analysis." *Social Forces* 32: 323-30.

Frey, William. 1979. "Central City White Flight: Racial and Non-racial Causes." *American Sociological Review* 44: 425-48.

Friedrichs, Robert. 1970. *A Sociology of Sociology*. New York: Free Press.

Frisbie, W. P., and Poston, D. I., Jr. 1975. "Components of Sustenance Organization and Non-metropolitan Population Change: A Human Ecology Investigation." *American Sociological Review* 40: 773-84.

————. 1978a. *Sustenance Organization and Migration in Non-Metropolitan America*. Iowa City: University of Iowa Press.

————. 1978b. "Sustenance Differences and Population Redistribution." *Social Forces* 57: 42-56.

Galaskiewicz, Joseph. 1979. "The Structure of Community Organization Networks." *Social Forces* 51: 1346-64.

Galaskiewicz, Joseph, and Marsden, Peter. 1978. "Interorganizational Resource Networks: Formal Patterns of Overlap." *Social Science Research* 7: 98-107.

Galpin, Charles. 1915. "The Social Anatomy of an Agricultural Community." *Research Bulletin* 34. Madison: University of Wisconsin Agricultural Experiment Station.

Gamson, William. 1966. "Rancorous Conflict in Community Politics." *American Sociological Review* 31: 71-81.

Gans, Herbert. 1952. "Urbanism and Suburbanism as Ways of Life." In *Human Behavior and Social Processes*, edited by A. M. Rose, pp. 625-848. London: Routledge and Kegan Paul.

————. 1962. *The Urban Villagers*. New York: Free Press.

————. 1967. *The Levittowners*. London: Allen Lane.

————. 1968. "Regional and Urban Planning." In *International Encyclopedia of Social Sciences*, edited by David Sills, vol. 12, pp. 129-37. New York: Macmillan.

————. 1975. "The Failure of Urban Renewal: A Critique and Some Proposals." In *The Manipulated City: Perspectives on Spatial Structure and Social Issues in Urban America*, edited by Stephen Gale and Eric Moore, pp. 199-212. Chicago: Maaroufa Press.

Gardner, Hugh. 1978. *The Children of Prosperity: Thirteen Modern American Communes*. New York: St. Martin's Press.

Garfinkel, Harold. 1967. *Studies in Ethnomethodology*. Englewood Cliffs, N. J.: Prentice-Hall.

Gerson, Elihu, and Gerson, M. Sue. 1976. "The Social Framework of Place Perspectives." In *Environmental Knowing*, edited by Gary Moore and Reginald Golledge, pp. 196-205. Stroudsburg, Pa.: Dowden, Hutchinson, and Ross.

Gerth, Hans, and Mills, C. Wright, eds. and trans. 1958. *From Max Weber*. New York: Oxford University Press.

Glaser, Barney, and Strauss, Anselm. 1967. *The Discovery of Grounded Theory*. New York: Aldine.

Goffman, Erving. 1959. *The Presentation of Self in Everyday Life*. Garden City, N. Y.: Anchor Books.

————. 1963. *Stigma*. Englewood Cliffs, N. J.: Prentice-Hall.

————. 1967. *Interaction Ritual*. Garden City, N. Y.: Anchor Books.

Gordon, David, ed. 1971. *Problems in Political Economy: An Urban Perspective*. Lexington, Mass.: Heath.

————. 1978. "Capitalist Development and the History of American Cities." In *Marxism and the Metropolis*, edited by William Tabb and Larry Sawers, pp. 25-63. New York: Oxford University Press.

Gottlieb, B., ed. 1981. *Social Networks and Social Support in Community Mental Health*. Beverly Hills, Cal.: Sage.

Gough, Kathleen. 1968. "Anthropology: Child of Imperialism." *Monthly Review* 19: 12-27.

Gould, P. R., and White, R. R. 1974. *Mental Maps*. Harmondsworth, England: Penguin.

Gouldner, Alvin. 1970. *The Coming Crises of Western Sociology*. New York: Basic Books.

Granovetter, Mark. 1973. "The Strength of Weak Ties." *American Journal of Sociology* 78: 1360-80.

————. 1974. *Getting a Job*. Cambridge: Harvard University Press.

Gras, N. S. B. 1922. *An Introduction to Economic History*. New York: Harper.

Greer, Scott. 1962. *The Emerging City*. New York: Free Press.

Gubrium, Jaber, and Buckhold, David. 1977. *Toward Maturity*. San Francisco: Jossey-Bass.

Guest, Avery. 1977. "The Functional Reorganization of the Metropolis." *Pacific Sociological Review* 20: 553-67.

————. 1978. "Suburban Territorial Differentiation." *Sociology and Social Research* 62: 523-36.

Gusfield, Joseph. 1975. *Community: A Critical Response*. New York: Harper & Row.

Hall, Edward. 1966. *The Hidden Dimension*. Garden City, N. Y.: Doubleday.

Harris, Chauncey, and Ullman, Edward. 1945. "The Nature of Cities." *Annals of American Academy of Political and Social Science* 242: 14.

Hatt, Paul. 1946. "The Concept of Natural Area." *American Sociological Review* 11: 423-27.

Hawley, Amos. 1941. "An Ecological Study of Urban Institutions." *American Sociological Review* 6: 629-39.

————. 1950. *Human Ecology: A Theory of Community Structure*. New York: Ronald Press.

————. 1968. "Human Ecology." In *International Encyclopedia of Social Sciences*, edited by David Sills, vol. 4, pp. 328-37. New York: Macmillan.

————. 1981. *Urban Society: An Ecological Approach*. New York: Wiley.

Hawley, Willis, and Wirt, Frederick, eds. 1968. *The Search for Community Power*. Englewood Cliffs, N. J.: Prentice-Hall.

Heaton, Tim; Clifford, William; and Fuguitt, Glenn. 1981. "Temporal Shifts in the Determinants of Young and Elderly Migration in Non-Metropolitan Areas." *Social Forces* 60: 41-60.

Hill, Richard Child. 1974. "Separate and Unequal: Governmental Inequality in the Metropolis. *American Political Science Review* 66: 1557-67.

————. 1978. "Fiscal Collapse and Political Struggle in Decaying Central Cities in the United States." In *Marxism and the Metropolis*, edited by William Tabb and Larry Sawers, pp. 213-40. New York: Oxford University Press.

Hillery, George. 1955. "Definitions of Community: Areas of Agreement." *Rural Sociology* 20: 111-23.

————. 1968. *Communal Organizations: A Study of Local Societies*. Chicago: University of Chicago Press.

Hobbs, Thomas. 1651/1958. *The Leviathan*. New York: Macmillan.

Hollingshead, August. 1947. "A Re-Examination of Ecological Theory." *Sociology and Social Research* 31: 194-204.

——— . 1949. *Elmtown's Youth.* New York: Wiley.

Holzner, Burkart. 1968. *Reality Construction in Society.* Cambridge: Schenkman Publishing.

Homans, George. 1950. *The Human Group.* New York: Harcourt Brace.

——— . 1961. *Social Behavior: Its Elementary Forms.* New York: Harcourt Brace.

Hoyt, Homer. 1939. *The Structure and Growth of Residential Neighborhoods in American Cities.* Washington, D.C.: Federal Housing Administration.

Huber, Joan. 1973. "Symbolic Interaction as a Pragmatic Perspective: The Bias of Emergent Theory." *American Sociological Review* 38: 274-84.

Hunter, Albert. 1971. "The Ecology of Chicago: Persistence and Change, 1930-1960." *American Journal of Sociology* 99: 425-44.

——— . 1974. *Symbolic Communities.* Chicago: University of Chicago Press.

——— . 1975. "The Loss of Community: An Empirical Test Through Replication." *American Sociological Review* 40: 537-52.

Hunter, Floyd. 1953. *Community Power Structure.* Chapel Hill: University of North Carolina Press.

——— . 1980. *Community Power Succession: Atlanta's Policy Makers Revisited.* Chapel Hill: University of North Carolina Press.

Husserl, Edmund. 1913/1931. *Ideas: General Introduction to Pure Phenomenology,* translated by W. R. Boyce Gibson. New York: Macmillan.

Jackson, Pamela Irving. 1978. "Community Control, Community Mobilization, and Community Political Structure in 57 United States Cities." *Sociological Quarterly* 19: 577-89.

Jacobs, Jane. 1961. *The Death and Life of Great American Cities.* New York: Vintage.

James, William. 1892. *Psychology.* New York: Henry Holt.

Janowitz, Morris. 1951. *The Community Press in an Urban Setting.* New York: Free Press.

Kadushin, Charles. 1966. "Friends and Supporters of Psychotherapy; On Social Circles in Urban Life." *American Sociological Review* 31: 786-802.

Kanter, Rosabeth Moss. 1972. *Commitment and Community.* Cambridge, Mass.: Harvard University Press.

Kapferer, Bruce. 1969. "Norms and the Manipulation of Relationships in a Work Context." In *Social Networks in Urban Settings,* edited by J. Clyde Mitchell, pp. 181-245. Manchester: University of Manchester Press.

Karp, David; Stone, Gregory; and Yoels, Williams. 1977. *Being Urban: A Social Psychological View of City Life.* Lexington, Mass.: Heath.

Kasarda, John, and Janowitz, Morris. 1974. "Community Attachment in Mass Society." *American Sociological Review* 39: 328-39.

Kass, Roy. 1977. "Community Structure and the Metropolitan Division of Labor: Impact of Key Functions on Community Social Characteristics." *Social Forces* 56: 218-39.

Katznelson, Ira. 1975. "Community Conflict and Capitalist Development." Paper presented at the Annual Meetings of the American Political Science Association, San Francisco, September 26, 1975.

Killworth, P., and Russell, B. 1976. "Information Accuracy in Social Network Data." *Human Organization* 35: 269-86.

Kitagawa, Evelyn. 1963. *Local Community Fact Book, Chicago Metropolitan Area, 1960*. Chicago: Chicago Community Inventory.

Krase, Jerome. 1979. "Community, Morality, and the Inner City." *Humanity and Society* 3: 35-52.

Kromwall, John. n.d. "Zenda." Unpublished manuscript.

Kuhn, Manfred, and McPartland, Thomas. 1954. "An Empirical Investigation of Self Attitudes." *American Sociological Review* 19: 68-76.

Kuhn, Thomas. 1962. *The Structure of Scientific Revolutions*. Chicago: University of Chicago Press.

LaGory, Mark. 1979. "Twentieth Century Urban Growth: An Ecological Approach." *Sociological Focus* 12: 187-202.

LaGory, Mark, and Nelson, James. 1978. "An Ecological Analysis of Urban Growth Between 1900 and 1940." *Sociological Quarterly* 19: 590-603.

Laska, Shirley Bradway, and Spain, Daphne, eds. 1980. *Back to the City: Issues in Neighborhood Renovation*. New York: Pergamon Press.

Laumann, Edward, and Pappi, Franz. 1976. *Networks of Collective Action: A Perspective on Community Influence Systems*. New York: Academic Press.

Laumann, Edward; Marsden, Peter; and Galaskiewicz, Joseph. 1977. "Community Elite Influence Structures." *American Journal of Sociology* 83: 594-631.

Lenin, Vladimir. 1917/1966. "Imperialism, the Highest Stage of Capitalism." In *The Essential Works of Lenin*, edited by Henry Christman, pp. 177-270. New York: Bantam.

Levy, Marion. 1968. "Structural-Functional Analysis." In *International Encyclopedia of the Social Sciences*, edited by David Sills, vol. 6, pp. 21-29. New York: Macmillan.

Liebow, Elliot. 1967. *Tally's Corner*. Boston: Little, Brown.

Lincoln Park Conservation Association. n.d. "Lincoln Park Conservation Association." (pamphlet). Chicago: printing courtesy of The Berger Reality Group.

Lindesmith, Alfred; Strauss, Anselm; and Denzin, Norman. 1977. *Social Psychology*. New York: Holt, Rinehart and Winston.

Lofland, Lyn. 1973. *A World of Strangers: Order and Action in Urban Public Space*. New York: Basic Books.

Logan, John, and Sterns, Linda Brewster. 1981. "Suburban Racial Segregation as a Non-Ecological Process." *Social Forces* 60: 61-73.

Long, Norton. 1958. "The Local Community as an Ecology of Games." *American Journal of Sociology* 64: 251-61.

Lynch, Kevin. 1960. *The Image of the City*. Cambridge, Mass.: M.I.T. Press.

Lynd, Robert. 1929. *Middletown in Transition: A Study in Cultural Conflicts*. New York: Harcourt, Brace, Jovanovich.

Lynd, Robert, and Lynd, Helen. 1937. *Middletown*. New York: Harcourt Brace.

Lyon, Larry; Felice, Lawrence; Perryman, M. Ray; and Parker, Stephen. 1981. "Community Power and Population Increase: An Empirical Test of the Growth Machine Model." *American Journal of Sociology* 86: 1387-1400.

Macionis, John. 1978. "The Search for Community in Modern Society: An Interpretation." *Qualitative Sociology* 1: 130-43.

Madge, Charles. 1968. "Planning, Social: Introduction." In *International Encyclopedia of Social Science*, edited by David Sills, vol. 12, pp. 125-28. New York: Macmillan.

Malinowski, Bronislaw. 1936. "Anthropology." *Encyclopedia Britannica*, vol. 1, p. 132. London and New York: William Benton.

Manis, Jerome, and Meltzer, Bernard. eds. 1978. *Symbolic Interaction*, 3d ed. Boston: Allyn and Bacon.

Manning, Peter K. 1973. "Existential Sociology." *Sociological Quarterly* 14: 200-25.

Markusen, Ann. 1978. "Class and Urban Social Expenditure: A Marxist Theory of Metropolitan Government." In *Marxism and the Metropolis*, edited by William Tabb and Larry Sawers, pp. 90-112. New York: Oxford University Press.

Marshall, Harvey. 1979. "White Movement to the Suburbs: A Comparison of Explanations." *American Sociological Review* 44: 975-94.

Marshall, Harvey, and Stahura, John. 1979a. "Determinants of Black Suburbanization: Regional and Suburban Size Category Patterns." *Sociological Quarterly* 20: 237-53.

———. 1979b. "Black and White Population Growth in American Suburbs: Transition or Parallel Development?" *Social Forces* 58: 305-28.

Marx, Karl. 1859/1904. *A Contribution to the Critique of Political Economy*. New York: International Library.

———. 1867/1946. *Das Kapital*. New York: Modern Library.

———. 1904/1969. "Introduction to the Critique of the Political Economy." In *Marx and Modern Economics*, edited by David Horowitz. New York: Monthly Review Press.

Marx, Karl, and Engels, Friedrich. 1848/1958. *The Communist Manifesto*. New York: International Publishers.

Mayer, Harold, and Wade, Richard. 1969. *Chicago: Growth of a Metropolis*. Chicago: University of Chicago Press.

McBride, Sarah. 1890. Untitled Reminiscences, December 25, 1890, furnished by Bobbi Pankonin.

McGee, Leo, and Boon, Robert. 1977. "Black Rural Land Decline in the South." *Black Scholar* 8: 8-11.

McKenzie, Roderick. 1924. "The Ecological Approach to the Study of the Human Community." *American Journal of Sociology* 30: 287-301.

———. 1926. "The Scope of Human Ecology." *American Journal of Sociology* 32: 141-54.

———. 1927. "The Concept of Dominance and World Organization." *American Journal of Sociology* 33: 28-42.

———. 1933. *The Metropolitan Community*. New York: McGraw-Hill.

———. 1968. *On Human Ecology*, selected and edited by Amos Hawley. Chicago: University of Chicago Press.

McLuhan, Marshall. 1964. *Understanding Media*. New York: Signet.

Mead, George Herbert. 1934. *Mind, Self, and Society*, edited by Charles Morris. Chicago: University of Chicago Press.

Meltzer, Bernard; Petras, John; and Reynolds, Larry. 1975. *Symbolic Inter- actionism*. London: Routledge and Kegan Paul.

Mercer, Blaine. 1956. *The American Community*. New York: Random House.

Merton, Robert. 1949. *Social Theory and Social Structure*. Glencoe, Ill.: Free Press.

————. 1967. *On Theoretical Sociology*. New York: Free Press.

Michelson, William. 1974. "The Reconciliation of 'Subjective' and 'Objective' Data on Physical Environments in the Community: The Case of Social Contact in High Rise Apartments." In *The Community Approaches and Applications*, edited by Marcia Pelly Effrat, pp. 147-73. New York: Free Press.

Milgram, Stanley. 1967. "The Small World Problem." *Psychology Today* 1: 61-67.

Miller, Zane. 1981. *Suburb*. Knoxville: University of Tennessee Press.

Mills, C. Wright. 1963. "The Social Life of a Modern Community." In *Power, Politics, and People*, edited by I. L. Horowitz, pp. 34-52. New York: Ballantine.

Mitchell, J. Clyde. 1969. "The Concept and Use of Social Networks." In *Social Networks in Urban Situations*, edited by J. Clyde Mitchell, pp. 1-50. Manchester: University of Manchester Press.

————. 1973. "Networks, Norms, and Institutions." In *Network Analysis*, edited by Jeremy Boissevain and J. Clyde Mitchell, pp. 15-36. The Hague: Mouton.

Molotch, Harvey. 1976. "The City as Growth Machine: Towards a Political Economy of Place." *American Journal of Sociology* 82: 309-32.

Moore, Gary, and Golledge, Reginald, eds. 1976. *Environmental Knowing*. Stroudsburg, Pa.: Dowden, Hutchinson, and Ross.

Mullins, Nicholas. 1973. *Theories and Theory Groups In Contemporary America*. New York: Harper & Row.

Newby, Howard. 1979. "Urbanization and the Rural Class Structure: Reflections on a Case Study." *British Journal of Sociology* 30: 475-99.

Nisbet, Robert. 1953. *The Quest for Community*. New York: Oxford University Press.

————. 1966. *The Sociological Tradition*. New York: Basic Books.

Nye, Lowell Albert, ed. 1968. *History of McHenry County, Illinois, 1832-1968*. Woodstock, Ill.: McHenry County Board of Supervisors.

Nye, Norman H. 1970. *S.P.S.S.: Statistical Package*. New York: McGraw-Hill.

O'Brien, Robert. 1942. "Beale Street, Memphis: A Study in Ecological Succession." *Sociology and Social Research* 26: 430-36.

O'Connor, James. 1973. *The Fiscal Crises of the State*. New York: St. Martin's Press.

Orleans, Peter. 1973. "Differential Cognition of Urban Residents: Effects of Social Scale on Mapping." In *Image and Environment*, edited by R. M. Downs and D. Stea, pp. 115-30. Chicago: Aldine.

Pahl, R. E. 1974. "Instrumentality and Community in the Process of Urbanization." In *The Community: Approaches and Applications*, edited by Marcia Pelly Effrat, pp. 241-60. New York: Free Press.

Pampel, Fred, and Choldin, Harvey. 1978. "Urban Location and Segregation of the Aged." *Social Forces* 56: 1121-39.

Park, Robert. 1929. "Urbanization as Measured by Newspaper Circulation." *American Journal of Sociology* 35: 60-79.

——— . 1936. "Human Ecology." *American Journal of Sociology* 42: 1-15.

——— . 1952. *Human Communities.* Chicago: University of Chicago Press.

Park, Robert, and Burgess, Ernest. 1921. *Introduction to the Science of Sociology.* Chicago: University of Chicago Press.

Park, Robert; Burgess, Ernest; and McKenzie, Roderick. 1925. *The City.* Chicago: University of Chicago Press.

Parsons, Talcott. 1937. *The Structure of Social Action.* New York: McGraw-Hill.

——— . 1949. *Essays in Sociological Theory.* Glencoe, Ill.: Free Press.

——— . 1951. *The Social System.* Glencoe, Ill.: Free Press.

——— . 1960. "The Principal Structures of Community." In *Structural Processes in Modern Society*, edited by Talcott Parsons, pp. 250-79. New York: Free Press.

——— . 1966. *Societies: Evolutionary and Comparative Perspectives.* Englewood Cliffs, N.J.: Prentice-Hall.

Pearce, D. M. 1979. "Gatekeepers and Homeseekers: Institutional Factors in Racial Steering." *Social Problems* 26: 325-42.

Phillips, Derek. 1975. "Paradigms and Incommensurability." *Theory and Society* 2: 37-61.

Polsby, Nelson. 1963. *Community Power and Political Theory.* New Haven, Conn.: Yale University Press.

Poplin, Dennis. 1979. *Communities: A Survey of Theories and Methods of Research.* New York: Macmillan.

Popper, Karl. 1945/1962. *The Open Society and Its Enemies.* New York: Harper.

Poulantzas, N. 1968. *Pouvoir politique et classes sociales de l'État capitaliste.* Paris: Maspero.

Proshansky, Harold. 1978. "The City and Self-Identity." *Environment and Behavior* 10: 147-69.

Quinn, James. 1950. *Human Ecology.* New York: Prentice-Hall.

——— . 1934. "Ecological Versus Social Interaction." *Sociology and Social Research* 18: 565-70.

——— . 1940. "Human Ecology and Interactional Ecology." *American Sociological Review* 5: 701-34.

Radcliffe-Brown, A. 1958. *Method in Social Anthropology*, edited by M. N. Srinivas. Chicago: University of Chicago Press.

Reckless, Walter. 1926. "The Distribution of Commercialized Vice in the City." *Publications of the American Sociological Society* 20: 164-76.

Redfield, Robert. 1941. *The Folk Culture of Yucatan.* Chicago: University of Chicago Press.

Reiss, Albert, Jr. 1951. "Functional Specialization of Cities." In *Cities and Society*, edited by Paul Hatt and Albert Reiss, pp. 555-75. New York: Free Press.

Reps, John. 1965. *The Making of Urban America: A History of City Planning in America*. Princeton, N. J.: Princeton University Press.

Resources for the Future. 1960. *Metropolis and Region*. Baltimore: Johns Hopkins University Press.

Rex, John, and Moore, Robert. 1967. *Race, Community, and Conflict*. London: Oxford University Press.

Ritzer, George. 1975. *Sociology: A Multiple Paradigm Science*. Boston: Allyn and Bacon.

Rodwin, Lloyd. 1960. "The Roles of the City Planner in the Community." In *Social Science and Community Action*, edited by Charles Adrian, pp. 43-55. East Lansing: Michigan State University Press.

Roof, Wade Clark, and Spain, Daphne. 1977. "A Research Note on City-Suburban Socioeconomic Differences Among American Blacks." *Social Forces* 56: 15-30.

Ross, H. Laurence. 1962. "The Local Community: A Survey Approach." *American Sociological Review* 27: 127-34.

Ross, Murray. 1967. *Community Organization: Theory and Principles*. 2d ed. New York: Harper & Row.

Rossi, Peter. 1960. "Power and Community Structure." *Midwest Journal of Political Science* 14: 390-401.

Sale, Kirkpatrick. 1978. "The Polis Perplexity: An Inquiry into the Size of Cities." *Working Papers for a New Society* 6: 64-74.

Sanders, Irwin. 1958. *The Community: An Introduction to a Social System*. New York: Ronald Press.

Sanderson, Dwight. 1939. *Locating the Rural Community*. Ithaca: New York State College of Agriculture.

Saunders, Peter. 1981. *Social Theory and the Urban Question*. London: Hutchinson.

Schnore, Leo. 1958. "Sociology Morphology and Human Ecology." *American Journal of Sociology* 63: 631.

———— .1964. "Urbanization and Economic Development." *American Journal of Economic Development* 23: 37-48.

———— . 1967. "Measuring City-Suburban Status Differences." *Urban Affairs Quarterly* 3: 95-108.

Schulze, Robert. 1958. "The Role of Economic Dominants in Community Power Structure." *American Sociological Review* 23: 3-9.

Schutz, Alfred. 1971. *Collected Papers*, vol. 1. The Hague: Martinus Nijhoff.

Schwartz, Barry. 1978. "The Social Ecology of Time Barriers." *Social Forces* 56: 1203-20.

Seeley, John; Sims, Alexander; and Loosely, Elizabeth. 1956. *Crestwood Heights*. New York: Harper & Row.

Sennett, Richard. 1970. *The Uses of Disorder: Personal Identity and City Life*. New York: Vintage.

Shaw, Clifford. 1930. *The Jack Roller*. Chicago: University of Chicago Press.

Sheffield Neighborhood Association, Garden Walk Program Book Committee. 1981. *Sheffield Thirteenth Annual Garden Walk*. Chicago: Sheffield Neighborhood Association.

Shevky, E., and Bell, W. 1955. *Social Area Analysis*. Palo Alto, Cal.: Stanford University Press.

Shevky, E., and Williams, Marilyn. 1949. *The Social Areas of Los Angeles: Analysis and Typology*. Berkeley: University of California Press.

Shlay, Anne, and Rossi, Peter. 1981. "Keeping up the Neighborhood: Estimating Net Effects of Zoning." *American Sociological Review* 46: 703-19.

Simmel, Georg. 1950. *The Sociology of Georg Simmel*. Translated and edited by Kurt Wolff. Glencoe, Ill.: Free Press.

———. 1956 *Conflict and the Web of Group Affiliation*. Translated and edited by Kurt Wolff. Glencoe, Ill.: Free Press.

Simpson, Richard L. 1965. "Sociology of the Community: Current Status and Prospects." *Rural Sociology* 30: 127-49.

Sjoberg, Gideon. 1960. *The Pre-Industrial City*. New York: Free Press.

———. 1965. "Community." In *Dictionary of Sociology*, edited by J. Gould and W. L. Kolb, p. 115. London: Tavistock.

Sly, D. E. 1972. "Migration and the Ecological Complex." *American Sociological Review* 37: 615-28.

Sly, D. E., and Tayman, J. 1977. "Ecological Approaches to Migration Re-examined." *American Sociological Review* 42: 783-95.

———. 1980. "Metropolitan Morphology and Population Mobility: The Theory of Ecological Expansion Re-examined." *American Journal of Sociology* 86: 119-38.

Sorokin, Pitirim. 1928. *Contemporary Sociological Theories*. New York: Harper.

Spencer, Herbert. 1885/1966. *The Works of Herbert Spencer, Volume 1: Essays Scientific, Political, and Speculative*. Osnabruck: Otto Zeller.

———. 1898/1967. *The Evolution of Society: Selections from Herbert Spencer's Principles of Sociology*, edited by Robert Carneiro. Chicago: University of Chicago Press.

Stacey, Margaret. 1969. "The Myth of Community Studies." *British Journal of Sociology* 20: 134-47.

Stahura, John. 1978. "The Evolution of Suburban Functional Roles." *Pacific Sociological Review* 21: 423-39.

———. 1979. "Suburban Status Evolution/Persistence: A Structural Model." *American Sociological Review* 44: 937-47.

Stein, Maurice. 1960. *The Eclipse of Community*. New York: Harper & Row.

Sternlieb, George. 1978. "The Small City: Vanguard of Remnant?" *Wisconsin Sociologist* 15: 131-36.

Stokes, Randall, and Hewitt, John. 1976. "Aligning Actions." *American Sociological Review* 41: 838-49.

Stone, Gregory. 1954. "City Shoppers and Urban Identification: Observations on the Social Psychology of City Life." *American Journal of Sociology* 60: 36-45.

Stoneall, Linda. 1974. "Integration Within a Commune." *Youth and Society* 5: 475-96.

———. 1978. "How is Z a Community? The Phenomenology of Community." Ph.D. dissertation, Michigan State University.

———. 1981. "Cognitive Mapping: Gender Differences in the Perception of Community." *Sociological Inquiry* 51: 121-27.

———— . 1983a. "Where Are You From? A Case of Rural Residential Identification." *Qualitative Sociology 6.*

———— . 1983b. "Bringing Women into Community Studies: A Rural Midwestern Case Study." *Journal of the Community Development Society 14.*

Strasser, Hermann. 1976. *The Normative Structure of Sociology: Conservative and Emancipatory Themes in Social Thought.* London: Routledge and Kegan Paul.

Strauss, Anselm. 1961. *Images of the American City.* New York: Free Press.

———— . 1978. *Negotiations.* San Francisco: Jossey-Bass.

Suttles, Gerald. 1968. *The Social Order of the Slum.* Chicago: University of Chicago Press.

———— . 1972. *The Social Construction of Communities.* Chicago: University of Chicago Press.

Sutton, Willis, and Kolaja, Jiri. 1960. "Elements of Community Action." *Social Forces* 38: 325-31.

Sutton, Willis, and Munson, T. 1976. "Definitions of Community, 1954-1973." Paper presented at the Annual Meetings of the American Sociological Association, New York, August 1976.

Tabb, William. 1978. "The New York City Fiscal Crises." In *Marxism and the Metropolis,* edited by William Tabb and Larry Sawers, pp. 241-66. New York: Oxford University Press.

Taeuber, Karl, and Taeuber, Alma. 1969. *Negroes in Cities.* New York: Atheneum.

Taub, Richard. 1979. "Lincoln Park." Unpublished report.

Taub, Richard, et al. 1977. "Urban Voluntary Associations: Locality Based and Externally Induced." *American Journal of Sociology* 83: 425-42.

Thatcher, Harry. n.d. "Zenda." Unpublished manuscript.

Theodorson, George, ed. 1961. *Studies in Human Ecology.* Evanston, Ill.: Row, Peterson.

Thomas, W. I., and Thomas, Dorothy Swain. 1928. *The Child in America.* New York: Knopf.

Thompson, Laura. 1949. "The Relations of Men, Animals, and Plants in an Island Community." *American Anthropologist* 51: 253-67.

Thorne, Barrie, and Henley, Nancy, eds. 1975. *Language and Sex: Difference and Dominance.* Rowley, Mass.: Newbury House.

Tilly, Charles. 1974. "Do Communities Act?" In *The Community: Approaches and Applications,* edited by Marcia Pelly Effrat, pp. 209-40. New York: Free Press.

Toennies, Ferdinand. 1887/1957. *Community and Society,* edited by Charles Loomis. East Lansing: Michigan State University Press.

Turbeville, Gus. 1949. "Religious Schism in the Methodist Church: A Sociological Analysis of the Pine Grove Case." *Rural Sociology* 14: 29-39.

Turner, Jonathan. 1978. *The Structure of Sociological Theory.* Homewood, Ill.: Dorsey Press.

Vickerman, R. W. 1979. "The Evaluation of Urban Change: Equilibrium and Adaptive Approaches." *Urban Studies* 16: 81-93.

Vidich, Arthur, and Bensman, Joseph. 1958. *Small Town in Mass Society*. Garden City, N. Y.: Doubleday.

Villemez, Wayne. 1980. "Race, Class, and Neighborhood: Differences in the Residential Return on Individual Resources." *Social Forces* 59: 414-30.

Walton, John. 1966. "Substance and Artifact: The Current Status of Research on Community Power Structure." *American Journal of Sociology* 71: 430-38.

———. 1974. "The Structural Bases of Political Change in Urban Communities." In *The Community: Approaches and Applications*, edited by Marcia Pelly Effrat, pp. 174-206. New York: Free Press.

Warner, Lloyd. 1959. *The Living and the Dead*. New Haven, Conn.: Yale University Press.

———. 1963. *Yankee City*. New Haven, Conn.: Yale University Press.

Warner, Lloyd, and Lunt, Paul. 1941. *The Social Life of a Modern Community*. New Haven, Conn.: Yale University Press.

———. 1942. *The Status System of a Modern Community*. New Haven, Conn.: Yale University Press.

Warner, Lloyd, and Low, J. O. 1947. *The Social System of a Modern Factory*. New Haven, Conn.: Yale University Press.

Warner, Lloyd, and Srole, Leo. 1945. *The Social Systems of American Ethnic Groups*. New Haven, Conn.: Yale University Press.

Warner, Lloyd, et al. 1949. *Democracy in Jonesville*. New York: Harper & Row.

Warren, Donald. 1978. "Explorations in Neighborhood Differentiation." *Sociological Quarterly* 19: 310-31.

Warren, Roland. 1965. *Studying Your Community*. New York: Free Press.

———. 1978. *The Community in America*, 3d ed. Chicago: Rand-McNally.

Webber, Melvin. 1963. "Order in Diversity: Community Without Propinquity." In *Cities and Space*, edited by L. Wingo, Jr., pp. 23-56. Baltimore, Md.: Johns Hopkins University Press.

Weber, Max. 1905/1930. *The Protestant Ethic and the Spirit of Capitalism*. London: Allen and Unwin.

———. 1922/1947. *The Theory of Social and Economic Organization*, translated and edited by A. M. Henderson and Talcott Parsons. New York: Oxford University Press.

———. 1958. *From Max Weber*, edited and translated by Hans Gerth and C. Wright Mills. New York: Oxford University Press.

———. 1905/1962. *The City*, translated and edited by Don Martindale and Gertrude Neuwirth. New York: Collier Books.

Weigert, Andrew. 1981. *The Sociology of Everyday Life*. New York: Longman.

Wellman, Barry. 1979. "The Community Question: The Intimate Networks of East Yorkers." *American Journal of Sociology*. 84: 1201-31.

———. 1981. "Community Networks and Mobilization of Resources." Paper presented at the American Sociological Association meetings in Toronto, August 28, 1981.

Whitten, N. E., and Wolfe, A. W. 1974. "Network Analysis." In *Handbook of Social and Cultural Anthropology*, edited by J. J. Honigman, pp. 717-46. Chicago: Rand-McNally.

Whyte, William Foote. 1955. *Street Corner Society*. Chicago: University of Chicago Press.

Whyte, William H. 1956. *The Organization Man*. New York: Simon and Schuster.

Wilhelm, Sidney. 1964. "The Concept of the 'Ecological Complex.'" *American Journal of Economics and Sociology* 23: 241-48.

Willer, David, and Anderson, Bo, eds. 1979. *Social Exchange and Social Networks*. New York: Elsevier.

Willis, William, Jr. 1969. "Skeletons in the Anthropological Closet." In *Reinventing Anthropology*, edited by Dell Hymes, pp. 121-52. New York: Pantheon Books.

Wirth, Louis. 1928. *The Ghetto*. Chicago: University of Chicago Press.

———. 1933. "The Scope and Problems of the Community." *Publications of the Sociological Society of America* 27:62.

———. 1938. "Urbanism as a Way of Life." *American Journal of Sociology* 44: 1-16.

———. 1944. "Human Ecology." *American Journal of Sociology* 50: 483-88.

Wirth, Louis, and Bernet, Eleanor. 1949. *Community Fact Book of Chicago*. Chicago: Chicago Community Inventory.

Wolf, Eric. 1970. *Peasant Wars of the Twentieth Century*. New York: Harper & Row.

Wrong, Dennis. 1961. "The Over-Socialized Conception of Man." *American Sociological Review* 26: 185-93.

Zipf, George. 1949. *Human Behavior and the Principle of Least Effort*. New York: Hafner.

Zorbaugh, Harvey. 1929. *The Gold Coast and the Slum*. Chicago: University of Chicago Press.

Index

AUTHOR INDEX

SUBJECT INDEX

accommodation, 16, 95

action, social, 270-74

adaptation, 14-16, 66n, 69-70, 73-78, 82-83, 87, 92, 101, 106, 108-12, 114-15, 120, 127-29, 135, 254, 256, 265-66

aggregates, 65-66, 69, 72, 76-78, 86-87, 100-1, 175, 253, 262-63, 267

alienation, 17, 144, 159, 162, 173, 268; definition, 162

analysis, 13, 16-18, 73, 147, 181, 191, 264, 267, 271

anthropology, 14, 104, 106, 111-12, 132, 214-15, 218, 223, 226, 248

Armitage Street, 49, 56, 79

attitudes, 14, 85-86, 222, 257, 259, 269, 273

authority, 8-9, 82, 131, 139-40, 149, 152-53, 163, 173, 231-32, 234, 274; definition, 233

axes, community, 110-11, 119; horizontal, 110-11, 123; vertical, 110-11, 123-24

banks, 44, 60-61, 67, 84, 99, 149, 196

biography, 16-17, 181, 188, 190, 198, 201-2, 210

biology, 23, 66, 73-74, 100, 103, 115, 127, 145, 252, 263

biotic, 68-70, 73

blacks, 50, 60, 91, 93, 157, 253; in Lincoln Park, 93-94, 150-51, 162, 272

bond, 3, 216-17

boundaries, 2-3, 5, 17, 20, 73, 88-90, 96-97, 121, 261, 266-67; boundary maintenance, 104, 131, 133, 218; boundary maintenance, defi-

nition, 131; of conflict theory, 114, 165, 172-73, 183-84; human-ecological, 99-101; network-exchange analytical, 221-22, 224, 247-49; social-psychological, 188, 192, 205, 208-10; structural-functional, 115, 117, 131-32

bourgeoise, 10, 137, 153, 156, 163

bureaucracy, 9, 15, 81, 99, 138-39, 156, 221, 260, 271

capitalism, 7-10, 136-39, 142, 148, 152-53, 160-66, 168, 172-73, 256, 258

census, 22, 71, 73, 76-77, 89-91, 147, 150, 173, 264

central business district, 78, 94-96, 99, 101

centralization, 91-92; definition, 90-91

change, 7-9, 11, 13, 19, 21-22, 65-66, 76, 80-81, 87-90, 92-93, 103, 107-9, 116-17, 127-33, 135-37, 139, 142-44, 146-47, 151-52, 157-59, 161-64, 168-69, 171-73, 190, 194, 205-6, 208, 218-19, 221-22, 228-29, 232, 240-44, 246, 254-56, 260-62, 265-74

Chicago, 13, 22, 26, 32-33, 36-38, 43-44, 48, 54-57, 59-63, 68-72, 78-79, 84-85, 87-89, 92, 96, 99-101, 121-23, 127, 130, 148-51, 153, 156, 158, 161, 166-68, 183-84, 192, 205, 207, 233, 253, 267; fire, 38, 54, 58-59, 93; Loop, 96, 120; *Tribune*, 50, 85

Chicago School, 12, 14, 68, 85, 253, 267

choice, 72, 148, 153, 186, 188, 192,

210-11, 222, 230, 246, 253-54

church, 7, 92, 108-11, 121, 149, 186, 192, 194, 208, 231, 234, 271; in Lincoln Park, 54-55, 58-61, 93, 159, 167, 242; Linn Presbyterian, 28, 32, 36-39, 41-42, 61, 98, 122, 124, 126, 128-29, 194-95, 228, 230-31, 239

cities, 2, 6, 9-11, 13, 20-22, 66, 68, 70, 72-73, 75, 81, 83-86, 88-90, 93-94, 96, 98, 114, 121-23, 126-27, 130, 135, 137, 140, 142-45, 149, 151, 153, 155-57, 164-66, 169, 172-73, 177, 182, 184, 186-87, 206, 208, 218, 222, 229, 233, 239-40, 252-53, 255, 269, 272-74; definition, 138; preindustrial, 96, 138; preindustrial, definition, 138

class, 10, 14, 16-17, 63, 82-83, 109, 111, 116, 120-21, 125-26, 133, 135-38, 142-44, 146-48, 150-65, 168, 170-73, 175, 222, 234-35, 240-42, 247, 253, 256-60, 265, 271-72; definition, 153-54

coalitions, 16-17, 154-55, 214, 224-25, 232, 234, 244, 265; definition, 234

cognition, 15-17, 175-76, 188; cognitive mapping, 182-84, 187-88, 206-10; cognitive mapping, definition, 183, 187; environmental cognition, 186-87, 210

cognitive psychology, 14, 175-76, 182, 210

collectivity, 3, 7, 106, 122, 130, 190, 246; collective action, 4, 253; collective behavior, 21, 149; collective consumption, 257-58; collective life, 14; collective movements, 21; collective needs, 19; collective rituals, 125-26, 189

commitment, 112-13, 116-18; definition, 112

communes, 112-14, 116-18, 131-32; definition, 112

communication, 12-14, 83, 88-89, 99-100, 108-9, 175-76, 178-84,

189-90, 192-94, 210, 219, 223, 236, 242

communist, 137, 139, 141, 255

community: classical approaches to, 6-11; conflict approach to, 133, 135-74; definition, 1-5, 20-21, 67-70, 108-10, 121, 182, 185, 214-15, 221; human-ecology approach to, 65-103; of limited liability, 175-211; loss of, 7-8, 11, 221, 262-63; network-exchange approach to, 213-49; plant and animal communities, 13, 73-76, 78, 88, 94, 101, 103; social-psychological approach to, 175-211; structural functional approach to, 103-33; tribal and peasant communities, 78, 82, 111

comparison, 15-17, 22-23, 63, 106, 115-16, 118-19; of case studies, 21-22; theoretical, 11-14, 262-68

competition, 12-13, 16-17, 65-66, 68-69, 74, 76-78, 82-83, 86-87, 90-93, 100-1, 103, 139, 160-61, 164, 225, 233, 244, 253, 256, 266; definition, 92

concentration, 80, 84, 90-92, 94-95

concentric zone theory, 69, 75, 96-98

conflict, 9-10, 14, 92-93, 116, 125, 128-29, 133, 135-40, 144-47, 150, 158-60, 168-69, 171-73, 228, 230, 233, 241-42, 253-59, 263, 266-69, 273; definition, 139

conflict theory, 10, 12, 14-17, 19, 23, 133, 135-74, 241, 262-73; criticisms of, 255-58, 268-72

connection, 12-17, 211, 213-14, 219, 221-25, 243, 248-49, 260-61

consciousness: class, 158, 162; false, 137, 141, 148, 160-61; raising, 138, 217

consensus, 2, 14, 16-17, 103-4, 110-11, 114-16, 124, 130-33, 135, 152, 254-55, 265-67, 271-72

construction, social, 14, 17, 175, 181, 184-85, 187-92, 198, 203, 206, 209-10

About the Author

LINDA STONEALL recently completed postdoctoral work in personality and social structure at the University of California, Berkeley. Until 1981, she was Assistant Professor of Sociology at Illinois State University, Normal, Illinois.

Dr. Stoneall has published widely in the area of sociology. Her current research is on the community lives of the mentally ill.

Dr. Stoneall holds a B.A. from Lawrence University, an M.A. from the University of Illinois, an M.A. from Northern Illinois University, and a Ph.D. from Michigan State University.